Entrepreneurship

Entrepreneurship

*Initiating and Developing
a New Venture*

Luke Ike

Copyright © 2018 by Luke Ike.

ISBN: Softcover   978-1-5434-9088-6
           eBook   978-1-5434-9089-3

All rights reserved. No part of this book may be reproduced or transmitted in any form or by any means, electronic or mechanical, including photocopying, recording, or by any information storage and retrieval system, without permission in writing from the copyright owner.

Any people depicted in stock imagery provided by Getty Images are models, and such images are being used for illustrative purposes only.
Certain stock imagery © Getty Images.

Print information available on the last page.

Rev. date: 06/11/2018

To order additional copies of this book, contact:
Xlibris
800-056-3182
www.Xlibrispublishing.co.uk
Orders@Xlibrispublishing.co.uk
778384

CONTENTS

AKNOWLEDGEMENTS xi
INTRODUCTION TO THE BOOK xiii

PART 1

ENTREPRENEURSHIP, THE ENTREPRENEUR AND THE ENVIRONMENT

Introduction..3

Chapter 1   WHAT IS ENTREPRENEURSHIP?.........................5
    1.1 Introduction...6
    1.2 Types of Entrepreneurship..8
        1.2.1 Social Entrepreneurship..8
        1.2.2 Cultural or Aesthetic Entrepreneurship 9
        1.2.3 Civic Entrepreneurship 10
        1.2.4 Intrapreneurship...11
    Further reading 14

Chapter 2   WHO IS AN ENTREPRENEUR?............................15
    2.1 Definitions...16
    2.2 Classifying Entrepreneurs..20
    2.3 Identifying Entrepreneurs By Actions To Wealth Creation...28
    Further reading 34

Chapter 3   ENTREPRENURSHIP AND SMALL BUSINESS ... 35

    3.1 Distinguishing Entrepreneurship and Small Business 36
    3.2 The Entrepreneur and the Small Business Owner / Manager ... 39
    Further reading 40

Chapter 4   INNOVATION AS KEY
                 ENTREPRENEURIAL ACTIVITY 41

    4.1 Introduction 42
    4.2 Innovation and Creativity 45
    4.3 Enhancing Personal Creativity 47
    4.4 Enhancing Organisational Creativity 48
    4.5 Creating Corporate Capacity for Innovation 49
    Further reading 53

Chapter 5   SIGNIFICANT ROLES OF
                 ENTREPRENEURS IN THE SOCIETY AND
                 ECONOMY 54

    5.1 Introduction 55
    5.2 Organising Resources and Creating Value and Wealth 56
    5.3 Creating Competition and Economic Stability 57
    5.4 Acting As Agent of Economic Change 58
    5.5 Creating New Ventures 59
    5.6 Job Creation 60
    5.7 Encouraging Women Entrepreneurship 61
    5.8 Mobilising Indigenous Entrepreneurship 64
    5.9 Bringing Innovation to Market 65
    Further reading 66

Chapter 6   BECOMING AN ENTREPRENEUR 67

    6.1 Anyone Can Be an Entrepreneur 68
    6.2 Forces That May Lead to Entrepreneurial Option 70
        6.2.1 Pull forces 71
        6.2.2 Push forces 74

6.3 Four Primary Types of Individuals
   Who Become Entrepreneurs..76
6.4 Limitations to Entrepreneurial Option 77
Further reading 78

PART 2

ENTREPRENEURSHIP AND NEW VENTURE INITIATION

Introduction..81

Chapter 7   INITIATING A NEW VENTURE 83

7.1 Introduction..84
7.2 Idea Generation...85
7.3 Idea Realisation 92
Further reading 113

PART 3

ENTREPRENEURSHIP AND NEW VENTURE DEVELOPMENT

Introduction... 117

Chapter 8   THE ENTREPRENEURIAL NEW
            VENETURE BUSINESS ENVIRONMENT.......... 119

8.1 Introduction...120
8.2 The Enterprise Culture..121
   8.2.1 Introduction...121
   8.2.2 Internal Factors Shaping Enterprise Culture 123
   8.2.3 External Factors Shaping Enterprise Culture 124
Further reading 142

Chapter 9 THE ENTREPRENEURIAL NEW VENETURE AND MANAGEMENT TASKS........143

9.1 Introduction..144
9.2 Entrepreneurial Planning...145
   9.2.1 Introduction..145
   9.2.2 Purposes of Planning New Venture Development.....147
   9.2.3 The New Venture Planning Process.......................149
   9.2.4 The Business Plan..160
9.3 Entrepreneurial Strategy...164
   9.3.1 Introduction..164
   9.3.2 Essential Components of Entrepreneurial Strategy...167
   9.3.3 The Strategy Planning Process...............................171
   9.3.4 Crafting Entrepreneurial Strategy..........................173
   9.3.5 Growth as A Strategic Objective For
         The New Venture..174
      9.3.5.1 Introduction..174
      9.3.5.2 Strategies For Growth..................................175
      9.3.5.3 Managing Growth.......................................183
   9.3.6 Achieving Competitive Advantage.........................194
      9.3.6.1 Introduction..194
      9.3.6.2 Sources of Competitive Advantage..............196
      9.3.6.3 Sustaining Competitive Advantage..............202
      9.3.6.4 Retaining Entrepreneurial Dynamics...........205
Further reading 207

Chapter 10 ORGANISING THE ENTREPRENEURIAL
             NEW VENTURE 208

10.1 Introduction..209
10.2 Entrepreneurial Organisation Structures......................211
   10.2.1 Introduction..211
   10.2.2 The Simple Structure..212
   10.2.3 Web and Cluster Structures.................................213
   10.2.4 The Cellular Structure...215
   10.2.5 The Shamrock Structure.....................................216
   10.2.6 The Extended Organisation................................217
   10.2.7 The Hollow Organisation...................................218

10.2.8 Teams 219
10.2.9 Virtual Organisation 220
10.2.10 Network Structure 221
10.3 Financing the New Venture 222
   10.3.1 Introduction 222
   10.3.2 Government Financial Assistance
          Programmes and Incentives 235
   10.3.3 Uses of Fund 239
   10.3.4 Factors to Consider When Financing the Venture 244
   10.3.5 How Investors Select Investment Opportunities 247
   10.3.6 The Questions Investors Need Answering 248
Further reading 252

Chapter 11 THE ENTREPRENEURIAL NEW
            VENTURE AND LEADING 253

11.1 Introduction 254
11.2 Leadership 255
   11.2.1 Introduction 255
   11.2.2 Leadership and Power 257
   11.2.3 Response to Power in Organisations 263
11.3 The Entrepreneurial Leader 264
11.4 Theories of Leadership 268
   11.4.1 Trait Theories (Classical theories) 269
   11.4.2 Style or Behavioural Theories 270
   11.4.3 Contingency/Situation Theories of Leadership 277
   11.4.4 Helping, Coaching and Resolving Conflicts 281
   11.4.5 Leadership Development 283
11.5 Group and Team Building 284
   11.5.1 Groups in Organisation 285
   11.5.2 Group Development 287
   11.5.3 Entrepreneurial Team Working 292
11.6 Motivation 295
   11.6.1 Introduction 295
   11.6.2 The Entrepreneur Motivation Challenges 296
   11.6.3 Motivation Theories 300
Further reading 321

Chapter 12 THE INTREPRENEURIAL NEW
            VENTURE CONTROL 322

    12.1 Introduction..323
    12.2 Control Methods..327
    12.3 Control Systems 329
        12.3.1 Financial Control 330
        12.3.2 Budgetary Control 332
        12.3.3 Performance Appraisal Systems.............................335
        12.3.4 Total Quality Control..337
        12.3.5 Information Systems for Management Control 339
    Further reading 342

REFERENCES...343

AKNOWLEDGEMENTS

This book is dedicated to the memory of my beloved father Hyacinth, my beloved mother Eunice and my beloved sister Philomena.

Luke Ike

INTRODUCTION TO THE BOOK

The growing interest in entrepreneurship is spreading across nations regardless of level of development, resulting in a high level attention been given to entrepreneurship – new venture initiation and development.

Entrepreneurship is now regarded as a key element in many societies and national governments are finding it very difficult to ignore the impact it has on their individual society and economic development. The impact of entrepreneurship is always brought about through change - a result of creativity and innovation) in the economy and society.

Entrepreneurship has now become significant as an instrument of change in many societies. Change has always been a part of social and economic revolution, but what is new is the nature of contemporary change that presents both opportunities and problems. The opportunities come in the shape of new possibilities of a better future and problems lie in managing the uncertainty these possibilities create. It is not only necessary to accommodate change but there is the need to be able to respond to the challenges of change that requires the capability to anticipate and initiate it - what entrepreneurship and entrepreneurs can offer - anticipating and initiating change.

By responding to challenges of change, entrepreneurs take advantage of the opportunities needed for continuous economic growth and improvement in national income and standard of living of individuals. Hence, the world is demanding both entrepreneurship and entrepreneurs, to provide the needed improvement in socio- economic dynamism. This is the fundamental responsibility of entrepreneurship and entrepreneurs that make this happen.

To make sense of this responsibility of entrepreneurs and entrepreneurship, and how this is managed, the reader needs to have an insight and understanding of entrepreneurship in all its important aspects.

This book aims to provide this much needed insight and understanding of the subject matter by providing the fundamental knowledge into entrepreneurship – initiation and development of a new venture. The book is valuable to practicing entrepreneurs, University and College students who will become entrepreneurs of the future, as well as individuals interested in entrepreneurship.

PART 1

ENTREPRENEURSHIP, THE ENTREPRENEUR AND THE ENVIRONMENT

INTRODUCTION

To be able to understand the process of initiating, developing, and sustaining a new venture, the reader needs to conceive essential concepts associated with entrepreneurship, the entrepreneur and the environment. This part is organised to provide detailed information to this respect and includes chapters 1, 2, 3, 4, 5, 6, of the book.

Chapter 1 introduces the nature of entrepreneurship and types of entrepreneurship. In chapter 2, the nature of entrepreneurs as well as various ways of identifying them are introduced and explained. Chapter 3 presents entrepreneurship and its relationship with the small business, while chapter 4 further introduces entrepreneurship and its relation to innovation. Chapter 5 explains the significant roles entrepreneurs play in a society and the economy and chapter 6 describes the many reasons why people decide to become entrepreneurs.

CHAPTER 1

WHAT IS ENTREPRENEURSHIP?

Aim

To introduce the nature of entrepreneurship.

Objectives

After studying this chapter you should be able to:

- Understand the meaning of entrepreneurship.
- Explain the significance of entrepreneurship.
- Understand different types of entrepreneurship.

1.1 Introduction

Entrepreneurship is a rich and complex phenomenon. As such it is difficult to pin it down to a single universal definition.

This is the reason why entrepreneurship has been defined in many ways by many scholars, and there is no agreed consensus on what constitutes entrepreneurship:

- Entrepreneurship is simply what the entrepreneur does. This occurs when an individual develops a new venture, a new approach to a business, a new idea or a unique way of giving a marketplace a product/ service by using resources in a new way under condition of risk (Jones 2006).
- Entrepreneurship is about making a change. Only those who innovate and develop are entrepreneurs (Kao 2004).
- Entrepreneurship is an economic process of creative destruction, in which wealth is created when entrepreneurs introduce new products or service. As such entrepreneurship is the source of change. (Schumpeter 1939, 2001).
- Entrepreneurship is the ability to create and build something practically. It is initiating, doing, achieving, and building an enterprise or organisation, rather than just watching, analysing or describing one. It is the knack for sensing an opportunity where others see chaos, contradiction and confusion (Timmons 1989).
- Entrepreneurship is about creating and managing vision and communicating that vision to other people. It is about demonstrating leadership, motivating people, and being effective in getting people to accept change (Wickham 1998).
- Entrepreneurship is about connecting two spheres in society between which there exists a difference in value, and transferring value between them. Emphasis is on opportunity recognition, that may involve challenging some of the basic value in a community (Barth 1999),
- Entrepreneurship is about creativity, innovation and change (Ike 2017).

Confusion may come-up when people equate the term "entrepreneurship" sorely with small and private enterprise - as such, over- simplifying the concept. Clearly, the term "entrepreneurship" is much broader than that.

Entrepreneurship is not about the act of founding or owning a usually small business. It is important to recognise that, not all small business owner/managers are entrepreneurs, and not all large business are UN –enterprising. Entrepreneurs can found in all types of organisations - large, small organisations, public and voluntary sectors. Clearly, entrepreneurship is not confined to the world of business and entrepreneurs can be found in all works of life.

A number of other terms/concepts have also been derived from the idea of the entrepreneurship such as:

- Entrepreneurial - an adjective describing how entrepreneurs undertake what they do. The use of this adjective suggests that there is a particular style associated with entrepreneurship and to what entrepreneurs do, which aims at pursuing opportunities and driving change, through flexibility, creativity, and innovation.
- Entrepreneurial process - the process in which the entrepreneur engages is the means which new value is created as a result of the project: the entrepreneurial venture. It is the methodological way of starting a new venture typical of entrepreneurs, by constantly seeking opportunities and innovation and defeating forces of resistance.

1.2 Types of Entrepreneurship

1.2.1 Social Entrepreneurship

In a business context, entrepreneurship is traditionally associated with profit making activities. Social entrepreneurship however, involves the social dimension of entrepreneurship and the potential for structural change.

Social entrepreneurship is said to differ from the traditional because they do not have profit as their main aim instead, they concentrate on social, rather than commercial profitable outputs. They also differ in terms of time frames, being more concerned with long term capacity building than with short term outcomes. Equally, they are different in terms of their "scavenger- like" use of resources, recognising that most communities have under-utilised resources that need to be harnessed for the good of the society - requiring much innovative thinking and entrepreneurial action, particularly in an era when, a nation's welfare system does not, cannot, or will not meet such needs.

In many literatures social entrepreneurship may be referred to as Not- For- Profit or Public Entrepreneurship as it takes place in the domain where the profit motive and chance to make profit is non-existent or very limited, or in an area of rapidly growing interest. It concerns the adoption of entrepreneurial approach by individuals and groups in a Not-For-Profit manner - such like charity, faith organisations, etc.

1.2.2 Cultural or Aesthetic Entrepreneurship

The driving force for cultural or aesthetic entrepreneurship is usually traced to creativity.

Cultural or aesthetic entrepreneurship is usually created by people whose main driver is not wealth creation or business capability but creativity. Many cultural or aesthetic entrepreneurial businesses have been, and are created by such people.

Although creativity may be the driving force, it is possible that in the process, the cultural or aesthetic entrepreneur may make money out of their talent and become extremely wealthy, but monetary wealth is not their main motivation. Rather, it is the desire to produce original, imaginative and innovatory work.

The contribution of cultural or aesthetic entrepreneurs to the economy and society therefore, is not wealth creation parse, but to the enrichment of life by challenging convention, and by opening up ways of things and behaviours that previously did not exist. Such enterprises contribute to what may be called the "dream society."

1.2.3 Civic Entrepreneurship

Civic entrepreneurship is usually associated with the public service institutions.

Public service institutions are now discovering the advantages of entrepreneurship in relation to their service development and delivery. They are now realising the need to be entrepreneurial and innovative fully as much as any business does.

Many governments all over the world have begun to recognise the need for change in the way public services are resourced, organised and managed. This process of change from a largely bureaucratic supply-led organisation to more responsive customer oriented organisation is now becoming a part of the public service life although many are not finding this an easy task particularly, given the traditional philosophical beliefs that surround them, and the absence of relevant management skills.

What this means is that public sectors need to adopt a more innovative entrepreneurial approach to service delivery. This requires more consensus and commitment on the part of staff towards the need for change. This is achievable by creating an environment where staff feel valued and involved and take ownership of the innovation. It also demands setting realistic objectives and formulation of vision that is communicated, understood, and shared throughout the organisation.

On the whole, innovation in the public sector is unlikely unless the right conditions for this is established and sustained - a culture for change that includes interaction with internal and external environment, visionary leadership, people empowerment, etc –a culture that encourages and drives civic entrepreneurship.

1.2.4 Intrapreneurship

"Intrapreneurship" is a term developed around the larger organisations in relation to entrepreneurial activities going on in their businesses.

Because the word "entrepreneur" has been linked to small business, the term "Intrapreneurship" was coined to describe someone who behaves in an entrepreneurial fashion in larger organisations and to recognise the power of entrepreneurship in them.

The term "Intrapreneur" is also used to describe an entrepreneur who works within the confines of an established organisation.

Other related terms used to describe entrepreneurial behaviour in larger organisations and other organisations, than the small firms include:

- Organisational entrepreneurship - refers to entrepreneurship in established organisation irrespective of whether they are large corporation, government bodies, non-for-profit organisations or smaller businesses.
- Corporate entrepreneurship - as the process in which innovative products or processes are developed by creating an entrepreneurial culture within an organisation. It can take various forms, and there are several ways in which it can operate.

The intrapreneur's role in a large firm would parallel that of the entrepreneur, responsible for developing and communicating organisational vision, identifying new opportunities for the organisation, generating strategic options, creating and offering organisation wide perspective, facilitating and encouraging change within the organisation, challenging existing ways of doing things and breaking down bureaucratic inertia.

The intrapreneur could be described as an entrepreneur and a good corporate manager. Intrepreneurs are result oriented, ambitious and competitive. They are motivated by problem-solving and rational decision- making as well as by change and innovation, believing that reward is in the work as much as the pay. While they find bureaucratic systems frustrating and question the status quo, they understand that organisation can resolve conflicts. Intrepreneurs usually combine the qualities of the entrepreneur and the corporate manager and as such, they effect change in the organisation in which they work.

On one hand, Intrapreneushep is similar to traditional entrepreneurship already introduced earlier, in the sense that they both focus on innovation (new products, processes or management methods), on the creation of value – added products and require investment on risky activities for which the outcome is uncertain.

On the other hand, differences can be found in the fact that intrapreneuship is restorative (intended to counter stagnation within the organisation to restore the entrepreneurial culture), while entrepreneurship is developmental (creates a process, product or even a venture when none existed before). Also, the enemy of the entrepreneur in the marketplace is the market, whereas the enemy of the entrepreneur is the corporate culture. In addition the entrepreneur is concerned with overcoming obstacles to the market, while the entrepreneur is concerned with overcoming corporate obstacles. Whereas funding is often a constraint on the entrepreneur, the funding available to the entrepreneur is usually very considerable.

As already explained, Intrapreneuship is a term developed around the larger organisations in relation to entrepreneurial activities going on in there. Given the fast changing nature of world markets today, many large organisations are realising that they need to be more innovative and flexible than perhaps they had been in the past and as such, need to adopt a radical innovation agenda if they are to compete and perform. This demands among others, that the existing senior management systems in large firms must create space for entrepreneurs to operate - letting go of some degree of control creating room for change. However, it is possible that many senior management may not feel comfortable with change and may create some hindrance in this respect, since this requires that they will need to give up or at least share a part of their core power. Nevertheless, large firms now face the challenge of re-inventing themselves and their industries, not just in times of crisis but continuously. One way of doing this is to integrate the strengths of the entrepreneurial small firm (creativity, flexibility, innovativeness, closeness to market etc.) with the market power and financial resources of the large organisations. This would create the basis for Intrapreneurship.

There is a perception that small firms are more entrepreneurial than larger firms and the entrepreneurship theory (Kirby 2003) suggests that if established large organisations are to re-invent themselves a number of factors have to be in place:

- ✓ Adopt traditional corporate entrepreneurship model.
- ✓ Develop intrapreneurial culture.
- ✓ Develop a system to identifying intrapreneurial talents.
- ✓ Reward intrapreneurs.
- ✓ Establish system for administering and evaluating projects
- ✓ Commit organisation resources.

There are numerous reasons why large organisations have lost their entrepreneurial drive and have difficulties regaining it (including the inherent nature of large organisations, he need for short run profits, lack of entrepreneurial talent, inappropriate compensation methods, etc). Despite these limitations, there are large firms who are now exhibiting more sustained entrepreneurial tendencies. Some have deliberately tried to remain entrepreneurial by encouraging managers to innovate rather than administer (e.g 3M.) or urging their employees to behave more like entrepreneurs, and encouraging teams and project management, and corporate entrepreneurial developments such as downsizing, delivering, delegating of power to Strategic Business Units (SBU).

Further reading

Kirby, D. (2003), Entrepreneurship, London: McGraw Hill.

Kuratko, D. and Hodgetts, R. (2001), Entrepreneurship: A contemporary Approach (5th Edition), New York: Dryden.

Morris, M. (2000), "Revisiting "who" is the Entrepreneur", Journal of Developmental Entrepreneurship, Vol.7, No. 1, pp2.10.

Ovian, B. and McDougall, P.(2005), "Defining international entrepreneurship and modelling the speed of internationalisation, Entrepreneurship Theory and Practice, Vol. 29, No. 5, pp.537 -53.

Parker, S. (2002), "On the dimensionality and composition of entrepreneurship", Durham Business School Working Paper.

Westhead, P. Ucbasaran, D. (2005), "Decisions, actions and performance; do novice, serial and portfolio entrepreneurs differ?" Journal of Business Management, Vol. 43, No. 4, pp.393- 417.

CHAPTER 2

WHO IS AN ENTREPRENEUR?

Aim

To introduce the entrepreneur, classifications and identifications.

Objectives

After studying this chapter you should be able to:

- Understand the various definitions of the entrepreneur.
- Trace back the origin of the term entrepreneur.
- Describe different classifications of the entrepreneur.
- Identify an entrepreneur by actions to wealth creation.
- Identify an entrepreneur by the personality.

2.1 Definitions

Just like entrepreneurship, it is also difficult to come up with a universally accepted definition of an entrepreneur.

This is not because definitions are not available, but because they are many and varied, coming from different perspectives of the writer and as such, literatures are well served with suggested definitions and they rarely agree.

According to Jones (2007), an entrepreneur is an individual who establishes and manages a business for the principal purpose of profit and growth. The entrepreneur is characterised principally by innovative behaviour and will employ strategic management practices in the business.

Harwood (1982) suggested that an entrepreneur is someone who takes initiative, assumes considerable autonomy in the organisation and management of resources, shares in the asset's risk, uncertain monetary profit, and innovates in more than a marginal way.

Meredith et al (1982) sees entrepreneurs as people who have the ability to see and evaluate business opportunities; to gather the necessary resources to take advantage of them, and to initiate appropriate action to ensure success.

Lessom (1986) argued that there is, in fact, no such thing as an entrepreneur – no single individual who displays in equal degree, the full range of entrepreneurial attributes. Rather, he contends there are different types of entrepreneurs, each with different personality type and set of attributes and behaviours, that involves making choices and coping with future uncertainties.

J B Say, a French economist distinguished between the profits of those who provided capital and profits of entrepreneur who use it. He defined an entrepreneur as "someone who consciously moves economic resources from an area of lower to an area of higher productivity and greater yield." In other words, the entrepreneur takes existing resources, such as people, materials, buildings, and money and redeploys them in such a way as to make them more productive and give them greater value. This definition implies changing what already exists; it sees entrepreneur as instrument of change (Stokes 2000).

Peter Drucker (1980) defined an entrepreneur as "someone who always searches for change, respond to it, and exploited it as an opportunity". He thus made innovation a necessary part of entrepreneurship.

For Schumpeter (1939), an entrepreneur's role is to disturb the status quo (the general equilibrium) through innovation. Innovation may take various forms:

- ✓ The creation of new product.
- ✓ Alteration to the quality of existing product.
- ✓ Development of new process of production
- ✓ Opening up new market.
- ✓ Capturing a new source of supply.
- ✓ Developing a new organisation or industry, etc.

Some of the criteria used to define an entrepreneur may appear contradictory. They include:

- ✓ Risk taking.
- ✓ Founder of a new business.
- ✓ Maximise of investors' returns.
- ✓ Innovation.

The notion of risk is one that is often associated with the entrepreneur. But this fails to distinguish between entrepreneurs who take risks to progress new ventures and the investors who accept financial risks in backing those ventures.

Finding a new business has also been used to identify characteristics of an entrepreneur. However, many well known entrepreneurs have revitalised an existing organisation rather than building a new one from the scratch.

Some definitions emphasised the importance of entrepreneurs in providing economic efficiency that maximises investors' returns. It is important to note, that maximising investment is important objective, but it is not the only objective that entrepreneur pursue. Effective entrepreneurs work to reward all stakeholders in their ventures not just investors.

Innovation has also been suggested as a critical characteristic of an entrepreneur. However, innovation is an important factor in the success of all business venture, not just the entrepreneur's.

To be able to understand fully who an entrepreneur is, it is important to trace the origin of the subject matter. Its origin lies in seventeenth- century France, where an entrepreneur was an individual commissioned to undertake a particular commercial project by someone with money to invest.

The earliest use of the term "entrepreneur" reflected the sense of middleman who directed resources provided by others. In the middle ages, the word "entrepreneur" was used to identify someone who managed large projects on behalf of a land owner or the church such as building of a castle or cathedral.

In the 17th century the concept was extended to include some elements of risk and profit. Entrepreneurs were those who contracted with the state to perform certain duties, such as the collection of revenues or operation of banking and trading services. As the price was fixed, the entrepreneur could profit or lose from their performance of the contract.

In its earliest stages entrepreneurial activities usually meant an overseas trading project or large project on behalf of a land owner or the church- such as building of a castle or cathedral. Such projects were risky, both for the investor who could lose money, and for the entrepreneur who could lose a lot more. The inter-winning of the notions of entrepreneur, investor and risk is evident from the start.

Richard Cantillon introduced the word "entrepreneur" into economic literature in 1734 when he described three types of agents in the economy (Stokes 2000):

1. The land owner - who as the proprietor of land provided the primary resources,
2. Entrepreneurs - including farmers and merchants who organises resources and accepted risk by buying at certain price and selling at an uncertain price.
3. Hirelings - who rented their services.

Generally speaking, entrepreneurs take initiative, assume autonomy and innovate, and in the process they inevitably take risk. Doing anything that is new or different involves uncertainty or risk. Entrepreneurs also have the ability to see and assess opportunities and importantly, initiate the appropriate actions to ensure success. Indeed, it is probably this last factor that distinguishes them from the inventor.

The concept of risk was advanced through the work of Knight (1981) He distinguished between risk and uncertainty, and argued that in situation of risk it was possible to estimate the likely probability of an event, whereas in cases of uncertainty this was not possible. This theory of uncertainty helps establish the boundary between the manager and the entrepreneur - a manager becomes an entrepreneur when the exercise of his or her judgement is liable to error and he or she assumes the responsibility for its correctness – taking risk in period of uncertainty. Entrepreneurs possess the ability to direct others in conditions of uncertainty which require knowledge and judgement, foresight, superior management ability and confidence.

Entrepreneurs take initiative, assume autonomy and innovate. In the process they inevitably take risks, doing anything that is new or different involves uncertainty or risk. (Ike 2017). However, they also have the ability to see and assess opportunities and importantly, initiate the appropriate actions to ensure success. They make things happen.

2.2 Classifying Entrepreneurs

- **Introduction**

Classification of entrepreneurs into different types provides a starting point for gaining an insight into how different types of entrepreneurial ventures work and the disparate factors underlying their success.

Classification often complements definition. It can sort items so that defining characteristics become evident. Definition then enables allocation of particular items to specific categories.

However, classification can often be undertaken even if there is no clear definition available. This is so with the concept of the entrepreneur.

There are two main approaches- either to classify entrepreneurs themselves or to classify their ventures.

- **Classification according to those planning to start- up an initial venture**

Entrepreneurs can be classified based on those planning to start-up a new venture.

These types of entrepreneurs are usually identified as NASCENT ENTREPRENEURS:

- ✓ They are people engaged in creating new ventures.
- ✓ They are not classified as "real" entrepreneurs.

From the dictionary "nascent" has been defined as an adjective meaning "emerging", coming to "existence", starting to grow, or beginning to exist. If you connect this to entrepreneurship, it will mean that nascent entrepreneurship is an activity of uprising business.

Nascent entrepreneurs are individuals who are taking steps to find a new business but who have yet not succeeded in making a transition to new business ownership. Those who are self employed are more represented in nascent entrepreneurship.

- **Classification according to those running a single business**

Entrepreneurs can also be classified based on those running a single venture or business.

These types of entrepreneurs are called SINGULAR ENTREPRENEURS.

They include:

- ➤ NOVICE ENTREPRENEURS - Singular entrepreneur at the early stage of venture development when they are actively learning.
- ➤ OPPORTUNIST ENTREPRENEURS - who were interested in maximising their returns, (and sometimes called GROWTH ORIENTED ENTREPRENEURS, who pursued opportunities to maximise the potentials of their venture from short term deals).
- ➤ CRAFTSMEN - who attempts to make a living by privately selling their trade or products they produced to earn a stable living from their specialist skills (called INDEPENDENT ORIENTED ENTREPRENEURS), whose main ambition was to work for themselves, many preferred stability to growth, and willing to limit the scope of their ventures.

Craftsmen include:

- ✓ INCOME ORIENTED CRAFTMEN - those craftsmen whose main aim is to secure a steady income.
- ✓ EXPANSION ORIENTATED CRAFTMEN - those craftsmen who take the risk of expansion and face the challenge of changing their role from being craft operators to managers of craft operators.

The term CRAFT refers to not just to artisan but to any entrepreneur who uses a particular knowledge or skill in addition to general management skill that can deliver market value. So it will include independent management consultants, producers of arts and crafts, etc.

A further distinction could be made between craftsmen entrepreneurs whose expertise is based on traditional skills, and those whose expertise is scientific or technological or professional in nature.

- **Classification based on the individual entrepreneur and the venture.**

The American entrepreneurship academic Fredrick Webster presented classification schemes for both individual entrepreneur and their ventures. Four types of individual entrepreneurs are recognised within his scheme.

1. The Cantillon entrepreneur - named after 18th century French economist Richard Cantillon. This type of entrepreneur brings people, money and materials together to create an entirely new organisation. This is the classic type of entrepreneur who identifies opportunity and innovates to take it.
2. The industry maker - who goes beyond merely creating a new firm, but with innovation a whole industry, is created on its back (e.g Henry Ford).
3. The administrative entrepreneur – who is a manager who operates within an established firm but does so in an entrepreneurial fashion, usually occupying CEO position role called upon to be innovative during change.
4. The small business owner – who is an entrepreneur that takes responsibility for owning and running their own venture.

- **Classification based on venture's success and investors**

Webster (2006) further classifies entrepreneurial ventures by the ratio of the amount that is expected to be received as a result of the venture's success (the perceived payoff), and the number of investors involved (the principals).

Three types of venture are identified:

1. Large payoff: many participants - a major venture with the risk spread widely over a large number of investors.
2. Small payoff: few participants - a limited venture with the risk taken by a few key investors only.
3. Large payoff: few participants - I a major venture with the task taken on by a few key investors.

- **Classification based on innovation and risk taking**

Landau (1982) argued that characteristics of innovation and risk taking can provide basis for classifying entrepreneurs. He suggested that both factors are independent of each other and may be defined as high/low which gives a matrix that helps identify the following types of entrepreneurs:

- ✓ The gambler – (high risk bearing/ low innovativeness), is the entrepreneur (his/her venture) characterised by a low degree of innovation and high level of risk. The gambler arises from the fact that without a significant innovation, the entrepreneur is taking a big chance in being better able to deliver value than existing players in the field.
- ✓ The consolidator - (low risk bearing/low innovativeness), is the entrepreneur who develops a venture based on low levels of both innovation and risk. The risk and innovativeness is low because the venture delivers on the basis of a marginal improvement on what existing players are doing. As risks are low, so too must be expected return.
- ✓ The dreamer (low risk bearing/high innovativeness), is the entrepreneur who attempts to combine a high level of innovativeness with low risk. This is an ideal position that all entrepreneurs would like to operate but practically very difficult, since innovation by its nature, is normally associated with risk of the unknown.
- ✓ The true entrepreneur (high risk bearing/high innovativeness) – is where true entrepreneurs operate. They or their investors must tale risk to succeed and outperform in the

market place, but by understanding their innovation and why it appeals to the market, they minimise and manage the risks.

- **Classification based on technology and commercial viability**

Jones Evans (1995) offered technology based categorisation of entrepreneurs in relation to their technical and commercial experience prior to making the move to entrepreneurship:

- The "research" technical entrepreneur – those whose incubation has been in a research environment, they include pure research entrepreneurs (based in academic research environment with no significant commercial experience), and research-producer entrepreneurs (who while working in an academic or industrial research environment have had exposure to commercial decision making).
- The "producer" technical entrepreneur – those whose incubation has included an exposure to decision making in a commercial setting along with experience in technological development.
- The "user" technical entrepreneur – an individual whose main experience has been commercially based but has involved contact with, and the development of knowledge about, a technical development. This may be because they have been employed in its marketing or sales, or in procuring that technology for a business.
- The "opportunist" technical entrepreneur – is one who has no previous experience to technology but has seen a commercial opportunity in relation to it, and has pursued that with a new venture. Opportunist technical entrepreneurs may call upon a general technical knowledge base, and are keen to develop an understanding of the new technology and what it offers.

This technological approach to classifying entrepreneurs is useful for the following reasons:

✓ It indicates the type of support the entrepreneur will need in order to drive the venture forward as a successful venture.

The research and producer technical entrepreneur while in command of the technical aspects of what they are doing may need support with the commercial management of their ventures. User technical entrepreneur and the opportunist technical entrepreneur may call upon dedicated technical experts to underpin their commercial moves.

✓ It enables investors to judge the managerial balance of the ventures to which they are called upon to commit themselves.

An investor seeks not only good ideas but also one that has a clear market potential and is backed by managerial team that can not only invent but also deliver that invention to the customer profitably.

- **Classification based on employment, managerial, financial, technical, and strategic intents.**

Wai-Sum Sin (1996) examined types of new entrepreneur in China and basing his assessment on employment, managerial, financial, technical and strategic criteria identified five entrepreneurs:

1. The senior citizen – this type of entrepreneurs undertake a venture to keep occupied during his/her retirement. The business is small based on personal experience, privately funded with no long term strategic ambition.
2. Workaholics – this type of entrepreneurs include the retired, but who show ambition than senior citizens. They often possess administrative experience, with bigger business, and drawing on wider range of technical skills, and employees may be invited to make a personal investment in the future of the venture.
3. Swingers – these are younger entrepreneurs who aim to make a living from making deals. They are associated with limited industrial and technical experience, rely on networks of personal contacts, and their ventures are moderately large.

However, they tend not to have long term strategic goals. Their main aim is to maximise short term profits. They usually source fund from retained earnings, family contributions and personal loans.
4. Idealists —these are also younger entrepreneurs who run moderate sized ventures. They motivated to make short term profit, sense of achievement and independence that running their own venture gives them. They serve a variety of end markets and their ventures may be based on high technology products. They usually source funds through retained profits, family contributions and private investment.
5. High —flyers —this type of entrepreneurs are motivated in much the same way as idealists. The noticeable difference is that their ventures are much larger, reflecting success in the marketplace.

- **Serial (or habitual) entrepreneurs**

Serial (or habitual) entrepreneurs are those who, having led one business to success, move on to start another. They are usually driven by desire for autonomy, prestige and sense of achievement as much as the desire to make money.

Serial (or habitual) entrepreneurs may be subdivided into:

➢ Sequential entrepreneurs

These are entrepreneurs who start new businesses in sequence, only running one at any time.

➢ Portfolio entrepreneurs

Portfolio entrepreneurs are those who run several businesses simultaneously. Richard Branson has been identified as a type of this entrepreneur as he has diversified his business Virgin group into a number of different areas or portfolios.

Wright (2005) suggested that serial (or habitual) entrepreneurs might be classified in the following ways:

- Defensive serial entrepreneurs – are those who undertake subsequent ventures because of a forced exit from an ealier one. It could be because the venture was sold or floated on stock market to pay off venture capital investment.
- Opportunist serial entrepreneurs – are those who undertake subsequent ventures because they see or perceive the opportunity for financial gain, perhaps on a short term entry/exit basis.
- Group -creating serial entrepreneurs – are those who undertake serial entrepreneurship because creating a number of businesses is fundamental to the strategy they are pursuing in terms of deal making. Deal making serial entrepreneurs use acquisition as a major part of gaining new business deals) or organic growth, while organic growth serial entrepreneurs start-up new businesses from scratch and grow them into serials.

2.3 Identifying Entrepreneurs By Actions To Wealth Creation

Entrepreneurs can be identified by their particular set of actions or activities, aimed at creation of wealth with their ventures. In this respect, the entrepreneur can be identified:

- **As a manager undertaking a particular activity - the entrepreneur's task**

We can identify entrepreneurs in terms of the particular actions they perform and the way they undertake them – actions as managers. These actions involve entrepreneurs as managers undertaking a particular activity - the entrepreneurial task, such as:

✓ Owning organisations - in terms of owning and managing a specific entrepreneurial venture.
✓ Founding new organisations – engaging in either finding a new organisation or attempting to rejuvenate an existing one.
✓ Providing general leadership - entrepreneurs normally engage in general business management usually with eyes on the entire organisation, not just some aspect of it.

- **As an agent of economic change**

We can also identify an entrepreneur as an agent of economic change. This is due to change effects that the actions of the entrepreneur can bring to a nation's economic systems – creating new value.

As agents of change entrepreneurs do not leave the world in the same state as they found it. They play critical role in maintaining and developing the economic order we live under, and are significant because they have an important effect on the world economy.

Generally, entrepreneurs are known to be drivers of change in a society and economy which they accomplish through:

✓ Combining factors of production.
✓ Providing market efficiency.

- ✓ Accepting risk.
- ✓ Maximising investors' returns.
- ✓ Processing of market information.

By bringing people, money, ideas and resources together, accepting risk, providing market efficiency and maximising investors returns, entrepreneurs build new organisations and change existing ones. They are different from traditional managers, whose main interest is in maintaining the status quo by established organisation, protecting it and maintaining its market positions - an essential ingredient in the effective running of a wide variety of organisation, but it is not about driving change.

- **As an opportunist**

We can also identify entrepreneurs by their opportunist nature.

The description of entrepreneurs as "opportunists", involve their focus on taking advantage of opportunities when and where possible.

Entrepreneurs are noted to be attuned to opportunity, as they constantly seek the possibility of doing something differently and better to take advantage of opportunities. They innovate in order to create new values an d are more interested in pursuing opportunity than they are in conserving resources.

Entrepreneurs expose resources to risk but they also make them work, by stretching them to their limit, in order to offer a good return. This makes them distinct from managers in established businesses who all too often can find themselves more responsible for protecting scarce resources than for using them to pursue the opportunities that are presented to their organisation.

- **As individual with entrepreneurial personality**

It is also possible to identify an entrepreneur by his/her entrepreneurial personality.

Although there is no uniform standardised definition of "the entrepreneur" and there is no one stereotypical model as already indicated earlier, however, it is frequently contended that entrepreneurs display certain similar characteristics and pattern of behaviour (traits) that gives them a personality.

Despite the existence of the problem of no general agreement over how many there are, or what form they take, researchers have identified traits associated with entrepreneurial attributes they consider help to make up entrepreneurial personality (Hornaday 1982, Gibb 1990, Timmons et al, 1985). They include:

- Total commitment, determination and perseverance.
- Drive to achieve and grow.
- Orientation to goals and opportunities.
- Taking initiative and personal responsibility.
- Persistent in problem solving.
- Veridical awareness and a sense of humour.
- Seeking and using feedback.
- Internal locus of control.
- Tolerance of ambiguity, stress and uncertainty.
- Calculated risk taking and risk sharing.
- Low need for status and power.
- Integrity and reliability.
- Decisiveness, urgency, and patience.
- Team builder and hero maker.
- High energy, health and emotional stability.
- Creativity and innovativeness and opportunism.
- High intelligence and conceptual ability.
- Vision and capacity to inspire.
- Need for achievement.
- Desire for autonomy.
- Intuition.

These attributes and corresponding behaviours vary according to the situation in which the entrepreneur is founded, and can be learned or acquired. This suggests that entrepreneurs can be developed. In addition to above, a number of other writers (Wickham 2006, Carter 2006, Kirby 2008) have identified some noticeable characteristics of Successful entrepreneurs that include:

- ✓ Hard work.
- ✓ Self starting.
- ✓ Setting personal goals.
- ✓ Resilience.
- ✓ Confidence.
- ✓ Assertiveness.
- ✓ Responsiveness to new ideas.
- ✓ Information seeking.
- ✓ Eager to learn.
- ✓ Attuned to opportunity.
- ✓ Commitment to others.
- ✓ Comfort with power.

The claim that entrepreneurs have special or distinctive personality is something that can also be examined empirically and demonstrated to be right or wrong by using Wickham (2006) four methodological aspects:

1. Instrumentalisation of the concept of entrepreneurship - a methodological approach taken to defining, characterising, and measuring a variable that plays a part in some theoretical explanation of Entrepreneurial personality compared with that of non-entrepreneur. This method is useful because it is specific and quite easy to observe . . . However, it is very broad as it includes small business managers as well as entrepreneurs who start and develop large ventures.
2. Instrumenetalisation of personality – a methodological approach taken to identify entrepreneurial personality as something that can be determined independently of the individual's specific domain of entrepreneurial activity, otherwise there is the danger that the domain of activity predetermines personality allocations, once again making the theory self-fulfilling.
3. Ontology of personality.- concerned with the existence of many concepts of entrepreneurial personality that includes a realist view of personality (that claim that personality is something that individuals actually have and it is the responsibility of research programmes to describe it) a

positivist view of personality(that suggests only that which can be observed is real and that we should be suspicious of things we cannot observe), a personality might be regarded as a way of summarising consistencies and pattern of behaviour, but no more that a summary, not something directly observable.

Another important theory linking personality to entrepreneurship is its pragmatics. There are three positions to this.

1. Descriptive theory - based on independent observation of an individual's personality and their entrepreneurial inclination, behaviour and performance. It then describes correlation between the two. Descriptive theories require that personality be something observable and independent of entrepreneurial activity. They may be comfortable with a positivistic or instrumental ontology. Normative theories are not so dependent on observable counterparts of personality. A normative theory may claim personality to be something that cannot be revealed in a positivistic or even instrumental sense.
2. A normative theory - makes a claim that certain aspects of personality are necessary for effective entrepreneurial behaviour that can be based on empirical observation with a descriptive theory, but usually has an element of theoretical presumption that precedes empirical observation (for example, that entrepreneurs must be individuals who respond positively to change, whether or not this is actually observed). Normative theories direct descriptive theories in a particular direction, suggesting which factors are important and should be the basis of empirical study. Normative theories aspire to make predictions. Given a personality type, then success or otherwise of that type in an entrepreneurial career can be predicted to some degree. Personality testing of nascent entrepreneurs makes practical use of normative theories.
3. Prescriptive theories - suggest that if one wants to be a successful entrepreneur then one should have or adopt or develop a particular personality type. Prescriptive theories are usually based on the addicts of normative theories or findings of descriptive theories . . . Prescriptive theories suggest

pathways of development to entrepreneurs in that they suggest the personality characteristics entrepreneurs should acquire if they are to be successful. They are important in programmes for education of entrepreneurs. However, these theories differ in the way they instrumentalist the personality concept and the ontology they ascribe to personality.

Entrepreneurial Type

Entrepreneurship type	Personality type	Attributes
Innovator (Sir Terrence Conran)	Imagination	Originality, inspiration, love, transformation
New designer/enabler (Mary Quant)	Intuition	Evolution, development, symbiosis, connection
Leader (Sir John Harvey Jones)	Authority	Direction, responsibility, structure, control
New entrepreneur (Jack Dangoor)	Will	Achievement, opportunity, risk-taking, power
Animateur (Nelli Eichner)	Sociability	Informality, shared values community, culture
Adventure (Anita Roddick)	Energy	Movement, work, health, activity
Change agent (Steve Shirley)	Flexibility	Adaptability, curiosity, intelligence

Source: Lessem, 1986

Further reading

Cole, A. (1968), Entrepreneurship in Economic Theory, American Economic Review, Vol. 58, pp 64 -71.

Deakins, D. and Freel, M. (2003), Entrepreneurship and Small Firms (3rd Edition), London: McGraw Hill.

Drucker, P. (1985), Innovation and Entrepreneurship, London: Heinmann.

Kirby, D. (2003), Entrepreneurship, London: McGraw Hill.

Kuratko, D. and Hodgetts, R. (2001), Entrepreneurship: A contemporary Approach (5th Edition), New York: Dryden.

Morris, M. (2000), "Revisiting "who" is the Entrepreneur", Journal of Developmental Entrepreneurship, Vol.7, No. 1, pp2.10.

Ovian, B. and McDougall, P.(2005), "Defining international entrepreneurship and modelling the speed of internationalisation, Entrepreneurship Theory and Practice, Vol. 29, No. 5, pp.537 -53.

Westhead, P. Ucbasaran, D. (2005), "Decisions, actions and performance; do novice, serial and portfolio entrepreneurs differ?" Journal of Business Management, Vol. 43, No. 4, pp.393- 417.

CHAPTER 3

ENTREPRENURSHIP AND SMALL BUSINESS

Aim

To introduce entrepreneurship and relationship with small business.

Objectives

After studying this chapter you should be able to:

- Introduce small business and entrepreneurship.
- Describe small business and relationship with entrepreneurship.
- Distinguish between entrepreneurship and small business.
- Describe the entrepreneur and small business owner / manager.

3.1 Distinguishing Entrepreneurship and Small Business

Small businesses are always associated with entrepreneurship since small business triumph and entrepreneurship are closely related.

Although entrepreneurship is what makes small business successful, it is important to recognise that some distinctions exist between the two. This is best identified by making a distinction between entrepreneurial ventures and small businesses.

Distinguishing Entrepreneurship and Small Business requires drawing distinctions between them. Rather than trying to draw a distinction between the characteristics of entrepreneurs and small business managers, it is more valuable to differentiate what they manage, that is to differentiate between the small business and the entrepreneurial venture - that will give a clear picture of the differences.

Essential characteristics which distinguish the entrepreneurial venture and the small business are:

- Innovation.
- Potential for growth.
- Strategic objectives.

- Innovation

The successful entrepreneurial venture is usually based on a significant innovation that involves doing something new.

As explained earlier, not all small business owner/managers are entrepreneurs as most do not innovate or seek change in a continuous or purposeful way. Many small firms lack creative spirit. The majority of small business start-ups are based on established industries as majority struck to the same industry, and only few have products or techniques as many play safe staying with existing business or industry.

Once established, small firms can also lack innovative entrepreneurship. Small business owners/managers are invariably close to day to day problems of their business as it grows – often too close to see opportunities or the need to for change. They are usually involved in delivering an established product or services. This does not mean that the small business is not doing something new. However, a small business output is likely to be established and produced in an established way.

So while a small business may be new to a locality, it is not doing anything new in a global sense, whereas an entrepreneur is usually based on significantly new way of doing something. Nevertheless, it is important to recognise here that there are small business entrepreneurs who seek to exploit new ideas through continuous activities. But these are the exceptional as many small businesses are founded on existing ideas and practices.

- Potential growth

An entrepreneurial venture is likely to have more potential for growth than does a small business. This results from the fact that the entrepreneurial venture is usually based on a significant innovation. The market potential for that innovation will be more than enough to support a small firm.

The small business on the other hand operates within an established industry and is unique only in terms of its locality. Many small firms lack relative spirit needed to innovate. Majority of small business start-ups are based on established industries . . . Once established small firms can also lack innovation to grow as small business owner/managers are often too occupied by their day- to- day business activities in their firms to see opportunities or need to grow.

- Strategic objectives

Strategic objectives serve notice that management not only intends to deliver good financial performance but also to improve the organisation's competitive strength and long range business prospects. Most businesses have objectives. Objectives are common feature of managerial life in all businesses including entrepreneurial venture and small businesses although they may take a variety of forms.

Strategic objectives are those that concern a company's competitiveness and long term business position in its markets, and which achievement is essential to sustaining and improving the company's long term market position and competitiveness.

The entrepreneurial venture will usually go beyond the small business in the objectives it sets itself in that it will have strategic objectives – that relate to such things as growth targets, market development, market share, etc). However, it is important to recognise that not all entrepreneurial ventures will necessarily show an obvious innovation, clear growth potential or formally articulated strategic objectives and some small businesses may demonstrate these.

3.2 The Entrepreneur and the Small Business Owner / Manager

The term "entrepreneur "and "owner/manager" is often used to describe someone who is engaged in the management of small business. It is also used to describe those involved in running a small business. It encapsulates a condition which is typical of many small firms- the predominant role of the owner-manager.

The majority of small businesses are small as the name indicates, and owners of these firms are predominantly the managers as well, and likely to be the only manager. The owner-manager describes the reality for large number of small firms which are totally reliant and dominated by their owner. Although less confusing than entrepreneur to describe small business managers, owner- manager is also limiting term which implies a uniformity of management which does not exist in practice.

The diversity of types of owner-managers and entrepreneurs has led to many attempts to classify them. To reflect the differing backgrounds, and aspirations of these types, early studies by industrial sociologists simply split them into:

- Craftsmen – small business owners who make a living by privately selling their trade or products they produced to earn a stable living from their specialist skills (income oriented or expansion oriented).
- Opportunists - the archetypal (wheeler- dealer) who does deals, often by starting, growing and selling a small business in the pursuit of personal wealth.
- Professional owner/manager – the small business owner who adopts a more structured approach to building a small business.

This basic typology has been extended by other writers to lengths which indicate the great diversity of small business managers.

Further reading

Deacons, D. and Freely, M. (2003), Entrepreneurship and Small Firms (3rd Edition), London: McGraw Hill.

Drucker, P. (1985), Innovation and Entreprenurship, London:: Heinmann.

Kirby, D. (2003), Entrepreneurship, London: McGraw Hill.

Kuratko, D. and Hodgetts, R. (2001), Entrepreneurship: A contemporary Approach (5th Edition), New York: Dryden.

Morris, M. (2000), "Revisiting "who" is the Entrepreneur", Journal of Developmental Entrepreneurship, Vol.7, No. 1, pp2.10.

Ovian, B. And McDougall, P.(2005), "Defining international entrepreneurship and modelling the speed of internationalisation, Entrepreneurship Theory and Practice, Vol. 29, No. 5, pp.537 -53.

Westhead, P. Ucbasaran, D. (2005), "Decisions, actions and performance; do novice, serial and portfolio entrepreneurs differ?" Journal of Business Management, Vol. 43, No. 4, pp.393- 417.

CHAPTER 4

INNOVATION AS KEY ENTREPRENEURIAL ACTIVITY

Aim

To introduce innovation and significance to entrepreneurship.

Objectives

After studying this chapter you should be able to:

- Understand the meaning of innovation and its significance to entrepreneurship.
- Describe the relationship between innovation and creativity.
- Explain the need for enhancing personal creativity to achieve innovation.
- Explain the need for enhancing organisational creativity to achieve innovation.
- Understand how to create a corporate capacity for innovation.
- Outline some of the barriers to innovation.

4.1 Introduction

Innovation is a crucial part of the entrepreneurial process. It is the specific tool for entrepreneurs, the means by which they exploit change as an opportunity for different businesses or services.

Some difficulties surround the concept of innovation as the term "innovation" is not easy to define.

The Oxford Dictionary defines innovation as "making changes". However, some equates innovation only with invention, development of new products or technology, originality, a one - off inspiration. Innovation is linked to all these but practically, is more.

Innovation is strongly linked to invention, but although they overlap they are not the same. An invention is essentially a creative idea, but innovation takes that idea and puts it to work. Innovation actively encourages the development of new ideas and also turns them into useful products or services which customers need.

In a business sense, innovation can mean more than just developing a new product or new technology. It encompasses any new way of doing something so that value is created. Innovation does not stop at products/services, it embraces other new developments:-new markets, new marketing methods, new method of operating . . . This can also include:

- A new way of delivering an existing product or service.
- A new way of informing the customer about a product and promoting it to them.
- A new way of organising labour and capital in order to produce the product or service.
- A new approach to managing relationship with consumers and other organisation, etc.

Innovation is not always original. This is so because innovation does not take place in a vacuum – new ideas always have root on the old. They start with what already exist and become original from the unique way in which they combine or connect these existing ideas and knowledge. Creative thinking starts by trying to make connection between concepts that already exists but are too far apart for others to see. It has been said that the secret of the entrepreneur success is to use other peoples' brain.

Innovation is not always one -off inspiration – it is not a fib but a trend. Innovation does not rely on sudden flash of inspiration to give the blue print from new development. Innovation is a gradual process - which builds into something new and worthwhile over a period of time through a variety of stages.

According to Stocks (2003) some sources of innovation opportunity may include:

- The unexpected – unexpected success or failure often gives clues to underlying trends which can lead to innovation.
- The incongruous – described as a discrepancy between what is and what everyone expects. It is an important source of innovation because incongruity is a further sign that changes are taking place.
- Process need – the importance of need as a source of innovation is captured in the proverb "Necessity is the mother of invention".
- Industry and market structure – whole industry and market structure can change rapidly, sometimes after a long period of stability. Such changes offer exceptional opportunities to innovation and considerable threats to those who incorrectly read the changes.
- Demographic – such changes in the environment of an enterprise inevitably contain many possibilities for innovation – population births, deaths, diseases, age structure, employment, income, education etc, and the trends which these figures show . . .
- Changes in perception – this can leaded to innovation. For example, the fashion industry relies heavily on changes in perception.
- New technology – the most common innovation are often based on technology – new knowledge or invention.

Peter Ducker (2003) suggested that we can develop our innovation skills. He regards entrepreneurship and innovation as tasks that can be, and should be organised in a purposeful systematic way, as part of any manager's job. He presents entrepreneurs not as people who are born with certain character traits, but as managers who know where to look for innovation and how to develop it into useful products or services once they have found it. Entrepreneurship can thus be developed and learned and its core activity is innovation and a continuous purposeful search for new ideas, and their practical application.

Entrepreneurship can thus be developed and learned and its core activity is innovation and a continuous purposeful search for new ideas, and their practical application.

Innovation and entrepreneurship are engines of growth. Entrepreneurial innovation in production and business processes can lead to an increase in the productivity of labour and capital which further boost economic growth rates.

4.2 Innovation and Creativity

When relating innovation to creativity it is possible to see creativity as the ability to think new things, and innovation as the ability to do new things. These are two distinguishing features of the entrepreneur.

In today's fiercely competitive fast paced global economy, creativity and innovation are important both for start- up of new ventures, survival and for building competitive advantage.

Kirton (1976) has suggested that innovation takes two forms, involving different approaches to problem solving:

1. The highly creative solution- whereby someone comes up with completely new idea.
2. The adapted solution – whereby someone modifies an existing solution.

Creativity can be increased by adopting a systematic approach – the creativity process. This involves seven steps:\

1. Preparation – getting the mind ready for creative thinking that involves some formal training which provides the foundation for creativity and innovation.
2. Investigation – studying the problem and understanding its components.
3. Transformation – identifying similarities and differences in information collected.
4. Incubation – the subconscious need s time to reflect on the information collected.
5. Illumination – occurs usually spontaneously at some time during the incubation stage when all the previous stages come together.
6. Verification – may include experiments, building prototypes, etc.
7. Implementation – transforming the idea to reality.

Some barriers to creativity may include:

- ✓ Searching for the one right answer.
- ✓ Focusing on being logical.
- ✓ Blindly following the ruler.
- ✓ Constantly being practical.
- ✓ Viewing play as frivolous.
- ✓ Becoming overspecialised.
- ✓ Avoiding ambiguity.
- ✓ Fearing you will look foolish.
- ✓ Fearing mistakes and failure.
- ✓ Believing that you are not creative.

4.3 Enhancing Personal Creativity

Every individual is creative to some degree, although some are clearly more creative than others. Successful entrepreneurs are creative usually individuals or are associated with creative individuals or environment.

Enhancing personal creativity is crucial to innovativeness.

In order to get new ideas and become more creative, it is important to:

- ✓ Read widely.
- ✓ Join and attend professional groups and associations.
- ✓ Travel widely.
- ✓ Talk to anyone and everyone
- ✓ Scan newspaper, magazines and journals
- ✓ Develop a reference library/file.
- ✓ Spend time following natural curiosities.

Chell (2000) suggests that creative performance increase with intelligence. In contrast there are writers who argue that the creativity individuals' display would seem to have little to do with intelligence and appears to depend on the extent to which the right brain is developed or engaged. Nevertheless, it is an important part of creativity not just to be open to new ideas but to seek them actively.

Formal and structured ways of developing creativity may include:

- ✓ Brainstorming.
- ✓ Forced associations – list all areas where a person has particular interest against particular skills or competences to generate business proposals.
- ✓ Role play – innate a superhero and try to get inside the person and determine how he or she might approach a problem.
- ✓ Multiple uses – viewing things and people in terms of how they can satisfy their needs.
- ✓ Using metaphors and analogies- to develop ideas and creative thinking.

4.4 Enhancing Organisational Creativity

Creativity does not just happen in organisations– it has to be encouraged.

Organisations need to create entrepreneurial environment in which their own creativity can flourish as well as that of their employees. This can be done by:

- ✓ Expecting creativity by permitting employees to be creative.
- ✓ Expecting and tolerating failures.
- ✓ Encouraging curiosity – asking what if questions and taking a maybe we could attitude.
- ✓ Viewing problems as challenges and opportunities
- ✓ Providing creative training.
- ✓ Providing support.
- ✓ Rewarding support.
- ✓ Modelling creativity – setting an example by taking chances and challenging the status quo.

4.5 Creating Corporate Capacity for Innovation

While it might be possible to stimulate innovation through enhancing the external support structures, essentially the key is encouraging firms to develop their internal corporate capacity for innovation.

According to Peters (1987), this is encouraged by four strategic and principal management tactics as described below:

Key strategies:

- Using multifunctional teams for developing activities.
- Encouraging pilots- replace written proposals with pilots.
- Practicing creative swiping team to copy from the best with unique adaptation/enhancement as far as possible.
- Making word of mouth marketing – purchasers buy new products based principally upon the perceptions of respected peers who have already purchased or tried them.

Principal management tactics:

- Supporting committed champions – cherish those with a passionate enough attachment to a new idea.
- Modelling innovation (practice purposeful impatience – managers must demand innovation and personally symbolise innovativeness in their daily life.
- Supporting fast failures – in order to reduce the innovation cycle time, it is necessary to make more mistakes, and faster.
- Measuring innovation – since what gets measured gets done.

Corporate capacity for innovation can also be enhanced by:

1. Institutionalisation of change in organisations.
2. Reducing barriers to change in organisations.
3. Reducing barriers to Innovation.

1. Institutionalisation of change in organisations

Corporate capacity for innovation can also be enhanced by institutionalisation of change in organisations.

As already explained, innovation is about change. Change is constant and inevitable for any organisation to survive and prosper in today's fast changing business environment. It is now very essential that organisations should understand that they should not only accept change as part of the business essentials, but to initiate it, thereby institutionalising change in the organisation.

It is possible for an organisation to institutionalise change. This can be achieved by creating a culture where change is institutionalised within the organisation – the leaning organisation.

Organisational learning requires that when learning is acquired it is disseminated throughout the organisation. As a result there has emerged in recent years the notion of the learning organisation. The Japanese have done it through the concept of "Kaizen" – the notion of continuous improvement, and organisational learning and knowledge management are first cousins of continuous improvement.

2. Reducing barriers to change in organisations

Corporate capacity for innovation can also be enhanced by reducing barriers to change in organisations. According to Connor (1995, people resist change for the following reasons:

- ✓ Lack of trust.
- ✓ Belief that change is unnecessary.
- ✓ Belief that change is not feasible.
- ✓ Economic threats.
- ✓ Relative high costs.
- ✓ Fear of personal failure.
- ✓ Lack of status or power.
- ✓ Threats to values and ideas.
- ✓ Resentment of interference.

One of the major barrier to learning is the somewhat simplistic mental models that people hold in organisations and it is necessary to help them understand and change their assumption about how things work, help them increase their ability to learn, and solve problems and are not powerless, and can both individually and collectively change the organisation. Linked to this is the is the need to encourage people to adopt the principles and practices of system thinking – that acknowledges that problems may have multiple causes and solutions, and actions may have multiple outcomes including unanticipated side effects. The two concepts of learning organisation and continuous improvement are about getting better and not about being different. However, critics maintain that it is not knowledge that will create wealth but insight into opportunities for discontinuous innovation. It is radical linear innovation that is needed, and this can only be achieved if companies escape the shackles of precedent and imagine entirely novel solutions to customer needs.

3. Reducing barriers to Innovation

Barriers and concern for innovation are directly influenced by shortages of capital. The reasons for these are:

- ✓ Banks are not prepared to lend seed capital.
- ✓ Banks faced increased problems in risk assessment owing to increased uncertainty with respect to technology or high technology.
- ✓ Entrepreneurs may not be able to protect their investments through patents.
- ✓ Banks do not place any value on R&D in their balance sheet.

Special support have come in the form of parks and incubator centres varying with respect to sponsorship type, funding source, services provided, facilities tenant, composition and management schemes. It is based on the principle of sharing of resources and know how including typing, copying, computer, telephone, occupant space at reduced rates, building maintenance, conference/meeting rooms, reception facilities, furnishings etc, networking. As a resource provider intended to facilitate innovation the incubator offers specific input to support the growing firm that is resource – constrained and help with cash flow/property costs, suitable prestige premises and advice, brokers partnerships and alliance that are essential to firms by encouraging inter-tenant contact, acting as a gateway to other services. It is generally held that entrepreneurs are at a disadvantage, when compared with large firms in the innovation process. The cost of innovation could only be undertaken with the resources at the disposal of large firms. Economies of scale were believed to exist in research and development which meant that large firms could develop new products cheaply than small firms. Despite this it is believed that small firms are more efficient in the technological and innovatory process than large firms.

Further reading

Bacharach, S. and Lawler, E. (1980), Power and Politics in organisations, San Francisco, CA: Jossey Bass.

Baumol, W. (1968), The Entrepreneur: Introductory Remarks, American Economic Review, Vol. 38, pp 60 -3.

Cole, A. (1968), Entrepreneurship in Economic Theory, American Economic Review, Vol. 58, pp 64 -71.

Deakins, D. and Freel, M. (2003), Entrepreneurship and Small Firms (3rd Edition), London: McGraw Hill.

Drucker, P. (1985), Innovation and Entrepreneurship, London: Heinmann.

Kirby, D. (2003), Entrepreneurship, London: McGraw Hill.

Kuratko, D. and Hodgetts, R. (2001), Entrepreneurship: A contemporary Approach (5th Edition), New York: Dryden.

Morris, M. (2000), "Revisiting "who" is the Entrepreneur", Journal of Developmental Entrepreneurship, Vol.7, No. 1, pp2.10.

Ovian, B. and McDougall, P.(2005), "Defining international entrepreneurship and modelling the speed of internationalisation, Entrepreneurship Theory and Practice, Vol. 29, No. 5, pp.537 -53.

Parker, S. (2002), "On the dimensionality and composition of entrepreneurship", Durham Business School Working Paper.

CHAPTER 5

SIGNIFICANT ROLES OF ENTREPRENEURS IN THE SOCIETY AND ECONOMY

Aim

To introduce significant roles entrepreneurs play in the society and the economy.

Objectives

After studying this chapter you should be able to:

- Describe roles of entrepreneurs.
- Understand the significant roles entrepreneurs play in a society and the economy.
- Explain why these roles have continued to increase in recognition.

5.1 Introduction

Entrepreneurs are found to have been, and still playing important roles in any society and economy. It is in recognition of these roles that many nations (developed and developing), have increase their interest in developing and promoting entrepreneurship in their various nations to take advantage of these roles entrepreneurs can play in their national cultural development.

These roles could be categorised as follows:

- ✓ Organising resources and creating value and wealth.
- ✓ Creating competition.
- ✓ Driving structural change.
- ✓ Advocating innovation and change.
- ✓ New venture creation.
- ✓ Job creation.

5.2 Organising Resources and Creating Value and Wealth

As pointed out in chapter 1, entrepreneurship is frequently equated with new venture creation and small business.

Value is created by the entrepreneur by combing the factors of production (land, labour capital) in such as way to satisfy human needs. The components do not combine by themselves. They have to be brought together by individuals – the entrepreneur who combines other factors of production to create wealth. In this respect entrepreneurs are regarded as a fourth factor which acts on other factors of production to combine them in productive ways, playing a vital role of:

- ✓ Finding new combination of economic factors to meet human needs (to innovate).
- ✓ Organising resources effectively and profitably (to create new organisations).
- ✓ Creating wealth by adding value (generating employment).

5.3 Creating Competition and Economic Stability

Entrepreneurs through small business promotion and establishments can help maintain a competitive atmosphere in an economy, and help reduce monopolistic tendencies of the larger organisation. The existence and functioning of a market economy is in many aspects is due to small business enterprises, as they are important sources of intermediate goods for other industries, enabling the provision of a wider range goods and services in the economy at competitive prices.

Small businesses can also help maintain competition in any economic situation, even in a recession, as these businesses can survive even beside the large scale businesses because of their flexibility and adaptability, and such attributes can contribute significantly to the stabilization of the economy even during periods of economic instability- like in recession.

5.4 Acting As Agent of Economic Change

As earlier described, entrepreneurs are agents of economic change- they effect change in the economic and social system of any nation.

They play critical role in maintaining and developing the economic order we live under.

Entrepreneurs also create new value as managers of change – they do not leave the world in the same state as they found it. They bring people, money, ideas and resources together to build new organisations and to change existing ones by combination of economic factors, accepting risks, and creating change in economic growth and development.

Entrepreneurs contribute to the growth of any economy by creating new businesses. Many developed countries like USA, Germany, Unrepresented examples of economies where entrepreneurship has been a contributory factor to economic growth and development.

According to research undertaking in the 1980s and 1990s, by such bodies as the U.S Department of Commerce and the National Science Foundation (Jones 1999), small entrepreneurial firms were responsible in the U.S.A. for half of all innovation post World War II and 95% of all radical innovation; twice as many innovations per R&D Dollar spent than large firms; 24 times as many innovation s per R&D Dollar than the "mega firms" with more than 10,000 employees.

5.5 Creating New Ventures

As earlier noted, entrepreneurs have been described as creative individuals who are keen to take ownership of their own destinies. Accordingly, many create and own new ventures.

Successful entrepreneurs are known to possess the entrepreneurial attributes that have enabled them to present new ventures in such a way as to attract the support of investors. New ventures are also created through share option schemes.

A point of caution is necessary here because while above mentioned attributes may have the effect of making some firms appear entrepreneurial, in reality, it may not make them entrepreneurs. This is because many people who establish a film or new venture are only forced to create new ventures as alternative to employment and not out of entrepreneurial attributes. This is particularly true in period of recession and countries with high employment and societies where discrimination on many grounds (egg race, gender, etc), are high.

5.6 Job Creation

Clearly the creation of new ventures creates employment opportunities for both entrepreneurs and others.

The work of Birch (1979) in America revealed that new and small firms were a source of new job generation.

With unemployment increasing around the world many individuals are developing high interest in entrepreneurship and its related self –employment - to take advantage of employment generating opportunities provided by starting a new ventures.

The job creation cut across various demographics such as gender, age, marital statutes, ethnic groups and educational levels.

- ✓ Gender - Entrepreneurship is attracting many females into traditionally males dominated self employed professions like mechanics, window cleaners, builders, etc.
- ✓ Age - self employed is increasing among across age, For example, middle age men and women turning to new venture start-ups, due to various reasons that include: redundancy, early retirement, and likely experience that can be used for the purpose.
- ✓ Marital status - self- employment is much likely for single people and for people in other categories (married, widowed, divorced or separated). For example, marital condition can provides the support or push necessary to establish a new venture as an alternative for survival, and spouses are often partners in such enterprises
- ✓ Ethnic origin - in most high level advanced countries, there has been a significant increase in self-employment among ethnic minorities over the past years. It is a result of discrimination in the society, forcing people from ethnic minorities to seek employment opportunities through self-employment
- ✓ Education level - small ventures are now providing the means of entry into business for young and older educated entrepreneurial talents.

5.7 Encouraging Women Entrepreneurship

The growing interest among many countries in enterprise creation aimed at women results from the interaction of three important forces.

First, an increasing number of development economists and policy makers are validating enterprise creation strategies as an integral part of local economic development plans.

Second, the role of woman in the labour force has dramatically expanded. Women now appear in every role and occupation including small businesses.

Finally, policy maker are recognizing that women particularly, face unique barrios to achieving their entrepreneurial potential.

To attract resources to venture creation programmes for women, it is important to demonstrate that new business creation is a key component of local economic development and that programmes which support self-employment and venture expansion can facilitate business creation.

Women are the primary wage-earners in many developed countries. Since the World War II, women in developed countries have increased their labour force participation. Many women have joined the labour force because of economic necessity. Others have sought to exercise their right to an equal role with men in the world economy.

As women presence in the world economy has increased, governmental and intergovernmental units have established advisory bodies on the status of women to employment opportunities. These have made positive contribution to the status of women, but they have not made equal employment a reality. Gaps between male and female pay, employment and occupational status, though shrinking, exist in many developed countries. These labour market realities, both positive and negative, play a role in explaining the interest which women exhibit in self-employment and their entrepreneurial potential.

The women business owners are increasingly visible in many developed countries. The rapid rise in the number of women-owned businesses since 1970 represents one of the most significant economic and social developments in the world.

New technologies, advances in communication, greater acceptance of working women have created opportunities for women to start their own businesses.

While the growth in the number of women-owned small scale industries in the developed countries is encouraging, the size of such businesses remains small in terms of number of employees.

The European commission study of 17000 women reported in 1987 that more than one half had no employees, one fourth employed salaried workers and 21 per cent employed family members.

Similarly, a report from Great Britain indicated 60 percent of women-owned businesses have employees, while only 5 percent have more than 10. Ireland and Germany also indicated that most women-owned ventures have between 1-10 employees. In the U S., Bureau of Census data indicates that in 1982 only 9.8 per cent of women-owned businesses had employees and of these 2.5 per cent more than five. Similarity, a national research study of 468 women businesses found that the majority of the respondents had between 1-10 employees, while 18 percent employed 20 or more full time employees.

The above data indicate the increasing significance of small businesses in improving entrepreneurial talent of women in developed countries.

For the developing countries (DCs), major contribution small businesses can make to the economic development in the DCs is the improvement of the role of women in the economy. They will give to women, who are often socially disadvantaged, an opportunity to wage employment in the small business sector.

Engaging in small scale activities also will provide women with outlets for self fulfillment and personal development. In addition, they provide them with a convenient source of income and flexibility in working hours especially for house wives.

By providing employment or remunerative economic activates including supplementing income earned from regular jobs, small businesses also can contribute to a reduction of income disparities between socio-economic classes. The impact in stemming social discomfort and tension between these groups is not easily quantifiable, but has been increasingly recognized.

Women can play a considered role especially the rural small businesses. According to rough estimates produced by research form UNDP/ILO/UNIDO (2000), small scale industry is a supplementary source of income for an average of over 50% of women engaged in agriculture. Food processing, garments and crafts (including the promotion of basic household items) are among the most common activities.

5.8 Mobilising Indigenous Entrepreneurship

Another argument in favour of entrepreneurship and small businesses is that they serve as "training grounds" for developing new skills of industrial workers and entrepreneurs.

A small businesses owner is usually described as an entrepreneur because small business triumph and entrepreneurship are closely related. Therefore, entrepreneurship is seen as a key concept associated with small business development and performance. More important is the training and experience which they acquire in the operation of their enterprise s or for working in any. Their role as "incubator" for future Giant Corporation is suited as launching pad for indigenous industrial breakthrough.

In all societies, the traditional industry or sector has preceded the modern ones. There is ample evidence that the latter has evolved through a progressive transformation and modernization of the former. Often critical engines of these changes have been the small businesses.

In a developing economy such as in the developing countries (DCs), there is therefore, the need for entrepreneurship activities which could take the lead and initiate the highly needed breakthrough in industrialization. Today's turbulent economic climate requires that every one think and act like an entrepreneur. This applies throughout the business world ranging from existing business owner to anyone starting a career.

5.9 Bringing Innovation to Market

Small business entrepreneurs are known to provide the major source of innovations. They are usually more innovative than their larger counterparts because for them, working on new ideas that relate to their profit is motivated in a more direct way.

The larger business in most cases concentrates on products that have a steady or predictable demand leaving to SSIs the slower seller and more risky (pioneer) items. In addition, the large fixed capital of the large scale industries does not allow them the flexibility required for innovation. In many cases, only when the SSIs have already developed a steady market, do large businesses get interested.

The advantage of innovation through small business promotion can be very useful to the DCs through the very much needed development in various areas of economy.

Innovation is seen as key concept of small business entrepreneurial activity. Innovation is widely recognised as crucial factor in successful small business activities and contributions to any economy including that of developing countries (DCs).

The small business today is seen as playing an important role in the innovation of new products and processes as they are often regarded as being more innovative than large ones.

This is based on the advantage of small size that allows flexibility and adaptability and willingness to try new approaches reflecting their opportunist behaviour. The point is reinforced by well published success stories of innovative entrepreneurs who were forced to start their own new business when their ideas were rejected by large established companies. For example, Hewlett Packed turned down Steve Womack's invention of a small portable computer, so he took his idea to his friend Steven Jobs and together they began making Apple computers in a garage. The lack of policy and rules in a small, informal structure can provide a more creative environment than a large hierarchical organisation.

Further reading

Kirby, D. (2003), Entrepreneurship, London: McGraw Hill.
Kuratko, D. and Hodgetts, R. (2001), Entrepreneurship: A contemporary Approach (5th Edition), New York: Dryden.
Morris, M. (2000), "Revisiting "who" is the Entrepreneur", Journal of Developmental Entrepreneurship, Vol.7, No. 1, pp2.10.
Ovian, B. And McDougall, P.(2005), "Defining international entrepreneurship and modelling the speed of internationalisation, Entrepreneurship Theory and Practice, Vol. 29, No. 5, pp.537 -53.
Parker, S. (2002), "On the dimensionality and composition of entrepreneurship", Durham Business School Working Paper.
Westhead, P. Ucbasaran, D. (2005), "Decisions, actions and performance; do novice, serial and portfolio entrepreneurs differ?" Journal of Business Management, Vol. 43, No. 4, pp.393- 417.

CHAPTER 6

BECOMING AN ENTREPRENEUR

Aim

To introduce and explain reasons why people become entrepreneurs.

Objectives

After studying this chapter you should be able to:

- Understand the principles behind the assumption that anyone can be entrepreneur.
- Outline forces that may lead to entrepreneurial option.
- Describe four primary types of individuals who become entrepreneurs.
- Outline characteristics of the successful entrepreneur.
- Describe some of the imitations to entrepreneurial option.

6.1 Anyone Can Be an Entrepreneur

Generally speaking, it is believed that anyone can be an entrepreneur.

Clearly, there are the natural entrepreneurs, and there are also some people who are more temperamentally suited for entrepreneurship than others, but this does not necessarily rule the others out.

The point here is that anyone with the desire, who is willing to learn, take educated risk, and work hard, has self belief, can be a successful entrepreneur. Many successful entrepreneurs had to learn and change their beliefs to become successful entrepreneurs.

The possibility of becoming a success entrepreneur is open to everyone. This opportunity many be taken up by individuals, such as those who are inventors, the unfulfilled managers, the displaced managers, the young professional, the excluded, etc.

For many, that first huge step towards entrepreneurship might require a change in belief. In fact, changing one's belief is the biggest hurdle for the first time entrepreneur.

Although the stereotype entrepreneur is often portrayed as someone who prefers their own wits to education, this is not necessarily the case. Entrepreneurship education is critical for the business owner.

Many experts, such as Peter Ducker have suggested that the end of the traditional job is at hand. In his book "Managing In A Time of Great Change" (1999), Peter Drucker predicts the near future, that the traditional job will be replaced by work teams, which will be subcontracted out from project to project. This is now happening before our eyes at the present time. This observation points out that the trend towards self employment is not a temporary phenomenon, but a fundamental shift in the nature of work.

Today's turbulent economic climate requires that everyone think like an entrepreneur. As we move forward in the century and our economy evolves from manufacturing age into the information age, the requirement for entrepreneurial thinking and expertise has not just but increased demanding a better approach to doing business by individuals and groups. A better approach is to become more entrepreneurial. By learning and thinking individuals and groups can be liberated from the inherent risk in depending on one organisation for livelihood and well being. This requires that people from all works of life should take a hard look at themselves (in terms of their experience, resources, education and interests and skills) and assess them against today's market place in search of a fit - to create enterprises and entrepreneurs.

6.2 Forces That May Lead to Entrepreneurial Option

According to Kilby (2003), Making and a choice between more conventional career option and entrepreneurial career generally will be sensitive to four factors:

1. Knowledge of entrepreneurial option – the individual must know that entrepreneurial option exist and they must be aware of its potential of the business opportunity.
2. The possibility - the individual must have the possibility of pursuing the option. There must be no legal restriction.
3. The risks they present- the individual must have detailed knowledge of a business opportunity and access to the resources necessary to initiate it.
4. Valence – the way we are attracted to different options. Different people are willing to play off different needs against one another in different ways. Some people play safe and give priority to economic needs, other prioritise.

All these will affect the way in which the potential entrepreneur is willing to play off different needs against each other.

Specifically, a number of forces can lead individuals or groups to taking the entrepreneurial option.

These forces could be grouped into main categories:

- ✓ Pull forces.
- ✓ Push forces.

6.2.1 Pull forces

Pull forces encourage individuals to become entrepreneurs by attractiveness of the option that include:

- The freedom to pursue a personal innovation.
- The freedom of work for oneself.
- The potential to achieve personal goal.
- The sense of achievement to be gained from running one's venture.
- The financial reward of entrepreneurship.

- The freedom to pursue a personal innovation (the inventor)

The inventor is someone who has developed an innovation and who has decided to make a career out of presenting that innovation to the market. It may be a new product, or an idea for a new service. It may be high tech or may be based on traditional technology. The inventor often draws on technical experience of a particular industry in order to make his/her invention. However, the invention may be derived from a technology quite unrelated to the industry in which they work.

It may be based on technical expertise they have gained as a result of a hobby. Alternatively, the invention may result from a grey or gray research (research produced outside of the traditional commercial or academic publishing and distribution channels) programme carried out unofficially within the inventor's employer organisation or it may be the product of a private garden shed development programme.

It is an unfortunate fact that in general such inventors have a poor record in building successful businesses. This is not because their ideas are not good, their innovation are often quite valuable. More often than not, it is due to the fact that new products regardless of how many benefits it might potentially bring into the customer will manufacture and promote it.

Successful innovation calls for a wide range of management skills to innovate. The entrepreneur must establish a market potential for their innovation and lead an organisation which can deliver it profitably. They must sell the product to the customers and sell the venture to investors. Investors can often be impressed with the technical side of the innovation that they neglect the other tasks that must be undertaken. An example of an investor who combined technical insight with consummate business skills is James Dyson, who built up not one but two highly successful businesses to market innovative products.

- Freedom of work for oneself

People of all groups including young highly educated people with formal management qualifications are skipping the experience of working for established organisations and moving directly to work on establishing their own ventures to enjoy the freedom of working for themselves and take advantage of the success associated with entrepreneurship.

Young entrepreneurial talents are good drivers of economy growth of any nation. To a great extent, it is young people who are taking the lead and making the adaptations necessary to take advantage of the new possibilities these changes are offering.

- Achieving personal goals

The personal dimension relates to the potential to achieve personal goal. Entrepreneurs are motivated by a number of factors, and although making money may motivate some, it is not the only factor. Others may include -a sense of achievement of having created something, making an entire new world, challenge that the competitive environment presents. The approach to entrepreneurial process that will be desired here is based on four interacting contingencies. The entrepreneur is responsible for bringing these together to create new value. A contingency is something which must be present in the process but can make an appearance in an endless variety of ways. The four contingencies in the entrepreneurial activities include: the entrepreneur, a market opportunity, as business organisation and resources to be invested.

- The sense of achievement to be gained from running one's venture

Some people become entrepreneurs because they want to do things to make a meaning – to create a product or service to make the world a better place. The exploration of meaning and doing work that changes the world is something that drives some entrepreneurs. If you find yourself unsatisfied with life the relegates you to the sidelines or the background, entrepreneurship may well be the right part for you. Entrepreneurs learn by doing and explore with a voracious appetite. If the status quo is too simple for you, you understand one of the genuine reasons people choose entrepreneurship. Entrepreneurs don't want to change their lives – they want to change the world

- The financial reward of entrepreneurship.

Some people go into entrepreneurship because of the financial gain, probably being induced by successful entrepreneurs and their life styles as role models.

Going into entrepreneurship solely on financial gains is very risky because there is no financial guarantee. Entrepreneurial risks could be described as dynamic or Speculative risks are risks associated with a pure gamble or a carefully thought-out business venture - where three outcomes are possible – loss, no loss, or profit. However as we know "no risk- no success" as benefits may be derived from the exposure if the risk is taken. This is why avoidance to some extent, is regarded as an unsatisfactory way to handling business risks.

6.2.2 Push forces

Push forces- push individual into entrepreneurial venture due to unacceptable circumstances and lack of alternative option, and they include:

- Limitations from conventional job . . .
- Being unemployed in the established economy.
- The unfulfilled.
- The displaced persons.
- Being a "misfit" in an established organisation.

- Limitations from conventional jobs

Some people become entrepreneurs because they see it as mandatory journey to take. Their prior experience in the job market or achievements in the existing job makes them realise that working for others is no longer a life suited for them. Such entrepreneurs are driven with the need to succeed and control their own destiny.

Disagreement with previous employer or dissatisfaction with a particular job may also pus people into taking the entrepreneurship option. Such uncomfortable relations at work have pushed many people into starting their own small business.

- Being unemployed in the established economy

Redundancy has proved a considerable push into entrepreneurship particularly when accompanied by a generous hand shake in a locality where other employment possibilities are low.

A study reported that 25% of small business founded in UK in the late 1970s (Stoke 2006), were pushed in to taking this option being employed and having received a generous hand shake. Later research showed a figure of 50% when unemployment nationally was much higher.

- The unfulfilled

The unfulfilled in life may be forced to seek self satisfaction through the entrepreneurial option.

Such unfulfilled person may have taken up employment in the first instance and life as a professional or manager in an established organisation may bring many rewards (e.g a stable income, intellectual stimulation, status and degree of security). However, this is still not enough as the organisation may not offer a vehicle for all ambitions – the desire to make a mark on the world, to leave a lasting achievement, to stretch their existing managerial talents to their limits and to develop new ones. It may simply not let them do things their way. Such managers, confident in their abilities and unsatisfied in their ambitions, may decide to embark on an entrepreneurial career.

- The displaced persons

The increasing pace of technological and economic change means that many people are likely to make an increasing number of career changes during their professional lives.

Restructuring trends, such as downsizing and delivering mean that unemployment among professional groups is increasing many parts of the world. This increases the pressure on managers to work for them, and one possibility is to undertake an entrepreneurial routes. Many people approach redundancy positively, seeing it as an opportunity to achieve things they could not within the organisation. In effect, they recognise themselves as unfulfilled and feel grateful for the push they have been given into entrepreneurship option.

- Being a "misfit" in an established organisation- the excluded

Some people turn to entrepreneurial career because nothing else is open to them. This is not because such people are inherently entrepreneurial rather it is because for variety of social, cultural, political and historical reasons, they have not been invited to join the wider economic community. They do not form part of the established network of individuals and organisations. As a result they are pushed into entrepreneurship, forming their own business and using their own informal network to trade among themselves and, perhaps, with their ancestral countries.

6.3 Four Primary Types of Individuals Who Become Entrepreneurs

Miner (1997) suggested that four primary types of individuals become entrepreneurs:

1. The personal achiever- the individual who is driven and chooses the entrepreneurial option as the best means of doing this. This personal achiever is characterised by a clear objectives, hard work and dedication.
2. The emphatic super sales person - this type is characterised by a well developed ability to understand customer needs, to empathise with them and to communicate their offerings to them effectively.
3. The real manager - the entrepreneur who is motivated by having an organisation large enough to put demands on their managerial ability. They are motivated to build their own organisation because of the lack of existing organisation that can offer them the challenges they seek.
4. The expert idea generator – an individual who is motivated by the entrepreneurial option because it offers them a platform to develop and market an innovation they have created and to achieve the satisfaction of seeing it become a reality.

6.4 Limitations to Entrepreneurial Option

The number of entrepreneurs operating at any time will depend on the strength of the pull and push forces already explained as well as the strength of inhibiting forces acting against the forces.

If the forces acting for entrepreneurship are strong, then a large number of entrepreneurs will emerge. However, the supply of entrepreneurs will also be limited if inhibiting factors or inhibitors are operating.

Inhibitors are factors which prevent the potential entrepreneurs from following an entrepreneurial route, no matter how attractive an option it might appear.

Some important inhibitors include:

1. Inability to source capital.
2. High cost of start – up capital.
3. Risk presented by the business environment.
4. Lack of training for entrepreneurs.
5. Legal restrictions on business activity.
6. Lack of suitable human resources.
7. Personal inertia in following through business ideas.

Politicians and economic policy makers increasingly put the elimination of inhibitors to entrepreneurism at the top of their agenda. This is because they recognise the importance of increasing the number of entrepreneurs within the economy to stimulate growth.

Further reading

Deacons, D. and Freely, M. (2003), Entrepreneurship and Small Firms (3rd Edition), London: McGraw Hill.

Drucker, P. (1985), Innovation and Entrepreneurship, London: Heinemann.

Kirby, D. (2003), Entrepreneurship, London: McGraw Hill.

Kuratko, D. and Hodgetts, R. (2001), Entrepreneurship: A contemporary Approach (5th Edition), New York: Dryden.

Morris, M. (2000), "Revisiting "who" is the Entrepreneur", Journal of Developmental Entrepreneurship, Vol.7, No. 1, pp2.10.

Avian, B. and McDougall, P.(2005), "Defining international entrepreneurship and modelling the speed of internationalisation, Entrepreneurship Theory and Practice, Vol. 29, No. 5, pp.537 -53.

PART 2

ENTREPRENEURSHIP AND NEW VENTURE INITIATION

INTRODUCTION

In part 1, we have learnt about the meaning of entrepreneurship, different types of entrepreneurs, and classification and significance of entrepreneurs, as well as relationship to small business and innovation.

In this part we shall be looking at entrepreneurship and new venture initiation - the process of initiating new ventures. It is involves how entrepreneurs initiate new ventures to take advantage of opportunities. This includes the process of seeking new opportunities and analysing them to identify the right venture for the right customers, based on the uniqueness of the new venture – private, public or social enterprise.

New venture initiation is the dream of any entrepreneur as it signifies the beginning of the ownership of a new venture - business, enterprise, social enterprise, etc. It is suggested that entrepreneurship in the first instance is driven by a desire for creating change on the part of entrepreneur. This desire for creating change leads the entrepreneur to bringing together necessary resources in an innovative and dynamic way to initiate a new venture.

The entrepreneur has to mould the resources to hand to give the new venture its shape, and to ensure that those resources are appropriate for pursuing the particular opportunity. These interactions are the fundamental elements of the entrepreneurial initiation process, and together, they constitute the foundation of the strategy adopted for the new venture initiation and development.

The process of new venture initiation involves how the entrepreneur triggers wealth creation through the new venture. The entrepreneurial initiation process results from the action of the entrepreneur. It can only occur if the entrepreneur acts to develop an innovation and promote it to customers.

Understanding the process of new venture initiation is useful since this gives us a framework for understanding how entrepreneurs create new wealth. It also provides a guide for potential entrepreneurs when making a decision on new ventures initiation.

This part includes chapter 7 of this book that introduces us to the various elements necessary for initiating a new venture.

CHAPTER 7

INITIATING A NEW VENTURE

Aim

To introduce elements and processes necessary for initiating a new venture.

Objectives

After studying this chapter you should be able to:

- Understand the process of initiating a new venture.
- Outline and understand various elements involve an idea generation.
- Explain the need for idea realisation - new venture initiation - and various relationships involved in it.
- Understand sources of advice and assistance available to the entrepreneur.
- Understand ways of protecting a new Idea.

7.1 Introduction

Initiating a new venture is a serious and adventurous process.

The window of opportunity has to be identified or created and progressed to reality. This involves the process of venture initiation and starting a new venture.

Initiating a new venture is clearly a major decision for individuals pursuing the entrepreneurial option. Herron (2000) emphasised the primacy of the individual in the initiation, and went on to draw from behavioural psychology and organisation theory to develop a model of initiation decision. The primary inputs to this model are the individual's values, personal traits, and socio-economic context along the acquired skills, aptitudes, and training. In combination, these lead to the individual having a certain level of aspiration that may or not be met by their current circumstances. If the aspirations are not met, the individual will be dissatisfies and will start to explore alternatives. In this sense, initiating a new venture may not only be the start of the venture's existence, but also the end of initiation process as far as the entrepreneur is concerned.

A number of studies (Anderson 1999, Smith 2001, Thompson 2005) have examined whether the initiation process is relatively consistent or varies across different ventures. A positive correlation was observed: the higher the investment, the greater the extent of, and detail in, start-up preparations. Some entrepreneurs are found to first engage in a number of pre-launch preparation tasks in the process of new venture initiation. Others just launch into a new venture without adequate preparation.

The author believes, it is important to give more time in preparation period as far as new venture initiation is concerned. It is clear that this will provide the necessary background information and knowledge required to prepare the potential entrepreneur for every eventuality that may come up during venture operation.

Successful new venture initiation process usually includes the following:

- Idea generation.
- Idea realisation.
- Protecting the idea.

7.2 Idea Generation

Introduction

Being a successful entrepreneur requires having a good idea that can be turned into a new venture – (business reality), as well as understanding it in great depth.

The idea can come from various sources

- Hobbies.
- Experience.
- Skills.
- Qualifications.
- Sporting a gap in the market.
- Advice from friends, relatives, colleagues, an independent adviser, etc.

In all cases, fresh good ideas are inspirations from God Almighty. They are usually delivered fresh from the oven of heaven.

There are however, ideas that are simply the same as other existing businesses and the entrepreneur feels it can do better.

Ideas can also come out different. The new idea is different because an innovation has been made. This might take the form of offering a new product, or organising the company in a different way, etc.

Ideas can also come out better. The new idea is better because it offers a utility, in terms of an ability to satisfy human needs that existing products do not.

It is easy to get excited over a new idea. However, the best ideas are those inspired by a clear need in the marketplace, rather than those that result from uninformed invention.

Successful entrepreneurs put effort in identifying and clarifying a business idea and developing an understanding of its market potential. Many achieve this by working as part of an entrepreneurial team with an inventor who dreams of new ideas.

As introduced, entrepreneurs can base their ideas from many sources. Some entrepreneurs base their idea on skills, experience or qualification they have perhaps gained in a previous job or through a hobby.

Others sport a gap in the market - opportunities that are not being taken by existing business or not been met. These might come from identifying new fast growing market or identifying where customer needs that are being badly served by existing business.

There are many types of opportunities that the entrepreneur can addressee in different ways to create wealth – new venture - delivering new value to the customer.

In its details, every opportunity is different, but there are some common patterns in the way in which opportunity takes shape:

- ✓ New product.
- ✓ The new service
- ✓ New means of production.
- ✓ New distribution route.
- ✓ Improve service.
- ✓ Relationship building.

For an entrepreneur, opportunity sporting should not just be about getting an initial idea, it should be a way of life. It should cover every aspect and process of the entrepreneurial activities and venture business all the time, which include looking for opportunities all the time, seeking for improvement, and never being satisfied with performance. It is important to be constantly looking for new opportunities and constantly updating original ones. Opportunities come in many shape and sizes and they keep coming. They are like train leaving a mainline station. If you miss one there will be another one leaving at the same spot.

An opportunity could be seen as the possibility to do things both differently from and better than how they are being done at the moment. This opportunity could be created by a gap in the market or the opportunity of doing something both differently and better. An innovation presents a means of filling the market gap, i.e. a way of pursuing the opportunity. Successful entrepreneurs are always on the lookout for opportunities. They scan the landscape looking for new ways of creating value.

Identifying new opportunities demand knowledge of the customer needs and behaviour, the market place, the intended product and services, related technology, distribution channels, promotion, and competitors.

The nature of the opportunity pursued will define the shape the organisation must adopt. Every organisation built by an entrepreneur is different. The essential futures are the organisation assets (i.e. the things which the organisation posses, its structure, its processes, how it adds value and culture). To initiate a venture successfully, it is important that the entrepreneur should consider opportunity in terms of wealth creation and wealth distribution.

Methods of spotting opportunities

It is useful to be aware of the ways in which a market may be scanned for new opportunities, and of the techniques available to assist in this process:

- ✓ Heuristics – the word literally means serving to find out- that entrepreneurs call upon to generate business ideas, and can be seen to involve two types. The first is analysis heuristics which are the cognitive strategies that entrepreneurs adopt in order to gain and integrate new information and to spot market gaps. The second are synthesis heuristics which involves using a cognitive strategy to bring the ideas developed from analysis back together again in a new and creative way; generating a new perspective on customer needs and how they might be addressed.
- ✓ Problem analysis – entrepreneurs can spot ideas through problem analysis to identify the needs that individuals and organisations have and the problems that they face. These needs and problems may be either explicit or implicit. They may or manor be recognised by the subject. The approach begins by asking questions, "What could be better? Having identified the problem, the next question is "How this might be solved? An effective rewarding solution is represents the basis of new opportunity for the entrepreneur. The approach demands a full understanding of customer needs and the technology that might be used to satisfy them.

- ✓ Customer proposals – entrepreneurs can also identify or spot a new opportunity through customer proposals on the basis of recognition of their own needs. In this case, the customer offers the opportunity to the entrepreneur. Customer proposals take a variety of forms. At their simplest, they are informal suggestions; they can take the form of very detailed and formal brief.
- ✓ Creative groups – entrepreneurs do not have to rely on their own creativity. The best entrepreneurs are active in facilitating and harnessing the creativity of other people or creative group. An entrepreneur can use creative group that consists of small of potential consumers or product experts who are encouraged to think about their needs in a particular market area and to consider how those needs might be better served.
- ✓ Market mapping – this is a formal technique which involves identifying market opportunity dimensions defining a product category. These dimensions are based on the features of the product category. The characteristics of buyers may be used to provide a detailed mapping. The map defines the position of the product and market opportunity for the entrepreneur.
- ✓ Features stretching - involves offering something new and means looking for ways in which changes might be made. It involves identifying the principal features which define a particular product and then seeing what happens if they are changed in some way. The trick is to test each feature with a range of suitable adjectives such as "bigger", "faster", "stronger", "more often", "more fun" etc. and see what results from such tests. Anita Roddick's Body Shop provides a good example. Her initial inspiration was to provide good quality toiletries in packs much smaller than those offered. Environmentalism came later.
- ✓ Features blending – involves identifying the features which define particular products and blending individual features together from different product or services, instead of just changing the individual features. This technique is often used in conjunction with features stretching.
- ✓ The combined approach – effective entrepreneurs usually use combined approach of all techniques to spot and take

advantage of opportunities. They actively encourage creativity y thinking methodically about the market areas in which they have expertise. They also encourage people involved with them to be creative on their behalf. All these techniques already described are not mutually exclusive or each other. They may be used together.

Identifying real opportunities demand knowledge. Some important elements of this knowledge include knowledge of:

- ✓ The technology behind the product or service supplied.
- ✓ How the product or service is produced customer needs and buying behaviour they adopt.
- ✓ Distributors and distribution channels.
- ✓ The human skills utilised within the industry.
- ✓ How the product or service might be promoter to customers.
- ✓ Competitors who: who they are, the way they act and react.

This knowledge is necessary if good business opportunities are to be identified and properly assessed. Acquisition of this knowledge requires exposure to the relevant industry, an active learning attitude, and time.

Most entrepreneurs are actually experienced in a particular industry sector and confine their activities to that sector. Many have acquired this experience by working as a manager in an existing organisation . . . The incubation of period can be important to the development of entrepreneurial talent. However, industry special knowledge does not produce entrepreneurs on its own. It must be complemented with general business skills and people skills.

Scanning, screening, selecting and evaluation opportunities

Scanning opportunities require that the market and existing players must be scanned to spot the gaps in what the existing players offer to the market. This process demands an active approach to identifying new opportunities and to innovating in response to them.

Screening and selecting opportunities involves answering basic questions like:

- ✓ What is opportunity?
- ✓ Where is the opportunity?
- ✓ How large is the opportunity?
- ✓ What investment will be necessary if the opportunity is to be exploited?
- ✓ What is the likely return?
- ✓ What are the risks?

Evaluating opportunities and recognising the potential it offers to create new value means finding out how much the opportunity might be worth. This demands getting to grips with the market for the innovation, measuring its size, understanding its dynamics and trends, evaluating the impact the innovation might make in it, and ascertaining how much customers might be willing to spend on it, including the risks associated with it.

Delivering market opportunity

One thing is to identify market opportunities, another thing is to deliver.

The entrepreneur can deliver market opportunity by combining factors of production.

Entrepreneurship is about bringing change and making a difference. Entrepreneurs as innovators are people who create new. An innovation is a new combination of these factors of production. The entrepreneur is the person who organises factors of production and puts them to productive use and then present them to the market for assessment by consumers. The entrepreneur creates valuable innovation in the following areas:

- New products - creation of new products. This may exploit an established technology or may be the outcome of a whole new technology. The new product may offer a radically new way

of doing something, or simply be an improvement on existing ones that provides better benefits to customers.
- New services - a service is an act which is offered to undertake a particular task or solve a particular problem. Services are open to the possibility of new ideas - new production techniques, new operation practices, new means of informing the customer about the product, new ways of managing relationship within the organisation, new ways of managing relationship within the organisation, etc.

7.3 Idea Realisation
(The new venture start-up)

Introduction

Having identified, located and measured the idea, the next stage is to realise it – start a new venture.

Opening the window of opportunity is about turning the idea into reality. Once the window of opportunity is opened, then the entrepreneur can move through it by initiating the starting- up of the new venture.

Critical to this stage is the need to get stakeholders to make a commitment to the venture, to attract investors and employees, to develop a new set of relationships in the new network, and to establish the venture within its network.

The new venture and the entrepreneur drawing it must create a new set of relationship with the network of stakeholders. In effect, starting a new venture means redefining the relationship that stakeholders have with third parties and with one another in the market place, or network of relationships in the market place with the new venture.

The new venture must enter an existing network of relationship in the market place, and in doing so, modify the network of relationship. If the new venture is to enjoy long term success it must do this in a way that increases the overall value of the network of those who make it up and the business environment or stakeholders.

The entrepreneur needs to consider the new venture positioning in relation to essential elements and market playing factors in its internal and external business environment (internal and external stakeholders) such as:

- The type of venture – business venture, social venture, etc.
- Legal form – small business, large business, ltd, plc, etc.
- Relationship with investors.

- Relationship with suppliers.
- Relationship with distributors.
- Relationship with employees
- Relationship with customers.
- Sources of advice.
- Protecting the idea.

The type of new venture

The potential new venture entrepreneur should think and consider the type of new venture to set up - private, public, profit, non-for –profit, etc. The decision must be based on profit or social orientation of the entrepreneur.

As explained earlier, business ventures are normally associated with profit making activities. Social ventures are involved in the social dimension of entrepreneurship and the potential for structural change and they do not have profit as their main aim instead, they concentrate on social rather than commercial outputs. They also differ in terms of time – frames, being more concerned with long term capacity building that with short term outcomes. Equally, they are different in terms of their "scavenger- like" use of resources, recognising that most communities have under-utilised resources that need to be harnessed for the good of the society. Cultural or Aesthetic ventures have a different drive when compared to profit oriented and social entrepreneurship. They are usually created by people whose main driver is not wealth creation or business capability but creativity. Many businesses have been, and are created by such people. Civic ventures are usually associated with the public service institutions.

Legal form

When starting a new venture, it is important that whoever is starting it should understand the legal requirement for starting such as new venture at any particular business environment or area where the venture is to be started.

Knowing the legal environment is very important because it will help the potential entrepreneur understand the legal requirements for the new venture and make him/her give some thought to the legal problems that may need to be dealt with.

Although there may be some technically differences in the legal requirements for venture start –up between various locations but generally, there are three major forms of business organisations:

1. Sole trader.
2. Partnership.
3. Limited liability.

The simplest legal form of small business venture is the sole trader. This is the simplest and the most common form of private sector business and many small businesses are started as sole traders.

It is the simplest form of business start- up because it is easy to start.

Sometimes, this is referred as self employed especially in UK. This is the business owned by one person or individual.

In this legal form of business form, the individual is the business and the business is the individual. The two are inseparable.

However, the account of the business should reflect transaction of the business and not the individual. The owner runs the business and may employ any number of people to help.

Sole trader as a legal form of small business can be found in different types of businesses in various economic sectors:

- ✓ In the primary sector, many farmers and fishermen operate like this.
- ✓ In the secondary sector, there are small scale manufactures, builders and construction firms.
- ✓ In tertiary sector, we have small scale services like hairdressers, gardeners, retailers, etc.

Partnership exists when two or more people come together to form a business.

If two or more individuals start –up a small business together, they are said to conduct the small business as a partnership.

Partnerships are found in every economy or country although the technical definition and legal requirements may slightly differ.

In UK, a partnership is defined in the Partnership Act, 1990 as "the relation which subsists between persons carrying on business with common view to profit."

A Partnership is expected to have a maximum number of 20. The joint owners will share responsibility for running the business and also share profits.

Many small businesses are started or grow from sole traders to partnership after a period of time.

Generally, there are no legal formalities to complete when starting a partnership. A partnership can take the form of informal understanding or a formally drawn up partnership agreement. This depends on the legal requirement of a particular business environment.

Some business environment may legally require members of a particular profession to form partnership than limited companies so that they cannot limit liability for professional negligence. This is applicable such professions like Doctors, Accountants, Estate agents and Solicitors.

Generally, there are two main types of companies:

1. Private Limited Liability Companies (Ltd).
2. Public Liability Companies (Plc).

A small business can also be started or formed as a private limited liability company.

Generally, a company is usually a separate legal entity, distinct from the owners. This means that, it can sue and be sued in its own right and enters into its own contracts. There is also a divorce of management from ownership with a board of directors elected by shareholders to control the day to day operation of the business.

The number of people required to form a private limited company may depend on the legal environment but in UK there is only a minimum of only two shareholders and one director. With small business the owners are also directors.

In UK, many small businesses are started as private limited companies with two to five members, usually family members or friends, forming a private limited small business to take advantage of this type of legal form of business.

In UK limited companies must produce two documents:

1. THE MEMORANDUM OF ASSOCIATION.
2. THE ARTICLES OF ASSOCIATION.

MEMORANDUM OF ASSOCIATION - The memorandum set out the constitution and gives details about the company.

The company act 1985 states that the following details must be included:

- The name of the company.
- The name and address of the company's registered office.
- The objectives of the company, and the scope of its activities
- The liability of its members.
- The amount of capital to be raised and amount of shares to be issued.

A limited company must have a minimum of 2 members but there is no upper limit.

THE ARTICLES OF ASSOCIATION - It deals with the internal running of the company. They include details such as:

- The right of shareholders depending on the type of share they hold.
- The procedures for appointing directors and the scope of their power.
- The length of time directors should serve before re-election.
- The timing and frequency of company's meetings.
- The arrangement for auditing company accounts.

These two documents mentioned above, along with statements indicating the directors should be sent to REGISTRAR OF COMPANIES and if successful, will be issued a CERTIFICATE OF INCORPORATION.

Private limited companies are one type of limited companies. They tend to be smaller businesses and privately owned. They are usually family business. The directors tend to be shareholders and are involved in running the business. Their names end with limited. Shares can only be transferred privately and all shareholders must agree on the transfer. Many manufacturing firms are private limited companies.

Public limited companies on the other hand tend to be large. The company's name tend to ends in plc. The shares of these companies can be bought and sold by the public on the stock exchange. To become a public limited company, a memorandum of association, article of association and STATUTORY DECLARATION must be provided. STATUTORY DECLARATION - This is a document which states that the requirement of the Company Act has been met

When the company has been issued with certificate of incorporation, it is common to publish a PROSPECTUS- A document which advertises the company to potential investors and invites them to buy shares before floatation.

Going public is expensive because:

- ✓ The company needs lawyers.
- ✓ Publications.
- ✓ Financial institutions to process share applications
- ✓ Share issues have to be underwritten.
- ✓ Advertising costs.
- ✓ Minimum of share capital.

A plc cannot start trading until it has completed these tasks and received 25% payment value of shares.

It will then receive a TRADING CERTIFICATE and can begin operating and the shares will be quoted in the stock exchange. The stock exchange is where second hand shares are sold and bought and sold. A full stock exchange listing means that the company must comply with the rules.

Alternative Investment Market (AIM). AIM is designed for companies which want to avoid some of the high costs of full listing. However shareholders on AIM do not have the same protection as those with fully quoted shares.

Relationship with investors

The potential entrepreneur also needs to seek relationship with investors to start the venture going in the right direction.

Investors seek out opportunities to invest. They look for the best returns on the capital they provided, consistent with certain level of risk.

Because capital like any other factors of production is limited, investors are selective in the investment they choose to support. The potential entrepreneur must compete for the attention of investors.

If an entrepreneur offers an investor an investment opportunity, then they are limiting investment opportunity in other ventures by that investor.

Relationship with investors involves getting financial investment. The potential entrepreneur is interested in obtaining a variety of resources in order to progress their venture. To create the right relationship and maintain it, as well as start –up the venture successfully, the potential entrepreneur needs to consider the following factors carefully before going into any investment agreement:

- What level of investment is required?

This involves how much money will be needed to start the new venture. This will depend on the nature of the venture, the opportunity it is pursuing, the stage in its development, and the plans the entrepreneur has for the future of the venture. Initial investment levels are sensitive to the strategy the venture is pursuing in terms of initial scope the venture must have, and the potential for growth.

- Where the investment is to come from?

Sources of investment capital may include the entrepreneurs own money, bank loans, government loans, venture capital, share issues, business angels. The market for capital investment is fragmented. Different capital providers occupy different niches in the market. they are characterised by the way they look for different types of investment opportunity, accepting different levels of risk, expecting different types of returns, and assuming different levels of involvement in the running of the venture. They entrepreneurs need to understand these different markets and the way they work in order to manage the project of attracting funds and capital investment successfully (sources of finance is treated in details later).

- What the capital structure of the investment is to the capital structure of the venture?

This is simply the mix of different investments that are used in broad terms. It refers to the ratio of "equity" to "debt" capital., that is the mix of investors who expect a return that will be linked to the performance of the venture to those who expect a fixed return based on agreed interest rate whatever the performance of the business. The capital structure of the venture reflects the way in which the entrepreneur is sharing risk with the investors. Clearly, a secured loan exposes the investors to a lower level of risk than an equity share. At the same time, capital which exposes the investor to risk is more expensive than capital which does not. So by adjusting the capital structure, entrepreneurs can in effect, "sell off" the risk inherent in their venture to different degrees.

- How investors will be approached?

The potential entrepreneur and investors need to get in touch with each other before they can work together. Usually, the onus is on the entrepreneur to initiate the contact. That contact must be managed. Investors are human beings and are influenced by how things are said and done - especially with first impression. The way in which the entrepreneur first approaches an investor can have a bearing effect on the outcome of the contact. Three things need to be considered:

1. Who to contact – the entrepreneur must identify suitable sources of investment. That is the "who of the contact". This involves identifying organisations that provide investment capital. However, organisations do not make decisions, individuals do. The entrepreneur must find out which individual or individuals they should approach within the organisation. They must also consider the decision making structure within the organisation i.e. not only who actually

takes the investment decisions but also who influences them in that decision making, the way in which their decisions are policed and judged within the organisation.

2. How to contact – should it be formal or informal? Does the investor lay down a procedure for making contact? Most banks and venture capitalists do for example. Does the investor expect a written proposal or a verbal one? If verbal, do they expect one –to- one or face- to- face chat or a full presentation? If it is written do they have a format for the proposal or do they give the entrepreneur latitude in the way they communicate? Many investors will simply reject a proposal out of hand if they are not approached in the right way.

3. What to contact- what to tell the investor. At the initial stage, attracting investors' attention and interest is important as giving them information. The entrepreneur must also consider what exactly they are offering the investors i.e. what proposition is to be made to investors. Some of the critical dimensions are:

✓ The amount of investment required.
✓ How that particular investment fits with the overall investment profile for the venture.
✓ The nature of investment egg loan, equity, secured or unsecured
✓ Nature (egg liquidity of any security being offered).
✓ The degree of risk of exposure of capital invested the way in i.e. how the investment will be made, what amount of money, what time.
✓ Way out (i.e. how the investors will get their returns) or exist strategy.
✓ The degree of control the investors will be given, etc.

Relationship with employees

Entrepreneurial venture can be progressed only if the right human skills are in place. They demand productive labour, technical knowledge, business insight and leadership.

Human inputs are traded in markets. Some categories of human skills may be in short supply and the entrepreneur may compete to get hold of them. This competition takes the form of offering potential employees attractive compensation packages and prospects for development. Apart from this, the entrepreneur needs to define relationship with employees - to get the right human commitment. This requires providing answers to questions like:

- ✓ What human skills?
- ✓ Where will those skills be obtained?
- ✓ What will be offered to those who have those skills?
- ✓ How will potential employees be contacted?
- ✓ How will potential employees be evaluated?
- ✓ Should skills be in-house or hired externally?
- ✓ What type of leadership and motivation is required?

Relationship with distributors

The entrepreneur also needs to understand the nature of distributors as well as define relationship with distributors – to establishing the right presence in the distribution network and make the required sales and profits.

Conventional distribution channel is a channel consisting of one or more independent producer, whole seller and retailer. Each is a separate business seeking to maximise its own profit even at expense of the whole system as a whole. Historically, conventional distribution channels do not act as a unified system rather they constitute a loose collection of independent companies each showing little concern for overall channel performance.

The structure of distribution system has changed overtime. There has been growth in what is now called "vertical marketing system".

The vertical marketing system emerged to challenge the conventional marketing channels.

Unlike the conventional distribution system, the vertical marketing system is a distribution system in which producers, wholesalers and retailers acting as UNIFIED system.

The system is unified as one channel member may own the other, has contract with them, or has much power that they all cooperate.

Designing a channel system calls for:

1. Analysing consumer needs.
2. Setting channel objectives and constraints.
3. Identifying major channel alternatives.
4. Evaluating the major alternatives and choice.

The new venture entrepreneur also needs to consider a number of other factors when deciding which goods and distribution system to chose such as:

- ✓ The margin on the good – the difference between the price the good can be purchased and the price it can be sold.
- ✓ The rate of sale of the good – how many units will be sold in a period?
- ✓ The cost of storing and displaying the good for the period before it is sold.

Relation with distributors also requires the new venture entrepreneur managing distribution channel appropriately.

Channel management calls for:

- ✓ Selecting channel members.
- ✓ Motivating channel members.
- ✓ Evaluating channel members.

Selecting channel members requires a careful consideration.

When selecting channel members, the entrepreneur should determine what distinguish the better ones. He/she should evaluate channel in terms of:

- ✓ Numbers of years in business.
- ✓ Other lines carried.
- ✓ Growth and profit record.
- ✓ Competitiveness.
- ✓ Reputation.

Channel management also calls for careful motivation of members. The firm must sell not only through intermediaries but to them. Most producers use carrot and sticks approach.

CARROT - at times they offer positive motivation (egg higher margins, special deals, premium, cooperative advertising, allowances, display allowance, sales contest).
STICKS - at other times they use negative motivation (e.g threatening to reduce margin, to slow down delivery or end relationship).

Channel management also includes evaluating of channel members against standards such as:

- ✓ Sales quotes.
- ✓ Average inventory.
- ✓ Customer delivery time.
- ✓ Treatment of demand.
- ✓ Cost of goods or lost goods.
- ✓ Cooperation in company promotion and training programmes and services to customers.
- ✓ A company may periodically prequalify its intermediaries.

On the whole, managing channel members is about managing a relationship so that all in partners see that they are gaining from it.

Relationship with suppliers

To a supplier an entrepreneurial venture is a potential new customer.

At face value, this is good since a new customer offers the prospects of new business. However, the new venture may also complicate life for a supplier. The venture may be competing with existing customer of the supplier.

While the venture may be offering the potential for additional business, it may also be threatening to replace one set of business arrangements with another. The supplier may not always see the venture as a new business.

When approaching a supplier, the entrepreneur must be conscious not only of the new business they are offering them, but also of the way the relationship they are proposing to build will affect the existing relationships the supplier enjoys.

Relationship with customers

Customers are a key stakeholder group for the entrepreneur.

It is there interest in what the venture offers and their willingness to pay for it that ultimately provides the money which the entrepreneurial venture will use to reward all its stakeholder groups.

The best way to attract the interest of customers is to provide them with goods and services which generally satisfies their needs, solves their problems and meets their aspirations.

When starting new ventures, entrepreneurs are not just offering their products or services into a male of short term market exchanges, they are breaking and then reforming a pattern of relationship. Those relationships are governed by rules, some formal, some informal, some based on self interest, some are articulated openly, others are not even recognised until they are lost. Effective entrepreneurs understand those relationships and the rules that govern them, so that they can successfully manage their position within the network.

New venture initiation skills

The process of new venture initiation requires entrepreneurial skills

A skill is simply knowledge which is demonstrated by action. It is an ability to perform in a certain way.

In terms of new ventures initiation the turning of ideas into reality call for a number of skills:

1. General management skills - required to organise physical and financial resources needed to run the venture.
2. People management skills - needed to obtain the necessary support from others.

3. Entrepreneurial skills and spirit - to keep the venture innovative and adaptive to environment, as well as sustain the long term objective of the entrepreneur respectively.

General management skills include:

✓ Planning, organisational, leading and controlling Strategy skills.

People management skills include:

o Leadership skills.
o Delegation skills.
o Negotiation skills.

Traditionally it has been held that the entrepreneur is not a good manager and that a manager is not an entrepreneur.

There is evidence to suggest that successful entrepreneurial venture s is headed by entrepreneurs who are also effective managers.

Unlike the traditional manager who focuses on administrative efficiency, it would seem that the effective entrepreneurial manager needs to possess skills in building an entrepreneurial culture.

As has been shown already, the effective entrepreneurial manager needs to be able to:

✓ Recognise and cope with innovative.
✓ Take risks.
✓ Respond quickly.
✓ Cope with failure (absorb setbacks.
✓ Find chaos and uncertainty challenging and stimulating.

To do this effectively entrepreneurs need interpersonal/team working skills that involves the ability to:

✓ Create a climate and spirit conducive to high performance, including rewarding work well done and encouraging creativity, innovation, initiative and calculated risk taking.

- ✓ Understand the relationships present among tasks, and between the leader and followers.
- ✓ Lead in those situations where it is appropriate, including a willingness to manage actively, to supervise and to control the actions of others.

These interpersonal skills are normally termed "entrepreneurial influencing skills" since they have to do with the way entrepreneurial managers exert influence over others. They include leadership/ vision/ influence; helping, coaching and resolving conflict; and teamwork and people management. The aim is to organise resources efficiently and effectively for venture performance.

The fundamental task of the entrepreneur is to create or to change an organisation. Entrepreneurship is an economic activity. It is concerned first and foremost with building stable, profitable businesses which must survive in a competitive environment. If they are to thrive and prosper, they must add more value and deliver their value to buyers more effectively than their competitors.

The entrepreneur is task with the following functions:

- ✓ Resource- organisation configuration. Resources- the things that are used to pursue opportunity that include people, money, assets. In essence, organisation is a collection of resources.
- ✓ Resource- opportunity focus- the entrepreneur must decide what resources will make up the organisation. For example, its mix of capital, how this will be converted to productive assets and the nature and skills of the people that will make it up are matters to be decided by the entrepreneur in the first instance. If the organisation is the assets, structure, process and culture that will enable it to fit the opportunity then the resource mix must be correctly balanced.
- ✓ Learning organisation –the entrepreneurial organisation must be a learning organisation, that is, it must not only respond to opportunities and challenges, but reflect on the outcome that result from that response and modify future responses in the light of experience.

- ✓ Eldership - leadership must be applied constantly since organisations are fluid things. And left to themselves, they can lose their shape and sense of direction.

Sources of advice and assistance

There are many sources of advice and assistance to entrepreneurs, small business and their owners.

The type of advice and assistance available will depend on the location and economic development of the location or country and entrepreneurial culture. This usually reflects in the type of policy and institution set up or made available to advice and assist individual entrepreneurs and small business development.

Advice and assistance to entrepreneurs, and small business owners can come from:

- ✓ Individuals.
- ✓ Banks.
- ✓ Private advisory services.
- ✓ Government set up advisory services.
- ✓ Special advisory services.
- ✓ Companies.
- ✓ Government departments.
- ✓ Small business associations, etc.

Advice may be in the form of:

- ✓ A telephone number of a specialist who can help.
- ✓ A detailed discussion on the best way to run a business.
- ✓ Telephone numbers of organisations providing funds.
- ✓ Training videos or seminars.
- ✓ Specialist information on markets and types of business, etc.

Sources of Advice and Assistance for Small Business in UK

Individuals - it may be possible to get advice from people who have started their own business ad have been through the process of setting up and how they might do things differently.

Advice about specific skills for running a venture might come from:

- ✓ An accountant – who can give advice on accounts, book keeping, taxation, etc.
- ✓ A solicitor - who can give advice on the legal requirements of the business.
- ✓ A business consultant or an insurance advice – who can give advice on how to start, run or protect and cover equipment, employees, etc.

Banks - all the main commercial banks provide advice for potential business people. This ranges from information about sources of finance to helping to draw up a business plan. For example, the NatWest Start-up Service allows people to talk to a small business adviser at a local branch. The adviser can help to find out whether the business is entitled to government or EU grant. Many banks produce folders or publications with details and guidance on setting up a venture.

Training and Enterprise Councils (TECs) - these are government funded organisations which provide support and advise for businesses. TECs run Business Start-up Schemes. These schemes provide training and advice for businesses that are setting up such as with writing a suitable business plan and applying for funding. They also provide short –term finance for start-ups.

Business Links - the National Federation of Business Links offers a variety of help to businesses, such as technical assistance. It is an independent body. They help gain access to a wide range of information and advice from many sources, bringing support services together as a "one stop shop." They are found throughout UK. Their personal business advisers work with local businesses to identify growth opportunities and develop a support package, are central to the services offered. Business Links are intended to be self supporting as businesses are expected to pay for many of the services received. Whereas the government advise services had previously concentrated on start-ups, Business Links' aim particularly to help existing companies with the will to grow. They focus on small ventures usually with 10 to 200 employees.

Local Enterprise Agencies - local enterprise agencies are small, local advisory organisations, funded from private and public sources. A network of about 350 emerged during the 1980s, sponsored by local government, chambers of commerce, universities and colleges, and a mixture of private companies including banks and other financial institutions. The primary objective is to provide help and advice to local business communities.

Enterprise Agencies - these were created specifically by the government for small businesses. Most offer free advice on how to start and run a business, training courses, contacts and information on potential investors . . . Local authorities often help in their setting up.

The Department of Trade and Industry (DTI) - DTI runs amongst other things, road shows to areas of the country where consultants are available to help with business problems and a small business service offering advice on marketing, exporting etc. It also produces "A guild to help small firms" in the provision of information and advice.

Trade Associations - Trade Associations, such as British Travel Agents or the Booksellers Association can provide advice about certain types business or industry.

The Consumers' Association - Consumers Association is the publishers of "Which" that produce the which? Guide to Starting your own business.

The Small Business Association -The Federation of Small produces a "Be Your Own Boss" starter pack.

The Prince's Youth Business Trust - the Prince's Youth Business Trust gives training, advice and sometimes funds to young people starting a business.

Live WIRE - Live WIRE is a scheme started by Shell to encourage entrepreneurs between the age of 16 and 25.

- **Business Clubs** - these are regional organisations found all over UK . . . They are made up of businesses in the area and particularly useful for new firms. Often speakers from the Inland Revenue or insurance companies are invited to speak on tax, VAT, grants etc . . . A list of members is available and business provide and advice to each other . . . A certain amount of inter-trading also takes place . . . This helps new firms to make contacts and removes some of the risks when first trading.
- **Loan Guarantee Scheme (LGS)** - the Loan Guarantee Scheme is intended for small businesses not able to arrange loan under normal banking policies. It was introduced in 1981 to help small firms obtain finance from banks when they would not normally be able to do so because of lack of assets to use as security. In certain circumstances the government will agree to guarantee a bank loan, in return for which the borrowing firm pays an interest rate premium. The terms and conditions have varied considerably over the years.
- **The Business Expansion Scheme (BES)** - the Business Expansion Scheme was designed to attract outside investment in small businesses by UK tax payers, who could deduct up to a certain amount in any one year from their tax liability to match the size of their investment. The scheme not only attracts direct customers by individuals, but also portfolios offered by some financial institutions who select a range of businesses for investment.
- **Enterprise Investment Scheme (EIS)** - in 1994, the Enterprise Investment Scheme was introduced. Although similar to BES, alterations included: investment in private rented accommodation excluded. Investors could become directors and take some income from the business. Income tax relief is limited to a certain percent, although there is still no capital gains tax if the investment is held for five years. Individuals and companies can invest up to a certain amount (determinable with time).
- **Venture Capital Trusts (VCTs)** - introduced in 1995, VCTs are vehicles for private individuals to invest in smaller firms. VCTs are quoted on the London Stock Exchange (LSE). Investors in VCTs benefit from tax relief on income tax from dividends and capital gains tax on disposal of shares.

The Small Firm Service - one of the areas the government has sought to help small firms is in the provision of information and advice. On the recommendation of the Bolton committee, the Small Firms Service was set up in 1972 within the department of Department of trade and Industry (DTI), to provide information through 13 small firms Centres. This was further developed in 1978, by the addition of council ling service through over 100 Area Counselling Offices.

Protecting the Idea

You may feel the process of protecting your original ideas (sometimes referred to Intellectual Properties), the life blood of your business is time consuming and expensive. However, this may be your only source of competitive advantage.

Basically, there are four ways you can protect your idea:

- ✓ Patent (egg to protect invention).
- ✓ Copyright (e.g to protect against illegal copying).
- ✓ Registered design (e.g to protect shape, designs or decorative features).
- ✓ Trademark (e.g to protect symbols).

Legal issues relating to idea or Intellectual property may be found in areas like; abuse or neglect of International Property Rights. In a legal sense, the term property refers to a resource over which an individual or business holds a legal title - that is a resource that it owns. Resources include land, buildings, equipment, capital etc. Property rights also refer to the legal rights over the use to which a resource is put, and over the use made of any income that may be derived from that resource.

Property rights can be violated in many ways. This could be through private action- theft, privacy, blackmail, and the like by private individuals or groups. It could also be through public action and corruption - the extortion of income or resources from property holders by public officials, such as politicians and government bureaucrats. Entrepreneurs can protect intellectual property through: Patent, Copyrights, Trademarks, etc. Firms do operate well in business environment with legal systems that can quarantine protection of all business legal rights, and have the required machinery to enforce them.

Further reading

Bacharach, S. and Lawler, E. (1980), Power and Politics in organisations, San Francisco, CA: Jossey Bass.

Baumol, W. (1968), The Entrepreneur: Introductory Remarks, American Economic Review, Vol. 38, pp 60 -3.

Cole, A. (1968), Entrepreneurship in Economic Theory, American Economic Review, Vol. 58, pp 64 -71.

Deakins, D. and Freel, M. (2003), Entrepreneurship and Small Firms (3rd Edition), London: McGraw Hill.

Drucker, P. (1985), Innovation and Entrepreneurship, London:: Heinmann.

Kirby, D. (2003), Entrepreneurship, London: McGraw Hill.

Kuratko, D. and Hodgetts, R. (2001), Entrepreneurship: A contemporary Approach (5th Edition), New York: Dryden.

Morris, M. (2000), "Revisiting "who" is the Entrepreneur", Journal of Developmental Entrepreneurship, Vol.7, No. 1, pp2.10.

Ovian, B. and McDougall, P.(2005), "Defining international entrepreneurship and modelling the speed of internationalisation, Entrepreneurship Theory and Practice, Vol. 29, No. 5, pp.537 -53.

Parker, S. (2002), "On the dimensionality and composition of entrepreneurship", Durham Business School Working Paper.

Westhead, P. Ucbasaran, D. (2005), "Decisions, actions and performance; do novice, serial and portfolio entrepreneurs differ?" Journal of Business Management, Vol. 43, No. 4, pp.393- 417.

PART 3

ENTREPRENEURSHIP AND NEW VENTURE DEVELOPMENT

INTRODUCTION

As introduced in part 2, new venture initiation is about seeking new opportunities and analysing them - to realise the right venture for the right customers, based on the uniqueness of the new venture. Once the window of opportunity has been identified, assessed, analysed and realised, the entrepreneur needs to develop the new venture to make it viable in the marketplace, deliver the uniqueness and value satisfaction.

New venture development therefore, is about taking the new venture to the next level and making it presentable to the customer or the market place. This requires detailed understanding of the entrepreneurial new venture business environment by the entrepreneur, and the use of management principles of planning, organising, leading and controlling activities to achieve the desired development and performance.

This part includes chapters 8, 9, 10, 11, 12 of this book.

Chapter 8 will introduce the entrepreneurship new venture in relation to its business environment. In chapter 9 the process of entrepreneurial new venture planning will be introduced and explained. Chapter 10 will explain how the entrepreneurial new venture is organised, while chapter 11 will be about the entrepreneurial new venture and leading. Finally, chapter 12 will explain in details the various elements involved in entrepreneurial new venture controlling.

CHAPTER 8

THE ENTREPRENEURIAL NEW VENETURE BUSINESS ENVIRONMENT

Aim

To introduce the entrepreneurial new venture in relation to its business environment.

Objectives

After studying this chapter you should be able to:

- Understand the business environment of a new venture.
- Explain the importance of enterprise culture for new venture development.
- Describe internal factors shaping enterprise culture.
- Describe external factors shaping enterprise culture.

8.1 Introduction

Business environment could be described as all elements existing in and outside the organisation that have the potential to affect the organisation. The development of any new venture does not take place in a vacuum, but within a business environment.

The business environment is constantly changing and is a source of threats and opportunities to any new venture. The performance of any new venture will depend on how the entrepreneur takes advantage of the opportunities and cope with uncertainties associated with environmental threats.

Part of the entrepreneur's role will be to sense external forces accurately and then initiate suitable internal changes to handle them.

The right environment will encourage venture initiation and development, but the wrong environment will hinder it.

Successful entrepreneurs are able to identify the right environment and essential factors that facilitates venture initiation and development – the enterprise culture.

8.2 The Enterprise Culture

8.2.1 Introduction

The starting point for successful development of a new venture is the understanding of the business environment and essential factors that can help facilitate this development – the enterprise culture.

Planning, organising, leading and controlling human and material resources associated with the new venture development require the knowledge and understanding, as well as a thorough analysis of the internal and external business environmental influences on the new venture.

While the key to initiating the new venture lies within the individual entrepreneur seeking to introduce change and satisfy personal goals, its development is not only affected by the ability of the individual entrepreneur seeking change, but also the degree to which the spirit of enterprise exists in the society, or can be stimulated within the society in which the new venture is been developed. This relates to factors that stimulates or prevents individuals, groups and organisations from behaving entrepreneurial.

Entrepreneurs are not robots; blindly fulfilling an economic function. They can only pursue opportunities or strive for economic efficiency within the right enterprising culture. As human beings entrepreneurs operate within societies which define and to an extent, defined by enterprise cultures.

There is no agreed definition of the concept of an enterprise culture. However, the enterprise culture might be conceived as one, requiring individuals, groups and organisations to take responsibility for their own destiny (ownership), rather than been dependent on others. It is about being dependent on one-self. It is about a proactive culture that is encourages initiating, doing, achieving new ventures or enterprises.

According to the UK Department of Employment (1989), the heart of any enterprise culture is in the ability to innovate, recognise and create opportunities, work in a team, take risks and respond to challenges. Under such circumstances, it is to be expected that there exists a wide range and diversity of enterprise cultures. However, the one thing they appear to have in common is positive social attitude towards personal enterprise that enables and supports entrepreneurial activity.

It is important to note that there is no such thing as standard identifiable and universal culture that stimulates entrepreneurship. Rather, there exists the culture that stimulates entrepreneurship. Such culture is expected to contain factors that serve as incubator for entrepreneurship initiation and development. These factors can be grouped under:

Internal factors:

- ✓ Entrepreneurial culture.

External factors:

- ✓ Socio-cultural factors.
- ✓ Politico- economic factors.
- ✓ Institution or organisational factors

8.2.2 Internal Factors Shaping Enterprise Culture

The Entrepreneurial factor

The culture of any venture is influenced by the founder who imprints his/her values on it. Hence, if founded by true entrepreneur, the culture of a new venture might be expected to be entrepreneurial.

Entrepreneurial cultures are usually "adaptive "in values - receptive to creativity, innovation and change.

This leads to a consideration of the values that characterises adaptive cultures. Peter et al (2000) suggested there are three essential set of values which ensures adaptive culture such as:

- ✓ Bias for action - whereby the emphasis is on autonomous and initiative and employees are encouraged to take risks; managers are not simply involved in strategic decision - making but in the day- to-day operation of the firm
- ✓ Focus on both what it does best and, importantly on its customers - as a means of improving its competitive position
- ✓ Respects and motivates its employees.

The entrepreneur Michael Dell, founder of DELL company maintains his entrepreneurial values that keep his company as adaptive as possible through a customer service culture, achieved through decentralisation of authority and decision making, encouraging employees to get as close to the customer as possible to ensure both high quality and customer service in relation to customisation, and developing awareness and responsiveness of the firm to changes in the marketplace, to the much needed higher level, to achieve both customisation and performance.

The founder of Wal-Mart Sam Walton was able to develop the business to its success on the bases of business cultural values of hard work, constant improvement, and dedication to customers and grievance care for employees. His business's commitment to these values is deeply ingrained in its strategy of low prices, good values, friendly service, productivity through the intelligent use of technology, hard nose bargaining with suppliers.

8.2.3 External Factors Shaping Enterprise Culture

Political factors

Political factors can create or hinder culture of enterprise.

The right political factors that create good governance is a necessary condition for the emergence of vibrant entrepreneurial class.

One important political factor is the political system itself - which can directly or indirectly influence the way the economy is managed.

A political system can be described in terms of command or market or mixed economy and each has different influence on entrepreneurship and venture development.

By a political system we mean, the system of government in a nation that is shaped by its institutions, political parties and interest groups, as well as political norms and rules that govern business activities in the nation.

Entrepreneurial activities are strongly influenced by developments in a political system. The extent to which entrepreneurial activities are restricted or encouraged will depend on:

1. The degree to which the political system emphasizes collectivism or individualism.
2. The degree to which the political system is democratic or totalitarian.

"Collectivism" and "Totalitarianism" as forms of political systems are very much related as both deny freedom of individuals and private enterprise. Collectivism refers to a political system that stresses the primacy of collective goals over individual goals. When collectivism is emphasized in a society, the needs of the society as a whole are generally viewed as being more important than individual freedoms. In such circumstances, an individual's rights to do something may be restricted on the ground that it runs counter to the good of the society or to the common good. So is totalitarianism in many ways – a political ideology based on collective orientation that includes Authoritarianism, Fascism, Secularism, and Theocratic system. In a totalitarian system, a single agent (whether an individual, group or party), monopolises political power. All the constitutional guarantees on which representative democracy is built – an individual's rights to freedom of expression and organisation, a free media, and regular elections- are denied to citizens. Those who question the right of the rulers to rule may find themselves imprisoned or worse. Collectivism and totalitarian systems have one thing in common. They do not encourage free enterprise, and as such, not necessary conducive for business and management activities.

Individualism and democracy in most cases go hand in hand. Individualism refers to a philosophy that an individual should have freedom in economic and political pursuits. It stresses precedence of individual interests over the interests of the society as a group. There are emphases on the importance of guaranteeing individual freedom and self expression. This is the case with democracy – a political system in which government is by the people, exercised either directly or through elected representatives which includes individual rights to freedom of expression, opinion and organisation, free media, regular elections, etc. The tenet of both individualism and democracy is that the welfare of society is best served by letting people pursue their own economic self- interest, as opposed to some collective body such as government dictating what is in society's best interest. The central message therefore, is that individual economic and political freedom is ground rules on which society should be based. Countries with this political orientation encourage business to support the good of the community by providing fair and just competition - conducive for business and management activities.

For example, in non democratic system, entrepreneurship is not only discouraged, but not accommodated. There are varying degrees and types of direct state intervention that can affect the propensity for private enterprise development.

In a more egalitarian and democratic system, entrepreneurial attitudes and behaviours tend to be encouraged by the non-interventionist policies of the state. Where intervention takes place it is usually intended in creating business environment and incentives for creativity, self confidence, innovation -attributes for entrepreneurship. In countries where strong government interventions have no entrepreneurial objectives, the tendency is to produce persons who are lacking in entrepreneurial attributes – lacking in leadership, creativity, self reliance and self confidence.

Political systems also shape entrepreneurial activities, in as much as they determine government policies, regulations and legislations, including political institutions that shape the general business environment of any firm. Government could influence business decisions through government policies, laws and legislations, as well as government agencies, all of which may specify rules of the game – creating the framework within which companies operate.

Political institutions also have influences on business and entrepreneurial activities in a given business environment. Political institutions include government political parties, agencies and pressure groups whose activities and actions may have direct and indirect influences on the political environment, business and management behaviours.

The nature and complex dimensions of political variables identified in the general business environment usually constitute political risks. Political risks are associated with the possibility that political decisions, events, or conditions will affect a business environment in a way that will cost business existence or its performance. Sources of political risks may include:

- ✓ Expropriation or nationalisation.
- ✓ Internal war or civil strife.
- ✓ Unilateral breach of contracts.
- ✓ Destructive government action.
- ✓ Harmful action against people.
- ✓ Restrictions on repatriation of profits.
- ✓ Differing point of view.
- ✓ Discriminatory taxation policies.

All these can create entrepreneurial problems. However, the government can create culture of enterprise with the presence of good government policies - necessary condition for the emergence of vibrant entrepreneurial class.

Macro-economic factors

A number of macro-economic factors directed to encourage entrepreneurial conditions for all ventures can help create or encourage culture of enterprise. They include the following:

- Market economy

Entrepreneurship requires a market economy. This highlights advantages associated with market economy in relation to enterprise and new venture development. Economic freedom associated with market economy creates greater incentives for innovation. Any individual who has innovative idea is free to try to make money out of that idea.

- Economic stability

Although entrepreneurship can probably cope with uncertainty better than most and some are actually able to benefit from it, a stable macro -economic environment is believed to be crucial to the development of entrepreneurship such as - low inflation, low interest rate, stable exchange rates, etc.

- Level of bureaucracy

Apart from economic stability, macroeconomic policies intended to reduce the level of bureaucracy facing new ventures and small firms with respect to taxation and compliance are essential ingredients for conducive entrepreneurial culture. Therefore, the emphasis in the taxation system should be a shifted from direct tax to indirect tax, with corresponding reduction in the levels of personal taxation and increased paper work that usually affect small business ability to cope. Additionally, governments can simplify taxation regulation and move to the system of self assessment in an attempt to reduce compliance costs for small firms. The objective is to reduce the burden of taxation on small firms and to simplify the financial requirement in cost and paperwork in an attempt to create an environment more conducive for entrepreneurial business activities.

- Strategic alliance and support

Strategic alliance and support should be engaged through government policies to develop culture of enterprise. As access to market is very important for the health of small business sector, macroeconomic policies should be intended to create new market opportunities for small and medium enterprises- encouraging strategic and subcontracting between small and large businesses. Government departments and agencies can encourage and support small businesses through procurement and contract policies, including policies that assist new ventures and small business in securing market opportunities overseas - through international interventions as political alliances, trade mission's provision of advice, etc.

- Employment and recession

Employment can affect the predisposition of entrepreneurship in many ways. High level of employment may restrict entrepreneurship (i.e. new firm formation), while high level of unemployment encourages individuals to offer themselves for self-employment.

Traditionally, entrepreneurship and new venture creation has flourished when an economy has been in recession. Under such circumstances entrepreneurship represents a means by which the economy and the population can break out of the downward spiral of unemployment and low economic growth.

There does seem to have been a link between the rate of unemployment and entry into business ownership in many developing countries. The revival of self employment and small business ownership in developed countries coincided with a period of recession and high levels of unemployment from the late 1970s, through the early 1980s. Recession and resulting unemployment has pushed many reluctant entrepreneurs into self-employment, and provided the stimulus for others who had already considered starting their own business, but were reluctant to give up the security of their employment.

- Encouraging growth of the service sector

Over the past years there has been a very considerable shift in the structures of economics, with a movement from manufacturing into the service sector. While this is true in all economies, it is most noticeable in the developed economies. Various theories have been put forward to explain this development, but essentially the debate focuses on whether the growth in services is independent of, or causally linked to, the decline in manufacturing.

The growth of the service sector is part of a fundamental shift towards a post industrial society. This involves a move from blue collar job towards a white collar employment as a result of the increased demand in services, and the consequent evolution of economies from agrarian to industrial, then service activities.

Some argue that the changes do not signify the emergence of a new type of economy but rather, changes in an industry as it adjust in an era of what is often referred to as "late capitalism." Thus, they contend that the increases in service sector employment are the result of manufacturers contracting out services to cut costs, increase flexibility, and remain competitive . . . Whatever the reasons, there has been an increase not only in the number of smaller, more flexible small enterprises, but in mew opportunities for potential entrepreneurs

The vast majority of small firms operate in the service sector and construction sectors of the economy. According to Jones (2015) 85% of the UK firms employing less than 50 people are in the service sector and construction. There has been a strong structural shift in the economy from the manufacturing based industries and towards services. Services have expanded to over 70% of GDP – a measure of the total output of an economy. Hence, small firms are most active in the more dynamic sector of the economy.

Small businesses have competitive advantage in many service sector which account for their strong representation of this area of business.

Many services such as communication and professional advice services (e.g. advert, accounting, computer service, consultancy etc.) rely on personalised, tailor made service and very suited to flexibility and responsiveness of small business. Other services involve consumption at the point of purchase (e.g. restaurants, wine bar, freehouses) which favour small outlets requiring individual management.

- Flexible working

Work flexibility or the existence of flexible work environment that give the ability to get a job to work from home will influence entrepreneurship, encoring people to make a change and start new ventures - working from home.

- Network and multi-level marketing

Network and multi-level marketing involves a system of pyramid selling - multi-level, or network marketing based on the principle of self- employed distribution being encouraged to build a sales organisation of persons like themselves, by their own efforts.

Direct selling via network/multi-level marketing has become one of the fastest growing forms of self-employment and entrepreneurship for many people in many countries, especially developing countries . . . The system can create a culture of enterprise by attractions the possibility of self- employment, not the least the ability to start and build a new venture or small businesses without any previous experience or skills or any great capital investment, as distributors work from home. The people involved in the network are rewarded financially on the basis of the total sales of the distributors within the organisation developed by them and in this way are paid in proportion to their efforts with respect to both selling and sponsoring (recruiting) others. The downside relates to overenthusiastic, unethical, and occasionally illegal activities of distributors.

- Franchising

Franchising is the arrangement whereby the owner of a product, process or service (the franchisor) allows someone else (the franchisee), the right to use it in exchange of some sort of payment . . . The most common form of franchise occurs when a company allows a third party to operate a proven business system in a defined geographical areas using a common format for promoting, managing and administering the business- known as business format franchising. This type of business arrangement can foster culture of enterprise as it is a low-cost means of setting up a new venture for many people who become entrepreneurs.

Micro-economic factors

Apart from macro-economic factors introduced, a number of micro-economic factors relating to the development of hard and soft schemes, innovative policies, grants and awards, incubator units or offices, enterprise zones - directed to individual new venture and small firms - can also help create enterprise culture. Governments can introduce these to improve enterprises culture (correcting market failures), intended to help new ventures and existing small firms acquire the opportunities, skills, and resources they need to survive and grow. They can also be used to strengthen economic competitiveness in an economy, by creating a healthy, vibrant business sector which the entrepreneur is part of.

- Hard and soft support schemes

Hard support and soft support schemes can be provided by the government to encourage new ventures and entrepreneurs.

Hard support schemes may include tangibles such as money, building, equipment etc. and varies (provision of finance, physical infrastructure, etc).

Soft support schemes may include intangibles such as education, know- how, etc, - that may come in forms of training, advice, consultancy, helping potential entrepreneurs to acquire general business skills and expertise in business specialist subjects such as accounting, taxation, legal issues, marketing and exporting, etc. These may be provided through the education system or through specialist organisations in the public and private sector.

Both hard and soft support can be provided nationally, regionally, locally and can be targeted at all stages in the life cycle of a firm. They are intended to raise awareness of the opportunities for self employment, stimulate the birth of new ventures, and facilitate survival and growth.

Throughout Europe and USA the Chamber of Commerce has played an active role in this context and new technology sectors are normally encouraged and promoted. However, developing countries usually promote business efficiency in non technology sectors such as retail. Overall, many governments are subsidising or paying in full for these services for small firms to enjoy since many entrepreneurs are either unwilling or unable to pay for management consulting or for training and consulting,

- Micro policies to support innovation

Governments can also introduce macro policies to support innovation in technology. Such policies can be targeted at universities and government research departments or centres, and are intended to encourage commercialisation of research.

- Grants and awards

Grants and awards can also be used to focus on existing entrepreneurs and small business intended to stimulate new product and process development through grants and awards.

- Developing incubator units or offices

Many countries are now developing incubator units or offices and science parks intended to create clusters of new small businesses with similar needs and interests.

The aim is to help small businesses solve the problem with office space, and create an environment that encourages and foster entrepreneurship, new venture development and sustainability

In such environment, small businesses can benefit from economies of proximity and association as well as the provision of common support and advisory.

- Enterprise zones

The Enterprise Zone is a tax free haven where government bureaucracy is kept to the minimum particularly with respect to land use planning regulation.

The introduction of Enterprise Zone is modelled on Hong Kong,

The creation of Enterprise Zones is now becoming popular in many countries as a specialist form of macro support directed to entrepreneurship and small business development – Where they do not have to pay local authority rates and are exempt from certain regulatory restrictions, in particular planning constraints. Some countries use it to encourage export promotion.

Socio-cultural factors

Socio –cultural factors can also help create culture of enterprise. Some of the socio- cultural factors influencing the development of enterprise culture may include the following:

- Religion

Religious beliefs influence attitude to entrepreneurship and development. Such religion that does not oppose entrepreneurship is likely to encourage it.

Good examples are Christianity and Judaism. These religions do not opposed development of entrepreneurship. Christians especially protestants have work ethics that encourages wealth creation, and under such circumstances a culture is created that encourages a spirit of self –reliance, enterprise and innovation.

Where such belief thrives and is encouraged, there is the growth of enterprise culture and many new ventures are established. This is true in many developed countries such as UK.

- Education

Apart from religion, formal education can also determine to a great extent the level of entrepreneurship development and anti-entrepreneurial behaviour in a society or country.

It is possible for people in society or country to be ambivalent towards entrepreneurship as a result of their educational conditioning – that is either restrictive or creates ignorance.

People may be ignorant or unaware of entrepreneurship due to the education system they are evolved in that encourages seeking employment than creating employment, placing more premium on knowledge acquisition and retention thereby restricting creativity, competence building, capability and the ability to relate to others, and conditions young people to be dependent – restricting entrepreneurship.

Clearly, an education system that is not restrictive to entrepreneurship is one that places no premium on knowledge acquisition and retention, that does not restricts creativity, competence, capability and the ability to relate to others, and that does not conditions young people to be dependent on others for employment opportunities will surely promote enterprise culture.

- Family

Entrepreneurial behaviour can be related to family background or ethnicity.

Family attitudes can act as encouragement or barriers to enterprise culture, both by conditioning offspring to behave in an enterprise or un-enterprising manner, and by encouraging or discouraging them from exploring the concept of self employment either formally or informally.

Many successful new ventures started as family business and these entrepreneurs have expressed the fact that they owe their success to the support of their family (in terms of provision of funding, access to the market, moral support, role models, etc). The children of self-employed parents are usually the moss disposed to entrepreneurship than those of employed parents.

This the case of Indians as they are exclusive owners of many small corner shops in UK- with their children and relatives as apprentice, following the footsteps of their parents or family members in starting their own corner shops.

In a society where there are few entrepreneurs and few family businesses, there are likely to be few family role models, and entrepreneurship development is unlikely to be encouraged.

- History

Historical conditioning can impact upon the extent to which entrepreneurship characteristics exist within the population and the degree to which it is accepted as socially legitimate (e.g. command economy, market economy).

- Plosive role models

Positive role model entrepreneurs are important contributors to culture of enterprise in a society our country. They are likely to have positive impact in the development of culture of enterprise in a society or country.

The more successful entrepreneurs people can look up to, the more the young and even the old are s motivated to take entrepreneurship alternative, due to positive role models in this area.

- Formal enterprise culture

Clearly, culture plays a role in entrepreneurial behaviour.

At least this appears to be true in the sense of formal enterprise culture - the entrepreneurship culture that manifested itself in the creation of new small businesses. As indicated earlier, Indians have a developed formal enterprise culture – the culture of starting and owning their business than working for someone, which is evident in the number of Indians corner shops and other small businesses in UK.

Legal factors

Legal factors can determine business and enterprise start-up and development in a society or country and thereby shape enterprise culture.

Entrepreneurship does operate well in business environment with legal systems that can quarantine protection of all business legal rights, and have the required machinery to enforce them.

The legal environment is the dimension of the general environment that spells out the legal requirement and associated issues, a business need to consider and adhere to, while carrying out business in a given business environment. This could be discussed under the following:

- ✓ Legal systems.
- ✓ Government legislations and regulations.
- ✓ Business laws and regulation.

- ✓ Employment laws and regulations.
- ✓ Operational, strategic and intellectual legal issues.
- ✓ Implications for managers.

Legal system of a country refers to the rules, or laws that regulate behaviour, along with the processes by which the laws are enforced, and through which redress for grievances are obtained.

The legal system of a country is of immense importance to enterprise because, it provides the legal framework that regulates business practices, define the manner in which business transactions are to be conducted or executed, and set down the rights and obligations of those involved in business transactions. It is important to recognise that the law constitutes the "rules of the game" for business activity.

Entrepreneurs need to identify the legal issues in their business environment that could constitute strategic or operational benefits or threats to the new venture.

Operational legal issues in business may be found in areas like:

- ✓ Starting up a business.
- ✓ Hiring and firing employees.
- ✓ Task compliance.
- ✓ Making and enforcing contracts.
- ✓ Labour relations.
- ✓ Going under and getting out.

Strategic legal issues may also be found in areas like:

- ✓ Product safety and liability.
- ✓ Marketplace behaviour.
- ✓ Product origin and local content.
- ✓ Legal jurisdiction.
- ✓ Arbitration.
- ✓ Property rights.

Legal issues relating to Intellectual property may be found in areas like; abuse or neglect of International property rights.

In a legal sense, the term property refers to a resource over which an individual or business holds a legal title- that is a resource that it owns.

Resources include land, buildings, equipment, capital etc. Property rights also refer to the legal rights over the use to which a resource is put, and over the use made of any income that may be derived from that resource.

It should be recognised that without effective property right protection, businesses and individuals run the risk that the profits from innovative new venture effort will be expropriated, either by criminal elements or by state.

Property rights can be violated in many ways. This could be through private action- theft, privacy, blackmail, and the like by private individuals or groups.

It could also be through public action and corruption - the extortion of income or resources from property holders by public officials, such as politicians and government bureaucrats.

Entrepreneurs can protect intellectual property through: Patent, Copyrights, Trademarks, etc.

Private sector support

The level and effectiveness of private sector support for enterprise and development can help shape the couture of enterprise in a society or country.

Private sector supports can come from:

1. Financial service institutions.
2. Professional services.
3. Large organisations.
4. Small firm networks and alliances.

Financial service institutions like banks and other financial institutions can help create culture of enterprise by re-deploying the funds of their investors and savers, redirecting them to targeted, safer, new and longer established enterer prises. To achieve this, banks will have to train their staff on the principles of running of small business and set up special small business units offering advice and guidance in addition to money to targeted new and established enterprises.

New lending schemes had to be introduced to supplement existing ones in line demands of the enterprises to be served, and venture capital firms are to be encouraged.

Professional services need to be encouraged to create culture of enterprise. This will help increase in the availability of advice to small enterprises, especially in the private sector where the chief source of advice in the rank order are accountants, banks or solicitors and then business associations or consultants. It is important to recognise that the needs of enterprises are not confined solely to preparing annual accountants and assisting with contractual matters but they need general management knowledge for starting and running a new venture to sustain it.

Large organisations also have their role in creating culture of enterprise in a society or country. They can do this by forming local partnerships between themselves and the small firms in their region. This can involve helping small firm suppliers/contractors through the supply chain by creating strategic alliances or preferred supplier partnerships. They can also sponsor various initiatives intended to promote the creation and development of small enterprises, play important role in the establishment and management of local enterprise agencies as discussed earlier and established schemes to establish new businesses. For example, the British Coal established initiatives (British Steel plc and British Coal Enterprise Ltd) to assist people in creating new ventures in areas affected by losses in their industry. The assistance took the form of loans, managed workspaces, training and advice, etc.

Small firm networks and alliances developed in the private sectors can also promote culture of enterprise. This will help links with large organisations that are important. It will also help link the formal and informal networks. The help and guidance received from both formal network (banks, accountants, lawyers) and the informal networks (family, friends, business contacts) will influence the nature of the firm substantially and the entrepreneur's ability to identify, cultivate and manage a network partnership that is an essential condition for survival and success.

Public sector support

Apart from private sector support, the level and effectiveness of public sector support for enterprise and development can also add shape in the bid to develop the culture of enterprise in a society or country. Public sector support for entrepreneurship is meant to encourage the following:

- Raising awareness
- Facilitating entry
- Facilitating growth

Raising awareness through the public sector support may include:

✓ Measures channelled through education system to young people
✓ Measures intended to encourage the unemployed to consider self employment as an alternative to unemployment.

Among the former are such school based initiatives such as Young Enterprise, Achievement programmes, the Young enterprise projects: all intended to develop pupil understanding of how to run a small business. Similarly, in higher education, numerous programmes have been introduced that are intended to raise awareness among students of importance of entrepreneurship and self employment. In UK, perhaps of more relevance to entrepreneurship development is Department of Trade and Industry intention to develop more entrepreneurial cultures with Universities. This include the £60 million University challenge initiative intended to assist 15 Universities to provide local seed – funding to support the early funding and communication of research and 25 million Science Enterprise Challenge intended to create 12 world class entrepreneurial centres in the Universities by bringing business and entrepreneurial skills into sconce curriculum. Bringing renewed interest in entrepreneurship in the Universities.

Both hard and soft support should be made available by the public sector to support and facilitate easy entry to enterprise that will help entrepreneurs create new ventures. Hard support should range from finance to premises and space, such as the Enterprise allowance scheme, the Loan Guarantee Scheme. These provide government guarantees to banks. Among the initiatives should be to provide space and accommodation for new small firms were Enterprise Zones should be seen as "tax free" heavens where firms do not have to pay local authority rates and are exempt from certain regulatory restrictions, in particular, planning constraints, intended to foster growth in new ventures. Managed workspace and business incubators are row other forms of support intended to facilitate the birth and development of new ventures. Managed workspace is a form of property development that provides both space and support for conventional new businesses. Normally rents are subsidised and the support available is in the form of secretarial an office services, security and business advice. There are no entry conditions and there is no graduation policy. As a result the workplace is normally occupied by a wide range of businesses, attracted by the flexible rents and space, and tenants are encouraged to stay. This contrasts with incubators.

Public sector support should also be geared towards facilitating growth. This should mainly take the form of making available the requisite funding and know-how to enable expansion to occur such as the Business Expansion Schemes. More targeted assistance should be given to facilitate innovation in medium and small sized enterprises. Know-how schemes have to involve training and consultancy (e.g. NVQs). Government initiatives to promote know-how in small business should include consultancy initiatives and other measures intended to provide small firms with know-how to grow, targeted at opening up new markets, especially overseas.

Not for profit sector support

In addition to private and public sector supports, the Not for profit sector support can also contribute in shaping the culture of enterprise in a society or country.

Not for profit sector support can also contribute to enterprise culture by helping to increased social awareness and enlightenment in enterprise. The result can create a whole range of initiatives, including programmes to assist different sectors of the population in establishing their own business and/or finding employment in small enterprises.

In UK for example, non-for –profit initiatives like Instant Muscle has been able to provide younger manual workers with basic management skills. Project Full Employ has help edn minority group members set up their own business or find employment. Livewire and the Prince Youth Business Trust have also provided finance for promoting new businesses operated by young people. STEP – the Shell Technology Enterprise Programme enables undergraduates to experience employment in a small enterprise.

Further reading

Deakins, D. and Freel, M. (2003), Entrepreneurship and Small Firms (3rd Edition), London: McGraw Hill.

Ducker, P. (1985), Innovation and Entrepreneurship, London: Heinemann.

Kirby, D. (2003), Entrepreneurship, London: McGraw Hill.

Kuratko, D. and Hodgetts, R. (2001), Entrepreneurship: A contemporary Approach (5th Edition), New York: Dryden.

Morris, M. (2000), "Revisiting "who" is the Entrepreneur", Journal of Developmental Entrepreneurship, Vol.7, No. 1, pp2.10.

Ovian, B. and McDougall, P.(2005), "Defining international entrepreneurship and modelling the speed of internationalisation, Entrepreneurship Theory and Practice, Vol. 29, No. 5, pp.537-53.

Parker, S. (2002), "On the dimensionality and composition of entrepreneurship", Durham Business School Working Paper.

Westhead, P. Ucbasaran, D. (2005), "Decisions, actions and performance; do novice, serial and portfolio entrepreneurs differ?" Journal of Business Management, Vol. 43, No. 4, pp.393-417.

CHAPTER 9

THE ENTREPRENEURIAL NEW VENETURE AND MANAGEMENT TASKS

Aim

To introduce the entrepreneurial new venture management tasks.

Objectives

After studying this chapter you should be able to:

- Understand the meaning of management.
- Explain what managers do.
- Understand the use of entrepreneurial management tasks of Planning, organising, leading and controlling to achieve new venture development.

9.1 Introduction

The entrepreneurial new venture needs to be properly managed to achieve the desired development and sustainability.

Management generally is concerned with how managers get things done with the aid of people and other resources. This relates to what entrepreneurs must do as they engage in the process of the new venture development.

This chapter presents the four management tasks and how the entrepreneur can apply them in the process of new venture management involving entrepreneurial planning, organising, leading and controlling, essential for achieving new venture development.

The amount of management involved will vary with the venture and the entrepreneur. As managers, entrepreneurs need not perform these tasks in any particular sequence, but more or less simultaneously, switching rapidly between them as the situation requires. The successful application of these tasks will vary, as much depends on the level of management understanding of the entrepreneur, how much the entrepreneur understands the external business environment, and the internal capability of the new venture to deliver whatever direction the entrepreneur decides upon.

9.2 Entrepreneurial Planning

9.2.1 Introduction

The starting point for managing a successful entrepreneurial new venture development is the application of planning activities and processes that will help identify and activate essential areas needed for the venture development. In discussing planning, we shall include strategy and decision making as part of the planning process, and this will be discussed in detail.

Many new ventures are created without the requisite planning. Frequently, those who start new ventures possess the technical but not the managerial skills and understanding to make them work. They are convicted by their idea and believe that customers will want to buy their ideas.

Many new ventures fail especially within the first two years of starting up. The reasons for this are numerous but the ability of the entrepreneur to plan and manage the venture is paramount.

Planning has been described in many ways by many authors, researchers, and management scholars. According to Cole (2006) Planning is defined as "decision making process by which an organisation decides what it wants to achieve and how it intends to achieve it, in what manner, as well as the result". Daft (2008) described planning as "the management function concerned with defining goals for the future organisational performance, and deciding on tasks and resource use needed to attain them."

In general, planning is usually concerned with three impotent points:

1. What goals/objectives the organisation wishes to pursue and achieve?
2. What causes of action to adopt to attain these goals/objectives?
3. What best ways to use resources to attain goals/objectives of the organisation?

Strategic planning has gained popularity amongst many successful firms operating in today's fast changing business environment, as it considers the firm and its environment. Chandler (1962) described strategic planning as, "the process of developing and maintaining a strategic fit between organisation's goal and capabilities and its changing environment."

When a plan is clearly defined, and leaves no room for interpretation, it is said to be a specific plan. Specific plans work well in situations or environment of certainty. Specific plans are not flexible in nature in that, it has specific, unambiguous, mainly quantified objectives, and leaves little room for adjustments.

Entrepreneurial new venture plan is expected to be strategic as well as flexible, such as in the use of directional planning. Directional planning may be preferable because it gives a looser guidance-providing focus, but not locking the new venture managers into over-specific goals or courses of action. Entrepreneurship as already noted, is about creating change through creativity and innovation. This requires flexibility and close relationship to the external environment in order to achieve the right change. Changes in the external business environment create both opportunities and threats to the new venture position, but above all, create uncertainty. Entrepreneurial new venture directional planning offers a systematic way to cope with these uncertainties of the business environment, and helps the new venture adapt to business conditions. However, the flexibility inherent in any directional planning needs to be weighed against the loss of clarity that could be provided by specific plans.

9.2.2 Purposes of Planning New Venture Development

The purposes of planning the new entrepreneurial venture are many and varied. They relate to the corresponding use of planning as a significant management activity and associated benefits to develop the venture and lead it to successful operation.

According to David Simon, former chief executive of BP from 1992 to 1995, "if you do not target, you do not measure, and you do not achieve". A lack of planning or poor planning can hurt an organisation's performance. Winston Churchill said it best during the Second World War that, "he who fails to plan, is planning to fail". Planning if done well brings many benefits.

Planning is the primary management function because all other management functions derive from it. It is through planning that the entrepreneurial new venture describes where it is going and how to reach there, that helps the entrepreneur answer the questions of who, what, when, where and how? Planning develops any venture's direction. In the new venture, it is important that people involved in it know the road the venture is taking ahead, and the entrepreneur should share this with them, so that everyone involved with the venture can know how and when they get there. Planning establishes goals and standards that help the entrepreneur to monitor progress. Until goals and targets are clear, no entrepreneur can be sure whether or not they have completed the task.

Planning is an essential instrument that helps to identify the feasibility of the venture idea, or appreciate the difficulties involved in its operation. As planning deals with the overall direction of the work to be done in the new venture, it can clarify direction, as it includes forecasting future trends, assessing actual and potential resources, and developing objectives and targets for the future performance. The act of planning may in itself add value, by motivating all involved and improving their performance through participation, and ensuring that the entrepreneur makes decisions on the basis of a wider range of evidence than if there was no planning system. This enables the entrepreneur to compare actual progress against the goals, identify significant deviations, and either adjust the goals, or change the way resources are being used.

As already mentioned, changes in the external business environment create both opportunities and threats to the new venture position, but above all, create uncertainty. Planning therefore, offers a systematic way to cope with these uncertainties of the business environment, and adapting to environmental conditions.

9.2.3 The New Venture Planning Process

As explained earlier, strategic planning is the process of developing, maintaining a strategic fit between organisation's goal and capabilities and its changing marketing environment.

It relies on:

1. Vision.
2. Mission/purpose.
3. Goals and objectives.
4. Corporate, functional and operational strategies.

The entrepreneur needs to identify and establish the future direction of the venture in terms of the:

1. Entrepreneurial vision.
2. Entrepreneurial mission/purpose.
3. Entrepreneurial goals/objectives.
4. Entrepreneurial strategies.

- **The entrepreneurial vision**

An essential element in the process of effective development and successful implementation of the new entrepreneurial venture is the identification and understanding of the "entrepreneurial vision."

In general, "vision" could be described as an almost impossible dream. In business terms, this is associated with a business idea.

All successful new ventures started with an entrepreneurial vision - an idea or dream of one type or the other (what at that time looked like an impossible dream). For examples,- Sony's former president, Akko Morita, had a vision or dream of wanting everyone to have access to "personal portable sound" so his company created the Walkman and Portable CD. Fred Smith had a vision to deliver mail anywhere in the United States before 10:30 A.M the next day, so he created Federal Express. Thomas Monaghan had a vision to deliver hot pizza to any home within 30 minutes, and created Domino's Pizza. Sam Walton had a vision to bring modern discount principles to small town Americans, and he created Wal-Mart. Bill Gate 1980s vision for Microsoft was "a computer on every desk and in every home". Today, all these dreams, or visions, or business ideas by these great men seem uninspiring, even obvious. In those days when they were having these dreams, it seemed extraordinary or impossible.

Vision is the starting point for giving shape and direction to new venture. This usually exists in the tension between what is and what might be, and specifies a destination rather than a route to get there.

Vision develops from the idea that things might be different from, or better than they are currently.

A vision might present itself to the entrepreneur quite suddenly or might emerge slowly taking shape as the entrepreneur explores an opportunity and recognises its possibilities. It includes the understanding of the rewards that are to be earned by creating the new world and why people should be attracted to them. If it is to lead the business in the right direction, vision must be properly examined, defined and examined before being developed.

The entrepreneur's vision is a picture of the new world he/she wishes to create. It is the picture of the world into which the entrepreneur fits an understanding of why people will be better off, the source of the new value that will be created, and the relationships that will exist. This is very positive and the entrepreneur is drawn towards it, and is motivated to make the vision a reality.

Entrepreneurs are usually described as visionaries and managers.

As visionaries, they create visions - a mental image that entrepreneurs usually carry around in their head, as a very powerful tool for the starting, development and management of the new venture.

As managers, entrepreneurs manage the creation of a new world that offers the possibility that value will be generated and made available to the venture stakeholders. This value can only be created through change – change in the way things are done, change in organisation and change in relationships.

It is practical to say that any new venture not based on a clear vision is likely to perish. In other words, show me a new venture and I will show you its vision. Vision plays a very important role in the strategic direction of any new venture, as it provides a picture perspective, and acts as guiding touch light and motivating force for any new venture, and those involved in it. It also provides a projection of what the venture aims to achieve in the future, the articulation of clarity of purpose, a view of future direction, providing the entrepreneur the basis for venture direction, sense of encouragement, venture moral, content and instrument for attracting people or investors.

The author believes that visions are inspirations from Almighty God, designed and given for a divine purpose. The practical application however, depends on a person's spiritual orientation, intentions and understanding of the purpose to which it is given.

Successful visions are usually associated with innovation, as every market offering include a vision or basic idea at its core. For example, products and services we enjoy today originate from visions or business innovative ideas, from various people, translating innovative ideas into products or services -cars, trains, buses, banking services etc. - with underlying benefits as customers buy benefits not products and services.

- **The entrepreneurial venture – mission/purpose**

This is concerned with the development of a mission for the entrepreneurial venture.

What a new venture seeks to do and to become or what it wants to accomplish in a larger environment, is commonly termed a venture's mission or purpose.

Every entrepreneurial new venture exists to accomplish something – to satisfy needs consistently.

A venture mission or purpose is at its best when guided by a vision.

Mission or purpose is a translation of the vision into reality and tends to be more concerned with the present (what venture now, what needs to satisfy now, and in what way?).

> Entrepreneurial new venture mission statement

Visions and Missions are expressed in mission statements.

A mission statement is a formal statement, defining the purpose of the venture and what it aims to achieve, its operations and scope, including its short term and long term objectives, aiming to distinguish it from similar ventures. It is a powerful communication tool which can both guide internal decision making and relate the venture to external investors and other stakeholders.

A mission statement reveals what the venture wants to be and whom it wants to serve.

Developing a formalised mission can be valuable to the entrepreneurial new venture for a number of reasons:

- ✓ It articulates the entrepreneur's vision - provide the entrepreneur with a way to codify the vision, to be clear about the difference the venture or change will make.
- ✓ It encourages analysis of the venture.
- ✓ It defines the nature of the venture- what it aims to achieve and how it aims to achieve it.
- ✓ It defines the scope of the venture – stakeholders.
- ✓ It provides guides for setting objectives.
- ✓ It clarifies strategic options.
- ✓ It facilitates communication about the venture to potential investors.
- ✓ It provides constant point of reference.

➢ Options for developing mission statement

The entrepreneur has the following options for developing mission statement:

1. Developing through consensus - the consensus approach involves getting everyone involved in the venture to contribute towards the development of the mission. The aim is to gather information, create ideas and gain many insights as possible for generating and evaluating the mission.
2. Developing by imposition - developing by imposition arises when:

- ✓ The entrepreneur feels that consensus is not the best way to generate the mission and decides that it is better to develop the mission self, or in consultation with a small group if they

exist, and then impose it on the whole people involved in the venture.
- ✓ The entrepreneur may see the mission as the articulation of his/her personal vision which may not be negotiable.
- ✓ The entrepreneur may be the only person who has sufficient knowledge of the venture and its situation.

The choice of approach or options for developing mission statement depends on the venture, how complex it is, the way in which it is developing, and the leadership style adopted by the entrepreneur.

> The process of developing a mission statement

The process of developing a mission statement for a new venture may involve searching and selecting several articles about mission statements and asking people involved to read them as background information. The entrepreneur may then prepare a mission statement for the new venture. In some cases, the statement prepared can be run through by other people involved in the new venture before the entrepreneur can come up with a single document.

The entrepreneur has the optioned of use of discussions groups to develop and modify the mission statement during the process of developing a mission statement. It is important to involve as many people involved in the new venture as possible in the process of developing a mission statement, because through involvement, people become committed to the new venture.

Because the mission statement is the most visible and public part of strategic management process, they are often displayed throughout a firms premises and distributed with company information to the marketplace. They are often displayed in business public places such as reception offices, and can be found in a firm's annual reports. Mission statement can and do vary in length, content, format and specificity, however, most exhibit the following components:

- ✓ Customer preferences.
- ✓ Product quality.
- ✓ Technological innovation.
- ✓ Concern for current growth and productivity.

- ✓ Management philosophy.
- ✓ Firm's self-concept.
- ✓ Concern for public image.
- ✓ Concern for employees as valuable assets of the firm.

> Expressing entrepreneurial vision effectively in the mission statement.

There are three distinct aspects involved in forming a well conceived entrepreneurial vision and expressing it in the new venture mission statement:

1. Good definition of the entrepreneurial new venture.
2. Communicating the entrepreneurial vision and mission.
3. Deciding when to alter the entrepreneurial vision and mission.

1. Good definition of the entrepreneurial new venture.

Arriving at good definition of the entrepreneurial venture usually requires taking some essential factors into account such as:

- Customer needs - what is being satisfied.
- Customer groups - who is being satisfied (i.e. the market).
- The technologies and functions performed-- how customer needs are satisfied.

Defining a venture in terms of what to satisfy, who to satisfy and how the venture will go about producing the satisfaction usually make a complete definition.

Defining and understanding customer needs and benefits - what is being satisfied - is very important. Just knowing what products/services a firm provide is not enough. Products/services parse, are not important to customers but when it satisfies needs or wants. Without the need or want there is no business.

Customer groups are relevant because they indicate the market to be served, the geographical domain to be covered and type of buyers a firm is going after.

The need to identify the technology and function performed is because it helps to indicate how the venture will satisfy the customers' needs and how much of the industry's production/distribution chain its activities will span. The new venture can concentrate or specialise in just one stage of an industry total production/distribution chain, or fully integrated spanning all parts of the industry chain. How broad or how narrow a venture's vision or mission is, usually relates to the resources and capabilities available to carry out the vision or mission.

2. Communicating the strategic vision

It is important to recognise here that having a good definition of the entrepreneurial new venture is not enough, but this must be communicated to interested parties in ways that is clear, exciting and inspiring.

Vision is, in the first instance, a personal picture of the new world that the entrepreneur seeks to create. If it is to be used to attract other people to the venture, then this new world must be communicated to them. They must be invited to share in what the venture can offer.

Communication is not just about relating information; it is also about eliciting action on the part of the receiver. It is not about getting people to know things as about getting them to do things.

Successful entrepreneurs endeavour that their vision can be used to motivate others. The first stage is to understand why people will find the vision attractive.

The particular strategy adopted by the entrepreneur will depend on the number of factors, some of the more important ones include:

- ✓ The nature of vision being shared - how complex is it? how much detail does it have?
- ✓ The entrepreneur's leadership style - collaborative, democratic authoritarian.
- ✓ The stakeholders to whom the vision is being communicated - who are they, how many?
- ✓ The nature of communication desired from them - stakeholders
- ✓ The stakeholder particular needs and motivation (economic, social, self development).

- ✓ The stakeholder's relationship to the entrepreneur.
- ✓ The methods of the communication - formal or informal.
- ✓ The medium through which the communication is transmitted - face to face, verbal, written, etc.

The entrepreneur needs to use possible diverse approaches to communicate the vision to interested individuals and groups – stakeholders.

By using diverse approaches to communicating this vision, the entrepreneur keeps it relevant, avoids being repetitive and keeps the message fresh to recipients.

The entrepreneur's ability to articulate the vision and communicate it to different stakeholders in a way that is appropriate to them and in a way that is right for the situation is the basis on which he/she builds leadership and power.

The entrepreneur must identify what the new venture (the new world) will offer stakeholders – both as individuals and as a group.

How to describe the strategic vision, word it in the form of a mission statement and communicate it to interested parties is very important.

A vision and mission couched in words that inspire and challenge, and help build committed effort from other people, and serve as powerful motivational tools, is very essential to venture success. Bland language, platitudes and motherhood and apple pie style verbiage must be avoided. They can be a turn-off rather than a turn-on.

Entrepreneurs need to communicate the vision in words that arouse a strong sense of venture purpose, build pride and induce people to buy-into the venture objectives. People are proud to be associated with a new venture that has a worthwhile mission and is trying to be world best at something competitively significant.

The best worded mission statements are:

- ✓ Simple and concise.
- ✓ They speak loudly and clearly.
- ✓ Generate enthusiasm for the firm future course
- ✓ Elicit personal effort and dedication from everyone in the venture.

A member of approaches to communicating vision have been such as, "I have a dream, storytelling", etc.

3. Deciding when to alter the entrepreneurial vision and mission

Deciding when to alter the entrepreneurial vision and mission is another important aspect in forming a well conceived entrepreneurial vision and expressing it in the new venture mission statement:

With regards to entrepreneurial new venture vision and mission or purpose, there is the need to appropriate it to the right time and conditions associated with the venture business environment.

Since times and conditions change (as nothing is static in life), it becomes imperative that the vision or mission of the venture may need to be changed or adjusted to environmental conditions such as:

- ✓ Shifting customer wants and needs.
- ✓ Emerging technological capabilities.
- ✓ Changing international trade conditions and other important signs of growing or shrinking.
- ✓ Business opportunities, etc.

Repositioning a venture in light of emerging developments and changes on the horizon lessens the chances of getting trapped in a stagnant or declining core or current activities or letting attractive new growth opportunities slip away because of inaction.

Entrepreneurs who keep sharp eyes to the changing environment attend quickly to user s' problems and complaints with the industry current products and services. They listen to customers and clues and information from them stimulate them to think creatively and strategically about ways to break new grounds.

- **The entrepreneurial goal /objectives**

The entrepreneurial planning process also requires converting vision, mission to goals and objectives.

Entrepreneurs rarely stumble upon success. Effective or successful entrepreneurs know where they are going and why. They are focused on the achievement of specific goals/objectives.

In many textbooks, goals and objectives are usually used interchangeably to mean the same, and for the purpose of space and time, this will be the case in this book.

Goals/objectives are important because:

- ✓ Organisation exists for a purpose and goals/objectives define and state that purpose, and how to achieve it.
- ✓ They are a source of motivation.
- ✓ They act as guide to action.
- ✓ They provide rational for decision.
- ✓ They also provide standard of performance.

Setting goals/objectives have strong motivational effect on the entrepreneur and people associated with the entrepreneurial venture.

Goal theory (Locke and Latham, 1990) has established that challenging goals lead to higher level of performance, than simple goals that are easy to attain. Difficult goals are sometimes called "stretch "goals because, they challenge people to try harder, although, if people believe the goals are impossible to attain, the effect is opposite.

Specific goals/objectives can lead to higher levels of performance than vague goals. Employees usually find it easier to adjust their behaviour when they have something precise to aim for, and they are less likely to become involved in distracting discussions about what a vague goal means. Entrepreneurial goals/objectives can be set for a number of reasons, some of which include:

- ✓ Profit maximisation.
- ✓ Growth.

The entrepreneur may set up a new venture for profit motives - to make much profit as possible, although the entrepreneur in practice is likely to have satisfactory level of profit as a goal. This is known as "satisfying", as limited information may restrain a venture's expansion and profit maximising capability. Some ventures especially, the small ones, (usually called Moms and Pops small business), may prefer to stay small and not want to expand to maximise profits. Also, a business venture may sacrifice short term profit maximisation for long term satisfying profit, to retain customers in the market.

As explained in part 1 of this book, an entrepreneurial venture has more potential for growth than does a small business. This results from the fact that the entrepreneurial venture is usually based on a significant innovation. The market potential for that innovation will be more than enough to support a small firm. The small business on the other hand operates within an established industry and is unique only in terms of its locality. However, there are also small businesses who aim for growth as a goal, especially where there are market potentials and the small business owner/manager is willing to take the advantage. He/she may belief the venture must grow in order to survive, so may pursue growth as the main goal, or that a failure to grow might result in loss of competitiveness, and eventual closure. Growth may also be seen as the main way of gaining from market opportunities, as well as reducing the risks and costs in business. Stakeholders especially, investors in the new venture are likely to favour growth, since they are likely to benefit from it.

9.2.4 The Business Plan

Introduction

A business plan is a plan that shows at a glance, key areas of the venture operations and management - the overall new venture mission, overview of key objectives, the market environment, strategy, financial forecast, operational activities, and people involved in the new venture that will make it succeed.

Many new ventures succeed because they completed a business plan before new venture start-up and development. Many others are unsuccessful because new ventures are created without the requisite business plan, with the entrepreneur having no established feasibility of the new venture success, or knowledge and skills required to manage the new venture, with the result that he/she has to learn the hard way by trial and error. Often, errors can be fatal.

If new entrepreneurial ventures are to succeed, it is important to establish their feasibility from the onset and to put in place the management activities that will help navigate them to success. This could be done through preparing a business plan.

The purpose of the business plan

Entrepreneurial new ventures usually need a business plan before start-up and development.

Preparing a business plan is considered by many management consultants as a very important step in launching any new venture or expanding an existing one.

The importance of a business plan for the entrepreneurial new venture cannot be over- emphasised. It is an essential tool for the potential entrepreneur.

Essentially, the purpose of the business plan is to help the business founder crystallise his/her ideas – to consider all aspects of the business and see how they fit together.

The business plan is something that cannot be taken too lightly. It is also something that needs not to be rushed. If it is, it is unlikely to be of any great use.

Developing a business plan is an invaluable exercise as, through it, it is possible to identify any mistakes that, if made in the marketplace, could prove fatal.

Once completed, the plan enables the entrepreneur to see where he/she is going and how to get there, establishing the feasibility of the new venture, determining the fiscal needs of the venture, and raising finance.

It also acts as a map showing what is expected to be done and when. Thus, not only does it check the commercial and technical viability of the idea, but it sets goals and objectives, and allows monitoring of actual progress.

In terms of determining the fiscal needs of the business, the business plan should show how much money is needed, what it is needed for, when and for how long it is required.

In terms of raising finance, this is a further, important function for the business plan – to persuade external financial institutions to fund the project. Often, it is seen as the only reason for producing the business plan. Some of the reasons why new ventures fail are under-capitalisation and problem with cash flow. Many fail with full order books because they lack the resources to service them. A soundly prepared business plan can help avoid such difficulties.

A good business plan should help the potential entrepreneur raise the requisite funding, assuming the project is viable, as it helps the entrepreneur to demonstrate his/her understanding of the business and managerial capability, give him/her the opportunity to present the idea and sell it in a way that potential financiers will be able to understand,

Potential financiers will want to see a plan for the proposed business and financiers are looking for the following evidence in the business plan:

- ✓ Evidence of market orientation and focus – the plan must demonstrate that the need of the potential customer has been recognised.

- ✓ Evidence of customer acceptance – it must provide a clear idea of how and to whom the product is to be sold and that it is likely to sell it in the numbers predicted.
- ✓ Proprietary position – potential financiers want to see that the competition is limited, at least initially, by protecting the idea – patents, copyright, trademark, etc.
- ✓ Return – the venture should be capable not only to service any loan but provide return on investment.
- ✓ Believable forecast – the forecast should be able to convince that this is an attractive proposition.

The activity of creating a formal business plan consumes both time and resources. Many entrepreneurs object to preparing plans because they feel their time would be better spent pushing the venture forward. They claim that they already know what it is in the plan and that no one else will read it.

If a business plan is to be undertaken well, there must be an appreciation of the way in which the business plan can actually be made to work as a tool for the business.

In principle, there are some mechanisms by which a business plan might aid the performance of the venture:

- As a tool for analysis.
- As a tool for synthesis.
- As a tool for communication.
- As a call for action.

If the performance of the venture varies from that identified in the business plan, the reason for this and the implications for the venture needs to be considered and any remedial action taken.

The format of the business plan

While there is no single generalised format of a business plan, and a plan intended for raising finance may be somewhat different from the plan designed to establish the feasibility of a project, normally a business plan may contain some or many of the following sections:

- Executive summary – this covers all the main points in the plan and is intended to convince the reader that the plan itself is worth reading.
- Description of the business – the mission and objectives of the business, the name of the business, the proposed legal status of the business.
- Key personnel and their roles- background of founders of the new venture, qualifications and relative experiences related to venture initiation, development and performance
- The market and the marketing plan – market review, marketing objectives, marketing strategy, action plan, the place where the product will be sold.
- Operation and production plan produced in house, sourced externally.
- Human resources plan. The number of personnel involved in venture start-up and development, their qualifications and positions and responsibilities.
- Capital resources plan – investment in equipment, plant and machinery, premises, etc.
- Financial plan – the projected profit and loss account, the projected cash flow statement, the projected balance sheet, sensitivity analysis, breakeven point and analysis.

9.3 Entrepreneurial Strategy

9.3.1 Introduction

As detailed in chapter introduction, the process of entrepreneurial planning also includes strategy as an important element.

All ventures operating in the competitive environment are affected by strategy and strategic issues.

Strategy links the new venture to the outside world. Entrepreneurs should be concerned about strategy, as they need to find ways to respond to competitors, cope with difficult environmental changes, and effectively utilize available resources.

A number of management scholars and researchers have come up with several perspectives in which strategy could be interpreted and understood.

For example, Kay (1996) sees strategy as "the match between the organisation's internal capabilities and its external relationship"- its suppliers, its customers, its competitors, and the social and economic environment within which it operates.

According to Chandler (1962), strategy is "the determination of the basic long term goals and objectives of an enterprise, and the adoption of courses of action and the allocation of resources necessary for carrying out these goals". Mintzberg (1998) suggested nobody can claim to own the word "strategy", as the word can be expressed in many ways such as:

- A plan – an intentionally adopted means of achieving a goal, with its progress monitored from start to a predetermined finish, or a consciously intended course of action. (A deliberate strategy).
- A ploy – a manoeuvre, intended to influence employees 'behaviours, outwit an opponent or competitors etc- a manoeuvre in a competitive game. For example a firm might add unnecessary plant capacity. The strategy is not to produce the goods but to discourage a competitor from entering the market.

- A pattern - associated with a pattern of behaviour in which progress is made by adopting a consistent form of behaviour. Unlike plans and ploys, patterns just happen as a result of the consistent behaviour. (Emergent strategies).
- A position – in terms of environmental fit and relationships with the markets or other organisations. A position strategy is appropriate when the most important thing to a firm is how it relates to, or is positioned with respect to its competitors, or its markets (i.e. customers). In other words, the organisation wishes to achieve or defend a certain position. A position might be a distinctive niche, whereby the firm makes distinctive products or services, or exploits a distinctive competence.
- A perspective - a unique way of looking at the world, of interpreting information from it, judging its opportunities and choices and actions. Perspective strategies are used by some firms to make their employees think in a certain way, i.e. change their perspectives.

While the field of strategic management and entrepreneurship have developed largely independent of each other, they are both focused on how firms adapt to environmental changes and exploit opportunities created by uncertainties and discontinuities in the creation of wealth.

Entrepreneurship is about creation, strategic management is about how advantage is established and maintained from what is created. As such several scholars (Chandler 1962, Kay 1996, Jones 2009), have called for the integration of strategic and entrepreneurial thinking. Researchers argue the two are really inseparable. They assert strategy must exploit an entrepreneurial mindset and thus have no choice but to embrace it, to seize opportunities, mobilise resources and act to exploit these opportunities, especially under highly uncertain conditions.

It is important to recognise that in studying strategic management practices, the role of entrepreneur is critical. Whether or not an effective process of strategy development is implemented, will be influenced by the entrepreneur, and his/her ability to comprehend and make appropriate use of sophisticated strategic management practices, which is a function of the entrepreneur's previous experience.

The underlying purpose of every new venture is to perform well. This raises the concept of central importance in discussing strategy, that of competitive advantage. The concept of competitive advantage is concerned with factors that give the new venture an edge over its competitors, and enable it to achieve higher levels of profitability. Strategy defined in this competitive sense – which seeks to identify and sustain sources of competitive advantage- is called competitive strategy. It is concerned with how entrepreneurs respond to forces in the competitive environment.

Mintzberg (1985) drew attention to the fact that some strategies are either "Deliberate" or "Emergent", or a combination of both.

Deliberate strategy (sometimes called planned or programmed strategy) is meant to happen. It is preconceived and usually monitored and controlled from start to finish.

Emergent strategy has no specific objective. It does not have a preconceived route to success. If it is successful, it is said that a consistent behaviour has EMERGED into a success, in contrast to PLANNED behaviour.

According to Mintzberg and Waters (1985), the pattern of entrepreneurial strategy tends to be more "emergent" than "deliberate. This is so because, for the venture to be entrepreneurial, the entrepreneur needs to constantly adjust and review strategies in light of prevailing circumstance and as such, the strategy emerges in the light of experience of what is happening in the marketplace, to become a behaviour - flexible enough to reflect venture needs for responding to events, and driving performance. This type of strategy:

- ✓ Encourages the entrepreneur to access and articulate the vision.
- ✓ Ensures auditing of the venture and its environment.
- ✓ Illuminates new possibilities and limitations.
- ✓ Provides venture focus and guides the structuring of the new venture.
- ✓ Acts as a guide to continuous decision making.

9.3.2 Essential Components of Entrepreneurial Strategy

Specifying the components of strategy helps the entrepreneur identify clearly the areas of strategy focus that reflects strategy formulation and implementation.

Ideally a good strategy should help the venture to perform in not only what it does best, but what it does better than other competitors.

What many functions a good strategy does for the venture is to be a boundary marker - that defines what the venture does and what it does not do.

The boundaries are defined by three basic elements:

1. Where do we compete? - (attractive market opportunities). External analysis id needed to identify this area and covers the tools and framework.
2. How do we compete or what unique value do we bring to the market? - (we need resources and capabilities to serve the market better than other s. This include tangible and intangible resources) Internal analysis is needed to identify this area.
3. How do we execute and sustainability?– (strategy implementation is needed in this area).

We can envisage strategy like a three legged stool. In order that the strategy should succeed, the three legged must stand firmly (i.e. 1. Scope, 2. Resource, 3. Competence /Implementation). If one of the legs is missing the whole venture will fall over. Thus, there is the need for strategic sustainability and therefore synergy is inevitable.

Chandler's definition of strategy presented earlier in this section is a good definition as it shows the three important components of strategy. This includes:

1. The determination of long term goals - concerns the conceptualisation of coherent and attainable strategic objectives. Without objectives, nothing else can happen. If you do not know where you want to go, how can you act in such a way as to get there?

2. The adoption of courses of action - refers to actions taken to arrive at the objective that has been previously set.
3. The allocation of resources - refers to the fact that there is likely to be a cost associated with the actions required to achieve the objectives. If the course of action is not supported with adequate level of resources, then the objectives will not be accomplished.

At any point in time the new venture will have strategy content, that is, a product range being sold to distinct group of customers with a particular approach taken to attract those customers within the marketplace. For Wickham (2006) the content of entrepreneurial strategy relates to three things:

1. The final product range - this covers the type and range of products that the venture business supplies to its market.
2. The consumers the venture serves or the market scope - the market scope defines the customer groups and market segments that will be addressed by the venture.
3. The advantage the venture seeks or competitive approach - competitive approach refers to the way in which the venture competes within its product market domain to sustain and develop its business in the face of competitive pressures.

The strategy content will evolve as the venture grows and develops. New products will be introduced and old ones dropped. The competitive approach may alter as the entrepreneur learns, and market conditions change.

Entrepreneurship and Strategy

Entrepreneurship is about creation, strategic management is about how advantage is established and maintained from what is created. Also, the art of strategic manage mint need to be entrepreneurial to succeed. As such several scholars have recently called for integration of strategic management and entrepreneurship. Researchers argue the two are really inseparable.

They assert strategy must exploit an entrepreneurial mindset and thus have no choice but to embrace it to seize opportunities, mobilise resources and act to exploit these opportunities especially under highly uncertain conditions.

It is important to recognise that in studying strategic management practices in new ventures especially the small business ventures, the role of entrepreneur is critical.

The Entrepreneur as Strategist

It is now important to consider who has responsibility for making strategic decisions in the entrepreneurial new venture.

In a new entrepreneurial venture especially the small ones, the entrepreneur as the business owner-manna is the ultimate strategist. Strategic management formulation and implementation of strategic management tasks is usually controlled by the entrepreneur who is normally the owner/manager- who sets the direction, areas, and basis for strategic formulation and implementation. The entrepreneur as business manager makes all strategic as well as operational decisions in the venture involving simultaneously in all levels of the venture strategic and functional decision making. The entrepreneur develops the vision and mission of the venture and thus formulates and implements the business strategies of the firm. The ability to deliver an effective process of strategy development and implementation will be influenced by the entrepreneur as the small business ventures' owner/manager, his/her knowledge, understanding and experience in the use and applications r of appropriate and sophisticated strategic management techniques. As a matter of fact, the personal ambition, business philosophy and ethical beliefs of the entrepreneur usually shape the venture's polices, practices, traditions, philosophical beliefs and ways of doing things, that combine to give it a distinctive culture, and the direction of strategy formulation and implementation.

As the venture grows larger, the ultimate responsibility for leading the task of formulating and implementing a strategic plan for the whole organisation usually rests with the top management at the top of the strategic management hierarchy, responsible for the entire organisation. Those responsible for strategy formulation in large firms may have such titles as president, chairman or chairperson, executive director, chief executive director, and executive vice president. They are usually members of the board of directors elected by the shareholders in a limited liability company. In large ventures, the ambitions, values, business philosophy, attitude of senior management towards work and ethical beliefs usually have important influences on strategy. Sometimes these influences are deliberate and sometimes unconscious. The strategic direction top managers take is often influenced by their vision of how to compete, how to position the enterprise, and by what image and standing they want the firm to behave – reflecting the firm's cultural traits and management values.

9.3.3 The Strategy Planning Process

The venture's strategy process is the way in which it makes decisions about the strategy content, implementation, as well as feed back to achieve competitive advantage and performance.

Strategic planning process is notably essential for business survival and success. This is a process and never a once for all event- it goes on and on, placing the need for continuous review in line with changing business environment. The strategic process usually contains distinct stages:

1. Strategic analysis.
2. Strategic selection/choice.
3. Strategic implementation.
4. Feedback.

Strategy process is embedded in the structure, systems and procedures that the venture adopts, as well as its culture and the leadership style of the entrepreneur running it.

As already explained, there is a distinction between planned or deliberate strategy and emergent strategy. Entrepreneurs constantly adjust and review emergent strategies in the light of experience.

The strategy content of the new venture will evolve over time. The way the business venture modifies its range of products, changes its customer base and develops its competitive approach will be the result of ongoing decisions and actions taken by the entrepreneur. These decisions and actions will evolve as most entrepreneurs do not have an explicit strategy to guide them. They are sometimes incremental and the result of short term pragmatic considerations, made in response to immediate market opportunity.

It is important to note that entrepreneurs make good strategies happen not through following a strategic planning process, but through entrepreneurial leadership. It is also important to recognise, that the entrepreneurial leadership approach to management is distinct at the level of strategy process, not in the content.

It is not what an entrepreneur does (the business they are in) that matters. What makes the leadership entrepreneurial is the way the entrepreneur organises the venture and use it to innovate and to deliver value to customers in a way existing players cannot. Leadership in this respect is associated with the entrepreneur and the zeal to effect change - that requires listening to people, learning from them and taking their ideas on board to achieve. It also means giving people the latitude to make their own decision and put their insight into the practice- creating and maintaining the spirit of entrepreneurship, as the way the people in the venture can learn and be flexible.

The strategy process adopted by the entrepreneurial new venture is defined by the way in which decisions about strategy content are taken. It is reflected in the relationship that exists between the existing strategy content, the strategy content desired by the new venture for the future, and the strategy content that is actually achieved. The results of these connecting decisions influence the investments made in the venture. Even though entrepreneurs are mostly the sole owners of the business venture they may be limited in the extent to which they can control the actions of the people who make up the venture organisation. The way in which entrepreneurs control the entrepreneurial venture and ensure that it delivers the strategy content they desire is dependent on a large number of factors such as:

- ✓ Their personal leadership style.
- ✓ The consensus they build for the desired strategy
- ✓ Their ownership of resources.
- ✓ The way in which they control resources.
- ✓ The control mechanisms and procedures they have established
- ✓ Their technical expertise.
- ✓ Their access to information and their ability to control that information within the organisation.
- ✓ The way they set objectives.
- ✓ The way in which they reward achievement or objectives.

9.3.4 Crafting Entrepreneurial Strategy

The task of crafting an entrepreneurial strategy begins with solid diagnoses of the venture's internal and external situations or environments.

Only armed with hard analysis of the big picture are entremets prepared to devise a sound strategy to achieve targeted strategic and financial results.

The entrepreneurial strategy making task involves developing a game plan or intended strategy and then adapting it as events unfolds inside and outside the venture.

Crafting an entrepreneurial strategy is an exercise that involve outside – in strategic thinking. The challenge is for entrepreneurs to keep their strategy closely matched to outside drivers as changing buyer preferences, the latest actions of rivals, market opportunities and threats and newly appearing business opportunities.

The venture strategies cannot be responsive to changing environment unless entrepreneurs exhibit entrepreneurial character of studying market trends, listening to customers, competitors and steering venture activities in new direction in timely manner. Good venture strategy is therefore inseparable from good venture entrepreneurial activities, managing change and innovation.

9.3.5 Growth as A Strategic Objective For The New Venture

9.3.5.1 Introduction

Business growth is critical to entrepreneurial success. The potential for growth is one of the factors which distinguish the entrepreneurial new venture from the small business. It is a defining feature of the entrepreneurial venture. The entrepreneurial new venture is characterised by its growth potential and there are a number of reasons why entrepreneurs wish to take advantage of that potential and grow their ventures. These may relate to:

- ✓ Desire to increase personal wealth through venture growth.
- ✓ Desire for achievement. In a sense, the size of the venture is a way of keeping the score.
- ✓ Desire to make a difference to the world - the larger the venture they create, the bigger the difference they have made.
- ✓ Desire for personal control. The bigger the venture, the greater the domain over which the entrepreneur can express their power, etc.

For these reasons growth is often an important objective for the venture. However, setting growth targets create challenges in relation to the venture's strategy, resources and risks to which it is exposed. If venture growth has to be achieved, it must be delivered by obtaining a greater volume of business driven by increased sales. The entrepreneurial new venture needs to have a strategy in place to develop sales base.

9.3.5.2 Strategies For Growth

- **Understanding the competitive environment**

Growth is needed to give the entrepreneurial new venture more resources to deal with the inevitable environmental changes.

The new venture needs to have a clear understanding of the environment in which it operates. That will help it reach a stage of financial viability as fast as possible, so that it can use its resources to deliver growth rather than being supported.

One characteristic that singles out growth businesses from lifestyle businesses is the fact that they think strategically- they think about the direction and scope of the business over the longer term.

Of fundamental importance to this is for the new venture to understand the nature of competition, and profitability of the venture in a business environment.

In his book on competitive advantage, Porter (1985) provided basis for structural analysis of industries, which he claims goes some way towards explaining profitability in a business environment. For him, the aim of any competitive strategy is to cope with and, if possible change, the rules in favour of the venture in any business environment it operates.

Unfortunately, new ventures especially small ones, are unlikely to be able to change those competition rules, so it pays to understand them in order survive, grow and expand. Porter claims five forces determine competitiveness in an industry:

1. The power of buyers.
2. The power of suppliers.
3. Substitute products.
4. The threats of new entrants.
5. The intensity of rivalry.

These five forces determine industry profitability and in turn are a function of industry structure- the underlying economic and technical characteristics of the industry. These can change over time but the analysis does emphasise the need to select industries carefully in the first place. It also provides a framework for predicting a prior, the success or otherwise of the entrepreneurial new venture. This enables the entrepreneur to find out what elements in the industry make the venture uniquely different from the competition.

- **Product /Market growth strategy grid by Ansoff**

Another strategy that the small business could apply to achieve growth and expansion is the product/market grid by an off.

In the search for growth, the entrepreneurial new venture has the following options:

1. It can stay with its base product or service.
2. It can develop related new products.
3. It can develop related new markets.
4. It can diversify into related or unrelated markets.

1. Market entry and penetration strategy
   (Existing product/ Existing market)

This is where the entrepreneur can see an opening in a market and use entry and penetration strategies to gain entry to the market with the same product within existing market . . .

Market entry is more likely to occur when certain conditions exit:

- Where the market is growing, can be made to grow, or had growth potential.
- There is likely to be sales potentials that existing business are unable or unwilling to fill.
- Where organisations leave the market, leaving unfilled demand for products.
- Where the new entrants has a real or perceived advantage- cost, price, quality, etc.
- Where existing operators are complacent or where there has been a fall in the level of quality or service.
- Where the entrepreneurial new venture is able to bring its reputation into the market place.

The entrepreneur can achieve market penetration by:-cutting prices, increasing advert, getting products into more stores, obtain better store display, point of display merchandising, increase usage by current customers, attracting competitors' customer, etc.

2. Market development and domination strategy
   (Existing product/New market)

The entrepreneur might consider possibilities of identifying and developing new markets for its current products.

He/she could review new demographics in the markets - children, senior consumers, and women, ethnic groups – to see if the group could be encouraged to have more of them.

The entrepreneur could also review new geographical locations.

It can try to develop the share of the market, in order to dominate it. Domination of the market can lead to economies of scale. This includes the ability to negotiate discounts with suppliers, attract the best staff, and find the best sites for the venture.

3. New product development strategy
   (New product /Existing market product)

The entrepreneur can also achieve growth by developing new products for its current markets. - offering modified or new products to current customers.

New products may also be created based on existing products - offering modified products to current market.

Current products could be offered in new styles, sizes, colours, or new lines, new brand. Market research may indicate the need for products that has not yet been developed.

Technological advances may also result in new products being developed that create a new market.

4. Diversification strategy
   (New product/New market)

The entrepreneur could also consider diversification.

Diversification strategies occur where the venture seeks to extend its current range of products or services. This may be by integration with other ventures or business, or through new product, or market development.

Diversification strategy has been found as basic requirement for growth in small business nice many new ventures start-up as small businesses. It has also been found that rising firm size is related to rising diversification of related products groups (Peterson 206).

Related diversification is where a venture diversifies into similar activities in the industry that it is currently offering. Similarities may happen in relation to existing provision, existing technology, related markets, complementing products, extension of production, new products, etc.

The entrepreneurial new venture can diversify into related markets through:

1. Forward integration - in which the it extends its activities to output activities (e.g distribution).
2. Backward integration - in which it extends its activities to sources of its inputs (e.g. suppliers of raw materials).
3. Horizontal integration - in which it moves into activities related to its current activities.

The entrepreneurial new venture can also diversify into unrelated markets described as:

- Consortia.
- Conglomerate.

The term consortia are often used when referring to an alliance that involves more than two organisations (often created for time limited projects such as civil engineering or construction developments).

The choice of the form of alliance will depend on the complexity of the alliance and the objectives of the two parties. Alliance partners tend to seek cooperation on the minimum number of areas that are needed indoor to avoid over exposure to the risk of one of the partners leaving abruptly or finding out too much.

Motivation for forming alliances may be as a result of international competitive pressure or capital pooling and Successful alliances usually involve:

- ✓ Complementary skills and capabilities of the partners.
- ✓ The degree of overlap between the parties markets are kept to a minimum.
- ✓ A high level of autonomy, with strong leadership and commitment from the parent organisation.
- ✓ The need to build up trust and not to depend solely on the on the contractual framework of the relationship.
- ✓ Recognition that the two partners may have different cultures.

Conglomerate diversifications on the other hand, seek new businesses that have no relationship to the company current technology, products or markets. If the new industry entered does not enable any existing competences to be leveraged and or there are no common links between new and existing, this is referred to as conglomerate development. Conglomerate companies are those containing broad range of business interests, many of which have no apparent link to each other, however, the risk is higher.

Generally, the theoretical explanation of linking diversification and performance stem mainly from efficiency gains due to economies of scale and scope of the products or services, organisational learning, risk reduction and top management strategic management.

- **Internationalisation strategies**

The entrepreneurial new venture can achieve growth through internalisation of its activities.

According to Masurel (2001), internationalisation is very important to any new venture that wants to expand and grow because of the tremendous potential exporting offers for enhancing sales growth,

Gankema et al (2000) identified five stages of internationalisation of small business ventures:

1. Domestic marketing.
2. Pre-export.
3. Experimental involvement.
4. Active involvement.
5. Committed involvement.

International market entry strategies of small ventures have also been found to include:

- ✓ Exporting.
- ✓ Licensing.
- ✓ Franchising.
- ✓ Joint venture and alliances.

For the entrepreneur, having access to foreign markets through exports enables the venture to be involved in international marketing activities and provides the much needed access to contracts for product distribution and sales and growth potentials in overseas, with less need for establishing operations overseas.

Licensing also enables the new venture the benefits from the technical expertise of other ventures. The licensing venture (licensor) can grant right to the partner new venture (licensee) to produce and/or sell a product in the host country and also provides assistance and other host of advantages in terms of technical expertise to the licensee. The entrepreneurial new venture (as licensee), pays the royalty payment for every unit produced/sold, lease cost, and risky associated with the license.

Franchising is one of the most popular forms of internationalisation of small businesses. A franchise is a system of distribution that can enable the new venture (as franchisee or supplier of products), to arrange for a distributor, and distribute a specific product or service under agreed conditions overseas. In a franchising agreement, the contractor (as franchisor) provides the licence with a preformatted package of activity. Normally the franchisor offers brand name and training services and the franchisee pays franchise fees as a percentage of the turnover. The entrepreneurial new venture can enjoy the benefits the franchise offers - in existing well known brand name and appeal, training service, and financial assistance provided by the franchisor.

The new venture can also achieve growth by a joint venture with an international partner. A joint venture involves entering into the foreign market strategy by joining with foreign partners to produce or sell a product or service. It is considered to be a successful strategy for internationalisation of new ventures. By pursuing joint venture strategy, a new venture with poor finance and lacking management skills can obtain the necessary resources to enter a new market. A joint venture also reduces political friction against foreign owned ventures in host market, and reduces venture risk in foreign investment through sharing of the venture project with a foreign partner

- **Niche strategies**

Entrepreneurs can improve their growth and competitive positions in the marketplace through niche strategy.

Niche strategy occurs when the venture focuses its activities on a narrow target market segment - a niche. This is a very attractive option for small business ventures as it helps them differentiate themselves and offers them the better chance of sustainable growth. The differentiation can be product or market based.

The key to differentiation is the ability to identify the unique benefits that a small firm product or service offers to potential customers. This may involve: - finding out what elements in the marketing mix are unique to the small firm, specialising in customers or products rather than methods of production, emphasising the non price elements of the mix such as quality, stressing the inherent strength of a small firm such as innovation, flexibility or personalised service.

Establishing a market niche is most effective when aimed at narrowly defined market segment. Sometimes this can involve concentrating on GAPs in the market place left by large firms.

- **Networking**

The idea behind promotion of new venture networking is the opportunity it provides for each members of the network to deliver growth through cooperation and flexibility, while retaining some advantages of economies of scale.

It has also been claimed that co-operation between networks of specialised businesses can make them even more competitive. This is especially the case for small business ventures (Peterson 2000).

Since many new ventures usually start –up small, they can take advantage of networking as a strategic instrument for competitive advantage and growth.

Some industrial districts have emerged in many countries in which independent small businesses operating in the same geographic area and industrial sector developed a network to perform one or more stages of the production process that help offer a highly competitive, flexible service to the market place (Jones 2004). These local economic networks of small businesses which can deliver flexibility, while retaining some advantages of economies of scale have been seen by some commentators as the natural successor to the old industrial model which depends on scale economies from the production of standardised products.

9.3.5.3 Managing Growth

Introduction

Managing growth is an important area in entrepreneurial new venture development. It is imperative entrepreneurs should understand the process of growth in their ventures and how this could be managed effectively.

In an innovative sense, the process of managing growth can be described in line with managing change. Managing change is not an easy task, and the more rapid the growth of the venture, the more difficult it is to manage. This is because, a number of complex changes happen during growth period which need to be managed.

In reality, few new ventures survive, let alone grow. There are numerous reasons why growth does not occur, and there have been many studies on the barriers to growth in new ventures and small business. According the Barber et al, (1989), these can be grouped into three categories:

1. Growth management and motivation – lack of management training, relatively low qualification, reluctance to delegate, the need for new management skills as the venture grows.
2. Resources –lack of access to finance, skilled labour, and technology needed to achieve and sustain growth.
3. Market opportunities and structure – in terms of market growth rate, size, frequency of purchases, degree of segmentation, opportunities for collaboration or merger, etc.

The study of more than 300 successful owner/manager firms and over a 10 year period, carried out by Canfield University (Barrow 2001), suggested that barriers to growth were linked to:

- ✓ Planning vacuum.
- ✓ Muddled marketing.
- ✓ Miss-management of change.
- ✓ Meddling and miss-spent time.
- ✓ Wrong objectives.

✓ No financial strategy.

However, there is one factor that has not been considered – the motivation of the founder - especially, in the case of a new venture or small firms. Often the founder does not wish to grow the business and Birley (2000) suggested that there are in fact, four types of owner/manager:

1. The protectionist – the owner/manager wants to maintain the business at its current size, thus protecting his/her investment.
2. The business oriented - the owner/manager wants to both grow and control the business in order to protect his/her income and investment.
3. The dynast - the owner/manager wants to grow the business in order to protect the investment and pass it on to the next generation.
4. The family business – the owner/manager wants to keep the business at the current size and pass it to the next generation.

There is the case of Mom and Pop businesses that never grow up with the reward of achieving personal goal that has not been possible while working for an employer.

These realities of growth barriers spell out the need for managing growth, and the understanding of some growth models in literatures.

Growth Models

A number of growth models have been developed which seek to describe how growth changes happen in ventures especially small ventures over time, and the impact to performance. The two most widely accepted models are:

1. The Greiner model.
2. The Churchill and Lewis model.

The Greiner Model

The Greiner model is a very useful model for understanding growth and management in small ventures because the model identified different levels of growth according to the industries that includes:

- ✓ Fast growing industries - identified with shorter growth period.
- ✓ Slower growth industries - identified with longer growth period.
- ✓ Growth stages (1–5) and problems, are characterised by crises to overcome before business can move on to sustainable growth

NOTE - only stages 1- 3 applies to small business.

- Stage1- Growth through creativity (with crises of leadership).

In the first stage, the venture achieves growth through creativity which is typified of an entrepreneurial new venture.

Here, the entrepreneurial ability of the individual - the leader and owner/manager is key as he/she is involved in all aspects of the business venture and entrepreneurial management style is required.

However, this initial growth success through creativity does not come without problems. It is usually associated with crisis of leadership.

The leadership problem is associated with the entrepreneur - operating as a solo - lacking the much needed management knowledge required to run the venture alone, as well as lack of additional capital required to operate large production runs and manage an increasing scale of the venture as a result of initial growth and change. There is the need for capital to be secured to underpin initial growth and financial control is no doubt required. The venture will also need additional hands in terms of personnel or employees, to help the entrepreneur meet up with additional organisational challenges and to achieve growth progress. The crises of leadership will demand leadership through direction.

- Stage 2- Growth through direction (with crises of autonomy).

At stage 2, the venture moves from stage 1 where growth comes through entrepreneurial creativity to stage 2 where growth results from strategic leadership or leadership through direction.

This second stage of growth success does not come without problems. It usually comes with crisis of autonomy.

At this stage line employees and line managers may become frustrated due to bureaucracy attendant upon a centralised hierarchy. Line staff is more familiar with markets and machinery than executives, and become torn between following procedures and taking initiative.

The passage from stage 2 (direction) to stage 3 (delegation) is marked by a crises of autonomy. The control mechanisms implemented to overcome the first crisis becomes less appropriate as the physical size of the firm increases.

Here, a declarative style is required. It becomes necessary therefore, for the venture to delegate to allow sufficient discretion in operating decision making.

- Stage 3 - Growth through delegation (with crisis of control).

At this stage growth is achieved through delegation with crisis of control as there is likely little co-ordination across divisions or functions.

Growth at this stage needs to be controlled and maintained. However, the entrepreneur as the top executive may perceive a loss of control resulting from excessive discretion or delegation to lower and middle managers employed to maintain growth in the venture.

Here, coordinative style is required. The entrepreneur as top executive manager needs to regain control through special co-ordination techniques, and stage 4 (co-ordination) is entered.

- Stage 4 - Growth through co-ordination (with crisis of red-tape).

By the time stage 4 has been reached, the venture is likely to have lost much of its entrepreneurial drive.

This stage is associated with crisis of red tape. There are probably set procedures for doing things and the watchdog approach is adopted by senior management together with the proliferation of systems and programmes that leads to a crisis of confidence and red tape.

The crises relates to too much coordination that leads to red –tape, the fact that problem arises with line managers objecting to excessive direction and senior managers viewing line managers as undo-operative and disruptive. Both groups are also unhappy with the cumbersome paper system that has now evolved to meet the management challenges. The venture has become too large and complex to be managed through an extensive framework of formal procedures and controls. Movement to stage 5 requires a shift to interpersonal collaboration.

- Stage 5 - Growth through collaboration (with crisis of???).

In this fifth stage, the organisation attempts to overcome the excessive bureaucracy of stage 4 by getting people to work together through a sense of mission or purpose.

The crisis associated with this stage in growth of the venture is usually described with???

Although crisis is expected to be eminent as venture activities evolves through, no consistent empirical evidence is available that points to the nature of the crisis into which stage 5 degenerates as venture activities shift into stage 6.

However, there is the hypothesis that crisis at this stage is expected to revolve around psychological saturation of employees, that will occur as a logical result of the information age.

Consequently, the venture will evolve with dual structures of habits and reflections, allowing employees to move periodically between the two periods of rest – or some alternative format where spent staff can refuel their energies.

It could be thought that this is the stage in which the venture revolts and begin to behave as they did when they were small. Here, a watchdog or participative style is required

The Churchill and Lewis Model

Churchill and Lewis developed a simple summary model of the key factors which affect success or failure of a venture or small business in the different stages of its life.

The model identified five stages of the business life. The model also identified strategies associated with each stage of the business life to overcome problems or accomplish successes. Four of these relate to the business owner or entrepreneur. They include:

- Stage 1- Existence

This is the stage where the venture or small business is born or comes into existence – the start-up. Main strategy here is centred on the achieving venture existence - to stay alive.

The concentration of the activities of entrepreneur as the owner/manager is on finding new customers and delivering products and services to satisfy customers and develop the customer based of the new venture. As such, the organisational structure of the new venture is usually simple - centred around the entrepreneur as the owner manager and given the fact that the venture is at its early stage of development, and in many cases with no or few employees. The entrepreneurs as business owner is also in charge of all business activities, running the business in his/her own style and it is usual that basic management activities(planning, etc) is minimal or likely to be none existent.

- Stage 2- Survival

At this the stage the venture having gone throne through the period of existence will try to survive.

The strategy here is centred on establishing existing customer base and product portfolio.

The venture has to demonstrate it has sufficient products and customers to be a viable business venture.

It has to control its revenues and expenses to maintain cash flow.

The organisational structure of the venture is still simple, and the entrepreneur as venture owner is still the business manager.

- Stage 3- Success

At this stage of the venture development, the venture has become a successful big venture with sufficient customers and sales to establish itself with confidence.

The entrepreneur as the owner/manager has now acquired functional managers and operations systems with some planning activities mainly in the form of operational budgets. The entrepreneur now has two strategic options.

1. To maintain its market niche and/or adapt to changing environment or circumstances, and stay in business for a long time. If not, either fold or drop back to survival stage.
2. To grow - if the entrepreneur consolidates the venture, clarifies his/her vision and ensures that resources are diverted into growth. Strategic management should be introduced to achieve that vision. The venture however, must remain profitable.

- Stage 4- Take-off

Having achieved success in the success stage, the venture can now take- off in the next stage on the basis of success achieved. This stage therefore, signifies the take – off stage for the new venture critical for the entrepreneur owner/manager performance and the venture further success.

The Strategy here is consolidating on performance because the entrepreneur as the owner/manager can ensure satisfactory financial viability and management since the venture has now become large enough to be managed effectively as an individual or legal entity. However, the opposite could happen and he venture may become a failure.

- Stage 5- Maturity

This stage signifies the maturity stage of the venture.

It is during this stage that the venture begins to develop the characteristic of a stable large venture (with decentralised management and formal information system). However, it could be noticed that as the venture passé through each stage of its development so far outlined, the entrepreneur as the venture owner also faces a roller coaster of human problems. The classic change/denial curve illustrates these changes and offer insights into the attitude of the owner at each stage (Burns et al 1996). The main concern at this stage is for the venture to retain the advantage of small size, including the flexibility of response and entrepreneurial spirit. The entrepreneur at this stage needs to learn to become more effective in taking in a new role and to adopt new attitudes, skills, and management style to be entrepreneurial and also adopting the right entrepreneurial structure at this level in the venture.

Since making new adoption involves change, it can take time and the entrepreneurs can also be faced with different phase or problems at this stage. As the business grows, the entrepreneur needs to understand the fact that he/she needs to spend less time doing and more time managing, which means he/she needs to delegate to other people who are required to take over some essential responsibilities in the venture. However, many entrepreneurs as owner/managers do find it difficult to let go and this explains why so few businesses are successful beyond the fourth stage. The three preceding stages are explained in terms of phases below:

In addition, the unfamiliarity of the entrepreneur as the venture owner with the new role expected of him/her makes them feel anxious about their contribution and so their effectiveness drops slightly. Within a short time, having become used to the role using previously successful skills and finding support to help them, their effectiveness improves and they do not believe that they have to change. As real demands are now being made and the entrepreneurism put under stress realising the need to develop new skills to keep up with the job creating a period of anxiety.

However, the testing period can be as frustrating as it can be rewarding. Mistakes can increase the low, but as the newly- learnt skills are brought into play effectively, the entrepreneur's performance improves and he/she can achieve a higher level of effectiveness than at the beginning stage - having developed a set of new skills alongside their old. However, failure to acquire new skills may make transition impossible.

Criticism of growth models

Since Greiner, Churchill and Lewis published their growth models and findings, other life cycle models have been produced.

All of them are similar but identify different stages and all have been criticised for the following reasons:

- Most new ventures or small firms experience little or no growth and are unlikely to reach stage 3, 4, 5.
- The actual sequence of issues or imperatives predicted BT the models is not supported by empirical research
- Growth models do not allow for backward movement or for the skipping of stages.
- Growth needs not involve crisis.
- Growth firms need not necessarily lurch from one crisis to the next.

It is important to mention here that their models are best uses as predictions of problems that the venture is likely to face as it grows and imperatives that the venture ought to have if it wishes to at different stages of development

Other factors affecting success in venture growth

From the model it is apparent that much of the success of the small firm is dependent on the skills of the entrepreneur as the venture owner/manager.

However, as the venture passes through each stage, the entrepreneur as owner/manager faces a number of individual human problems

Churchill and Lewis have developed a simple summary of the four of the factors that relate to the entrepreneur as the venture owner and the venture. The important point is the move from operational to strategic ability as the business grows.

Even when the business is established in the final stage, the ability of the owner of the business to think ahead is still critical to the development of the business. The business is therefore tied to the owner's aspiration for the business

Even when the business is established in the final stage, the ability of the entrepreneur as the venture owner to think ahead is still critical to the venture development. The venture is therefore tied to the entrepreneur's aspiration for the business

A study of growth companies- those companies that grew rapidly to a stock market quotation- by Ray and Hunch son (1983), underline some of the important differences between growth and "life style" or static businesses.

It is important to recognise that successful growth firms are considered to be more focused in their objectives, with strong emphases on forecasting financial data on a regular basis and timely basis- particularly cash flow, but also profit and sales. Also apparent is a very different style of management. These conclusions are underlined by a number of researches for example; a research conducted by the London Business School (2009), identified six common factors associated with successful growth businesses:

1. An experience manager - with a good knowledge of the market and industry: venture capitalists know that management buy-outs are less risky than start-ups. This is partly because they are then backing a number of managers, each with a good knowledge of their industry.
2. Close contact with customers and committed to quality of product and/or service – that; ears to higher profit margins achieved by competing on service rather than price or, and unique product.
3. Innovation and flexibility in marketing and technology - that makes the difference and gives differential advantage over competitors.
4. A focus on profit not sales, with good management systems controlling costs.
5. Attention to good employee relations, often backed by a bonus scheme.
6. Spotting opportunities that is something entrepreneurs are good at, although luck does play a part.

Growth firms are also found to have high levels of internal organisation- producing regular plans which contained objectives, strategies and budgets involving a management team. They also produce regular and timely financial reports which were compared to budgets are regular meetings of the team (Burns et al 1999).

In conclusion, it is right to assume there is no single formula that can guarantee successful growth of a small venture. However, it is important to recognise the significance of personal qualities of the entrepreneur as the owner-manager and their product/service idea or offering. These two elements are fundamental. The personal entrepreneurial attributes of the owner/manager is required to launch a new venture and application of effective management principles also vital that to help the entrepreneur focus on the needs of the customer and sustain venture growth. The role of the entrepreneur as the owner/manager needs to change as the business develops, but all too often they are not able to make the transition. However, there do seem to be fundamental differences in the characteristics of those owner-managers that launch growth businesses and those that set up life style businesses. The key difference is derived from their motivation for going into the business and innovation.

9.3.6 Achieving Competitive Advantage

9.3.6.1 Introduction

Competitive advantage is usually associated with the firm's position in the market, where it has chosen to operate in, and involves factors that give the firm an edge over its competitors, and enable it to achieve higher level of profitability, or other financial measure of performance.

Competitive advantage is seen as the overall purpose of business strategy. Some texts use the phrase superior performance to mean the same.

A business is said to possess competitive advantage if it is able to return higher profits than its competitors. When this superiority is maintained over time, we speak of sustainable competitive advantage.

Competitive strategy deals exclusively with management action plan for competing successfully and providing superior value to customers. A firm's competitive strategy usually consists of approaches and initiatives it takes to attract customers, withstand competitive forces, and strengthen market positions. The objective is to knock the socks off rivals ethically, honourably earn a competitive advantage, and respect of loyal customers. Strategy defined in this competitive sense is concerned with how managers respond to the Porter's five forces in the competitive environment.

Businesses often find it hard to access their competitive advantage as it requires answering three difficult questions:

1. What is the basis for the present advantages?
2. How valuable are these advantages?
3. Can these advantages be sustained?

Getting the right answers to these questions is very important for strategic performance and sustainability. It is important to note, that three tests can be used to evaluate the merits of one competitive strategy over another and to gauge how good a strategy is:

> The best fit test – a good strategy is well match to the firm's internal and external situations.
> The competitive advantage test- a good strategy leads to sustainable competitive advantage. The bigger the competitive edge, the more powerful and effective is the strategy.
> The performance test – a good strategy boosts company performance in relations to gains in profitability, and gains in business strengths and competitive position.

Successful organisations follow a strategy that describes the direction the organisation will pursue within its chosen environment, and guides the allocation of resources and effort. Without a strategy, an organisation is like a ship without a rudder, condemned to wonder aimlessly in response to winds, currents, and outside events. Since the outside pressures in a competitive market are seldom benign, the consequences of a poorly considered strategy can be disastrous. For the new venture, competitive advantage is located in both the entrepreneur and what is offered to the marketplace. A competitive advantage is present if the venture consistently offers the consumer something which is different from what competitors are offering, and that difference represents something valuable for the consumer. Competitive advantage is the reason why consumers spend their money with one entrepreneur rather than the others. The entrepreneur must therefore decide what type of competitive advantage they aim to pursue to attract customers and maintain perforce in the market place.

9.3.6.2 Sources of Competitive Advantage

The study of strategic management offers several explanations as to how competitive advantage can be achieved and sustained.

Here we focus on the major three sources of competitive advantage based on three schools of thoughts:

1. The competitive position school of thought - based on Porter's generic strategy framework.
2. The resource based school of thought -based on the development and exploitation of core competences by individual businesses.
3. The knowledge based school of thought -based on creation and development of knowledge through the process of organisational learning.

NOTE

These approaches can be seen as complementary and mutually enriching rather than mutually exclusive.

1. **The competitive position school**

The competitive positioning school of thought draws largely on the work of Porter's five forces of a competitive environment - the positioning of a firm in the competitive environment in relation to generic strategy framework.

Porter stressed the importance of industry in determining competitive advantage. According to Porter (1985), competitive advantage arises from selection of the generic strategy that best fits the organisation's competitive environment, and organising value adding activities to support the chosen strategy.

Managers are expected to identify and establish through the five forces analysis the right industry in which the firm should compete in relation to industry attractiveness and profitability.

Once the choice of industry is made, the manager then had to determine which generic strategy to pursue, the optimum configuration of the business value adding activities to support the chosen strategy. Porter offered some generic strategy alternatives – differentiation, cost leadership. Nevertheless, there are limitations of Porter's generic strategy:

- A business can employ a successful hybrid strategy without being "stuck in the middle."
- Cost leadership does not in itself, sell products.
- Differentiation strategies can be used to increase sales volumes rather to charge a premium price- a firm might choose not to charge a premium price but to increase sales and market share
- Price can sometimes be used to differentiate.
- A generic strategy cist not always the source of competitive advantage as competence-based strategy has arguably. Superseded the generic strategy framework.

2. The resource based school

Whereas Porter stressed the importance of industry in determining competitive advantage, the resource based approach suggests that the core competence of the organisation is of greater importance.

The resource based school (Rumelt 1984, 1991, Prahalad and Hamel 1990) emerged on the basis that competitive advantage results from the development and exploitation of core competences by individual business, whatever industry they are.

Heene and Sanchez (1997) argued that, it is the competences (abilities) of the business and the distinctive way that it organises its activities that determines its ability to outperform competitor.

The competence base theory is built upon the assumption that certain firms outperform others in the same industry. If this is the case, competitive advantage cannot be explained entirely by different industry conditions as proposed by competitive position approach.

Clearly, some organisations in the same industry are more successful than others, lending support to the view that competitive advantage is largely internally developed. For example, Philips development of optimal media including the lesser disc has led to a whole range of hi-fi and information technology products etc.

The approach is inside-out, suggesting that businesses seeking competitive advantage must first examine and develop their own distinctive resources, capabilities and competences before exploiting them in their environment.

According to Kay (993), distinctive capability results from one or more of the following:

- Architecture - unique network of internal and internal relationship which produces superior performance.
- Reputation - superior products, products quality, characteristics, design, and service.
- Innovation -R&D, designing, developing and marketing new products, improving design and organisation of its value-adding activities.
- Strategic assets - natural monopoly, patents, copyrights, etc.

The process of building new core competences or extending existing ones must take into account the following considerations.

- Customer perception - must be perceived by customers as better value for money. It should also provide greater perceived customer value to the business's products than that perceived in competitor's products.
- Uniqueness- must be unique to business.
- Continuous improvement.
- Collaboration - should result from building network.
- Organisational knowledge - must be based on organisational knowledge and learning, and improvement of the process by which organisation learns.
- Ability - should also have the potential to equip a business with the ability to enter and successfully compete in several markets.
- Be difficult for competitors to emulate.

Taken together, all these skills and resources represent ability of a firm to do more or do better (or both) than the competition. However, the competence based approach has an inherent danger of ignoring the environment which is essential for successful strategy formulation and implementation.

3. The knowledge based school

This school of thought suggests competitive advantage arises from creation and development of new knowledge through a process of organisational learning.

Organisational knowledge has been defined as "share collection of principles, facts, skills and rules which inform organisational decision making, behaviour and actions" (Storehouse and Pemberton 1999).

Knowledge can either be explicit or implicit/tacit. Explicit knowledge is knowledge whose meaning is clearly stated, details of which can be recorded and stored. Tacit knowledge is often unstated, based on individual experience and difficult to record and store.

The knowledge- based approach to competitive advantage encompasses the use of any conceptual framework that assist in the process of learning and in the creation of new knowledge that helps a firm be one or more steps ahead of the competition.

Competitive advantage however, is more likely to result from doing things differently from competitors and doing them better rather than from trying to emulate them. It is believed that if an organisation possesses superior knowledge to its competitors, then this can lead to core competences which in turn produce competitive advantage.

We have learnt earlier that the resource based school (Rumelt 1984, 1991, Prahalad and Hamel 1990) emerged on the basis that competitive advantage results from the development and exploitation of core competences by individual business, whatever industry they are. However, knowledge and organisational learning play a unique role in building and maintaining core competences because core competences can be based upon knowledge of customers and their needs, knowledge of technology and how to employ it in distinct ways, knowledge of products and processes etc, knowledge of business environment, of competitors, countries, etc.

In addition, superior performance is more likely to result from an informed knowledge of the firm, the environment in which it operates and the strategic alternatives available to it.

Learning organisations are able to transform themselves by anticipating change and discovering new ways of creating products and services; -they have learned how to learn . . . they use a number of ways such as:

- Openness - i.e. encourage, anticipate and accept changes.
- Creativity.
- Self efficacy - i.e. self belief in self ability.

4. **Other contributions**

John kay (1991) has developed a perspective on of competitive advantage which he identified as having its source in one of four distinct capabilities:

1. The architecture of the business i.e. its internal structure.
2. The reputation of the business.
3. The way the business innovates i.e. the ability to come up with new and valuable ideas.
4. The business strategic assets.

These four distinctive capabilities are general and apply to all business. They can be related to four specific sources of competitive advantage for the entrepreneurial venture making its presence felt in the marketplace such as:

1. Cost sources:

✓ Low input costs.
✓ Economies of scale.
✓ Experience curve economies.

2. Knowledge sources:

✓ Product knowledge - a special understanding of the product or service that makes up the market.
✓ Market knowledge – special insight into the ways the market functions.
✓ Technical knowledge – special understanding and competence in making and delivering the offering to the market place.

3. Relationship sources:

- ✓ Relationship with customers, suppliers, community, etc.
- ✓ A relationship establishes trust and trust add value by reducing the need for contracts and monitoring.
- ✓ A business may be able to build a competitive advantage on the basis of the special relationship it enjoys with stakeholders.
- ✓ Building relationship is essential if a business is to locate itself in a secure and supportive network.

4. Structural sources:

- ✓ Arises as a consequence not so much of what the business does as of the way it goes about doing things.
- ✓ Is a function not only of the business formal structure, the predefined way in which individuals will relate, but also of its informal structure, the unofficial web of relationship and communication links which actually defines it, and its culture which governs how those relationships will function and evolve.

9.3.6.3 Sustaining Competitive Advantage

Sustaining competitiveness of the Entrepreneurial venture means giving the venture some unique and valuable character, so that competitors cannot follow through the activities of the venture, and exploits the opportunity.

If this is not done, then the competitors will follow the entrepreneur through and exploit the opportunity as well. This will reduce the potential of the entrepreneur's business.

Closing the window of opportunity to stop competitors following through means creating a long term sustainable competitive advantage for the business.

As explained earlier, competitive advantage arises from planned strategies and opportunistic moves- emergent strategies. However, the rapid change of the environment means that competitive advantage is contestable rather than sustainable.

Identifying a competitive advantage - that is, something the customer finds different and attractive, and securing that on the basis of some aspects of the business costs, knowledge, relationship or structures in a way which provides a source for such advantage and differentiates the business from competitors - is a starting point for long term success. In order to secure that the entrepreneur must make sure the competitive advantage cannot be imitated and the profits it promotes can be eroded by competitors. The entrepreneur must decide not only what the competitive advantage of the venture t to establish also how the competitive advantage should be sustained. This could be through:

- ✓ Sustaining cost advantages – the key decision is how the venture keeps its costs lower than competitors.
- ✓ Sustaining knowledge advantages – knowledge advantage is based on the understanding of both the product and the market.
- ✓ Sustaining relationship advantages – his includes internal and external relationships in relation to stakeholders.

Superior performance is built and sustained through continuous organisational learning and result in a constant process of new strategy development and improvement in the way in which business activities are carried out - through creation of new business knowledge based upon continuous organisational learning. This is because:

- Price advantages are short- lived in mature industries in which purchasing patterns are established and product specifications are standardised.
- Allowing any disadvantage to persist for too long is in the interest of competitors. The inevitable erosion of advantage positions should be countered by continuous and creative search for new advantages.
- Advantages also erode as customer requirements change. This is especially evident in emerging markets in which initial advantage may be gained by providing superior systems and technical service that help the customer use unfamiliar products.
- Today's customers have the ability and flexibility to shop for benefits and customer retention demands continuous improvement.

Whether an advantage will endure depends on the resources, commitments, and strategies of competitors and the ease with which they can copy and nullify the advantage.

The most protected situations are patent –protected technologies or trade barriers. By investing in R&D, being the first to invest in emerging overseas markets, and having the largest sales force or superior order handling systems, the venture is able to reinvest the gains from its advantage into activities that will sustain these advantages.

When an entrepreneur can utilize positive feedback from customers established through a reliable customer complaint services, it is very difficult to unseat its competitive advantage, as the venture remains very close to its customers and continues to be proactive in the marketplace. Indeed, few competitors would consider a frontal attack on such a venture.

Sustainable competitive advantage requires that the venture outperform its rival over a long period of time. Although there is no recipe or formula that can guarantee superior performance, there are certain organisational behaviours that have been shown to make success more likely (Thompson 2006):

- ✓ Strategic intent – constantly stretching the organisation to its limits.
- ✓ Continuous improvement – continually trying to improve products and services, relationships with customers and suppliers, and the way in which activities are organised and carried out.
- ✓ Doing things differently from competitors – devising ways of doing business that are different from any better than the approaches adopted by competitors.
- ✓ Being customer oriented – always seeking to meet customer needs.
- ✓ Building knowledge based core competences and distinctive capabilities.
- ✓ Developing clear and consistent strategies that are understood by managers and by customers.
- ✓ Awareness of factors in the business environment, potential changes and their likely implementations for the business.
- ✓ Collaborating with other businesses and customers.
- ✓ Consideration in relation to relationship advantages – relationships are the glue that holds business network together. If relationships are long term and secure, then the network can be thought of as tight
- ✓ Consideration in relation to structural advantage – arises as a consequence not so much about what the venture does, but the way it goes about doing things. The entrepreneurial venture can gain structural advantage over others in the way its roles are flexible – which can lead to lower costs - by being more focused on the market and as such, more responsive to market signals and using those signals to make faster and better decisions about how to serve the market.

9.3.6.4 Retaining Entrepreneurial Dynamics

There is always the danger that the new entrepreneurial ventures can quite quickly lose its entrepreneurial dynamics as it grows, that is, the hallmark of its success.

In order to overcome such crises and to retain entrepreneurial spirit as the venture grows and develops, the entrepreneur needs to ensure that all employees involved in the venture are aware of:

- ✓ Customer needs.
- ✓ Why they purchase.
- ✓ The problems they face.
- ✓ Their specific needs and wants.
- ✓ The importance of improvement.

The very success of entrepreneur and the methods by which that success is often achieved can lead to bureaucracy and stagnation in the growing firm. It is therefore necessary that the entrepreneur should create an adaptive organisation – one capable of facilitating the character of the entrepreneur- namely to perceive and pursue opportunities, and to believe success is possible. To be able to perceive opportunities effectively, the ventures needs to be structured in such a way that:

- ✓ Levels and functions in the organisation know what the market is demanding and uses those market demands to structure its goals and objectives.
- ✓ Individuals in the organisation have a sense of ownership of the firm's broad objectives, rather than narrow objectives of their own functions specialism.
- ✓ No individual function becomes dominant and it is understood that success will be achieved only by balancing functional needs.
- ✓ Change becomes institutionalised and recognised as an organisational goal.

The key is to evolve an organisational structure and style of management that prevents the venture from developing inert culture. Indeed, this is precisely what Richard Branson has done with his Virgin group. Not only did he develop it as a cellular structure of individual, autonomous new and small enterprises, but he actually breaks up the larger enterprises as they begin to lose their entrepreneurial dynamic. For example, when the growth of Virgin Records began to show, Branson took the deputy managing director, the deputy sales director and the deputy marketing director and gave them responsibility for an entire new company. To pursue opportunities the firm needs to:

- ✓ Reward the pursuit of new ideas and encourage all its employees to try, especially as only a few will ever succeed.
- ✓ Recognise that the pursuit of new ideas needs patient, prostration and faith and create an environment where individuals are not afraid to innovate.
- ✓ Appreciate that in an era of change and uncertainty, plans need to be flexible and organisations need to adapt speeding to changed circumstances.

Further reading

Bacharach, S. and Lawler, E. (1980), Power and Politics in organisations, San Francisco, CA: Jossey Bass.

Baumol, W. (1968), The Entrepreneur: Introductory Remarks, American Economic Review, Vol. 38, pp 60 -3.

Cole, A. (1968), Entrepreneurship in Economic Theory, American Economic Review, Vol. 58, pp 64 -71.

Deakins, D. and Freel, M. (2003), Entrepreneurship and Small Firms (3rd Edition), London: McGraw Hill.

Drucker, P. (1985), Innovation and Entrepreneurship, London: Heinmann.

Kirby, D. (2003), Entrepreneurship, London: McGraw Hill.

Kuratko, D. and Hodgetts, R. (2001), Entrepreneurship: A contemporary Approach (5th Edition), New York: Dryden.

CHAPTER 10

ORGANISING THE ENTREPRENEURIAL NEW VENTURE

Aim

To introduce entrepreneurial organisation of the new venture.

Objectives

After studying this chapter you should be able to:

- Define the term "organising" and its functions in management.
- Introduce basic principles of entrepreneurial organisation.
- Introduce and explain theories of organisation structure.
- Introduce and describe the various entrepreneurial structural designs available to entrepreneurs.
- Understand how to organise finances for the new venture.

10.1 Introduction

Organising is one of the management tasks that help with the deployment of organisation's resources to achieve goals and objectives. It typically follows from planning and involves how managers try to accomplish plans. In other words, alongside planning, managers need to consider how they will achieve the direction chosen from the plan. In this sense, planning could be considered as providing the route map for the journey, and organising, as the means by which chosen destination is achieved.

Putting planned intentions of the new venture into effect requires purposeful activity, and this is where the organising task of management comes in. The process of organising usually involves:

➢ Determining grouping and structuring activities.
➢ Dividing and allocating roles arising from the grouping and structuring of activities.
➢ Assigning accountability for results.
➢ Determining details rules and systems of working, including those for communication, decision making and conflict resolution.

It is within this process that entrepreneurs can deal with detailed elements associate with principles of organising such as:

o Specialisation of roles and responsibility.
o Span of control.
o Degree of Standardisation.
o Degree of formality.
o Lines and levels of authority.
o Structural design and organisational design.
o Degree of delegation and accountability.
o Degree of collaboration, etc.

The purpose of entrepreneurial organisation of the new venture is to develop an organisation structure that is responsive to change.

The entrepreneur should develop an entrepreneurial organisation that is fit for the aims and objectives of the venture as well as opportunities and challenges in the marketplace. The entrepreneur also needs to organise the venture in such as way as to become an active learning organisation -. that will help it not only respond to opportunities and challenges, but reflect on the outcome that results from it, as well as modify future responses in the light of experience.

10.2 Entrepreneurial Organisation Structures

10.2.1 Introduction

There is no one form that typifies entrepreneurial structure.

Since entrepreneurship is about change, an entrepreneurial structure should be one with the necessary structural elements that fosters change – that allows creativity, flexibility, adaptability, innovation, etc.

The following organisation structures could be entrepreneurial:

- ✓ The simple informal structure.
- ✓ Web and cluster structures.
- ✓ Cellular structure.
- ✓ The virtual structure.
- ✓ Outsourcing structure.
- ✓ Licensing structure.
- ✓ Franchise structure.
- ✓ Network structure.

10.2.2 The Simple Structure

The simple structure could be used by entrepreneurs, at least in the early stages of their venture development. The birth stage of a new venture is usually characterised with informal structure since the new venture is just created. It is described as "simple" because everything is not in place - tasks are overlapping, there is no professional staff, no rules and regulations, and no internal systems for planning. Rewards or coordination, decision authority is centralised. With a simple structure, all of the key decisions are made by the entrepreneur usually the owner/manager, and everything of significance affecting the new venture is referred to him/her. He/she provides the entrepreneurial dynamic for the new venture and controls the venture at the onset.

This type of structure is associated with the benefits of creativity, flexibility, adaptability, innovation that it allows, to give the venture the needed entrepreneurial ability to innovate and change in line with internal and external business environmental demands. However, the structure is not without limitations. It is unlikely that the entrepreneur will have expertise in all aspects of the business which can be a limitation of this particular structure. Additionally, as the venture grows, it is equally inevitable that the decision making process will become too demanding and complex for one person – the entrepreneur, and there is pressure to relinquish some responsibility. This is the reason why Mintzberg (2005) maintained that entrepreneurial ventures characterised by simple structures and adhocracy, are frequently regarded as somewhat chaotic, as owner/managers usually find themselves going in many directions trying to seize multiple opportunities to establish a presence in all areas of the venture activities that may become overwhelming for a single individual.

10.2.3 Web and Cluster Structures

Handy (2001) looked at organisations in terms of their culture and identified four structures that supported the cultures he was describing:

1. A Web structure - (supporting power culture).
2. The Formal hierarchy or Greek temple structure – (supporting role culture).
3. A Matrix or Net structure - (supporting task culture).
4. A Cluster or Galaxy structure - (supporting person culture).

Handy's culture/structure typology exposed key aspects of structure which are significant to management such as:

- How power and /or control are handled by an organisation (i.e. centralised or diffused throughout the organisation).
- The type of power respected in an organisation (i.e. personal power, resource power, position power, expert power).
- The type of method preferred by an organisation (i.e. individualistic, collaboration, competitive).
- Relationship between people and structure - (whether people have to fit the structure or structure has to serve the people).

Handy's culture/structure typology also identified some structures that could be entrepreneurial such as webs and clusters.

A Web structure is characterised by control power dominated from the center – just like the simple structure described earlier. The centre power may be political or entrepreneurial resource power. The centralisation may be by an individual or a few key individuals trusted by the leader or the owner/manager. Few decisions are taken collectively, and work is carried out based on precedent and anticipating wishes and decisions of the central power source. This type of structure is often found in small businesses and have entrepreneurial benefits and limitations of simple structures already described. They may be found in some property, trading, and financial service small firms, etc.

Cluster or Galaxy structure represents a lose collection of individuals. In many cases, these are professionals sharing facilities but working as independent entities with separate goals and objectives. Power is not an issue since individual members are experts in their own rights. This type of structure is minimal as possible and serves the individuals. It may not be prevailing in many organisations, but may be seen where any kind of formal structure seems largely absent. It is simply to assist as administrative back-up for individual members, and thrives where rules, procedures and precedent are virtually non-existent as new ground rules is being broken all the time. Creativity is the watchword. The cluster will be successful where work is often very specialised, with each case unique, and where quick reactions to ever-changing and new events are needed, together with rapid risk taking and decision making - such as in small law firms, small architect firms, and some small management consultancy firms.

10.2.4 The Cellular Structure

The concept of the cellular structure (or firms within firms), is borrowed from biological science (Miles et al, 1992), as such, carries with it two important notions:

1. When cells combine, they create something (an organism) richer than the sum of the individual cells.
2. The idea of continuous evolution and growth.

As with living organisms, the entrepreneurial venture can create cellular (Cell units) that are self –governing, self-co-ordinating and self – initiating, enabling the venture to be entrepreneurial in terms of creative, adaptive and flexible ability to expand its resources.

Three characteristics that are integral to the success of the cellular organisation are:

- ✓ Acceptance of individual responsibility (taking ownership).
- ✓ Commitment to self-organisation and governance (permitting flexibility and strategic latitude).
- ✓ Principles of individual and collective profitability (profit sharing).

While each cell (unit) has individual autonomy, it must be working for the good of the venture as a whole. There is the principle of equality, as no cell is permitted to develop at the expense of another unless, as in the biological analogy, a cell is malfunctioning and needs treatment and or removal.

This is precisely what Richard Branson has done with his Virgin group when he develop it as a cellular structure of individual, autonomous new and small enterprises, breaks up the larger enterprises as they begin to lose their entrepreneurial dynamic when the growth of Virgin Records began to show.

10.2.5 The Shamrock Structure

Handy (1993) suggested that the shamrock structure has three components:

1. The core personnel - who maintain the strategy and core activities of the organisation.
2. Contracted associate staffs - which comes together when necessary to perform the organisation's activities.
3. Outsourced bodies (contracted groups) - that perform the support activities.

This type of structure has the clear potential to be entrepreneurial as it allows the venture to be flexible and adaptive to business environment with the aid of modern technology and electronic media.

The structure also brings the benefits of low operating costs, facilitating market entry and start-ups, flexibility, and ease of modification and growth potential. However, this type of structure is not without limitations as it is difficult to manage and not easy to sustain the relationship of all components involved. Usually, the agents whom the venture relies on for its core activities are free, often with portfolio careers and with little loyalty to the venture. Additionally, innovation can be problematic. Unless specifically contracted to do so, the associates rarely engage in essential research and development, normally acting as outworkers commissioned to carry out very specific activities.

10.2.6 The Extended Organisation

The extended organisation is one which uses the resources of other organisations in its network to achieve its goal.

This type of organisational structure can help the new venture gain cess to, and uses of resources of other organisations in its networks to achieve its goal by building long term, supportive and mutually beneficial relationship especially with suppliers who provide the venture the inputs it needs, associated organisations in the same business who can help manage fluctuations in demand, and distributors who can get firms goods and services to their customers.

The extended organisation has the clear potential to be entrepreneurial because it is:

- ✓ Easy to set up.
- ✓ Initial investment needed is very small and entry costs are low.
- ✓ Flexible and can easily be modified.
- ✓ Fixed costs are minimised.
- ✓ Allows the entrepreneur access to resources of other organisations.
- ✓ Growth is relatively easily to manage.

10.2.7 The Hollow Organisation

The hollow organisation is one which exists not so much to do things itself but with other organisations together.

In hollow organisation, all noncore operations are outsourced leaving the venture to concentrate on core activities.

The hollow organisation creates value by building a new network or making an existing one more efficient.

The hollow organisation is kept as small as possible - it may only be a single office. It sticks to essential or core activities. Example is one which simply markets products but does not involve in manufacture.

The hollow organisation enjoys the benefits just like extended and shamrock organisations and as such an attractive options for starting new ventures.

However, if they are to be successful, entrepreneurs must be sure of the strategy they are adopting. In particular, they must be confident about:

- ✓ Where the business will be located in the value adding chain.
- ✓ The value they are adding (i.e. why consumers will benefit from what the business has to offer).
- ✓ Why their product is different from others.
- ✓ How they will manage the relationship on which the business will depend and how they will sustain this relationship.

10.2.8 Teams

A team structure exists when management delegates significant responsibilities and authority, not to individual workers but to an identifiable team, which is then mutually accountable for the results. They are sometimes called "self managing teams" to emphasise the relative absence of hierarchical relationship.

The team may be from across functions, or from within a single area- in which case it looks like a small department.

For the entrepreneur team structure can be entrepreneurial as it offers the advantages flexibility, creativity, adaptability and faster response.

This is particularly true in ventures that depend on a steady flow of scientific developments and innovation to create new products.

Limitations may be found in some areas such as a team tendency to take on its own purpose and to spend much time in debate rather than action.

10.2.9 Virtual Organisation

Virtual organisation could be described as a temporary network.

It is the temporary arrangement among partners that can be easily reassembled to adapt to market change. The inspirations for this structural approach largely come from the Film industry.

Rather than seeking to control value chain activities through direct ownership of business, virtual organisation acquire resources or strategic capabilities by creating a temporary network of independent companies, suppliers, customers and even rivals and relies on information technology to create the links needed to share skills, costs and access to one another markets.

For the entrepreneur, virtual organisation can be entrepreneurial. The benefits are in the creative, adaptable and spontaneous environment which it creates in giving the entrepreneur the ability to organise people from various geographical destination of the world and assemble them as free agents who move from projects to projects, applying their skills in directing, search, customising, setting and designing venture activities as may be needed to achieve a particular objective in time.

10.2.10 Network Structure

A networked structure could be described as either a collection of individuals or units from within an organisation (intra-organisational networks) or collection of individual businesses (inter-organisational networks).

A network structure also exists when tasks required by one company are performed by other companies with expertise in those areas. It refers to situations in which organisations remain independent but agree to work together to deliver products or services. This usually happens when managers of is firm (or many firms) arrange for other firms to undertake certain activities on their behalf- usually those that they do not see as being core to the business, allowing the organisation to concentrates on setting strategy direction and managing the core units.

For the entrepreneur, networking can be entrepreneurial in terms of creativity, flexibility and adaptability which it creates for the venture.

There is the benefit derived from collaboration and the links between them are strengthened through interaction, although the individual members are independent, they recognise.

Also the intention is that by creating a system of loosely coupled units, the members can respond quickly to new opportunities in the marketplace. Thus, the network members have common objectives and it is this unified purpose that holds them themselves in reality.

In addition, networking enables the new venture to grow rapidly especially, the small business venture with limited capital expenditure if they can secure a network structure with large business, as specialist producers, suppliers and distributors.

However, networking has limitations. The network only responds as fast as the slowest member of the chain and it is found that the most suitable firms for membership of a network are those that make extensive use of teams and other lateral mechanisms, both within and between the firm and its partners, so that they are to shift resources to meet the demands of the environment.

10.3 Financing the New Venture

10.3.1 Introduction

One of the important functional areas of small business that needed adequate attention is the area of finance.

Finance is what every venture whether large or small need to worry about and new venture owner/managers need to finance them for the initial start-up and subsequent operations . . . Every venture needs finance – to get the business started and to get the business running efficiently and effectively.

Financial management can be defined as the management of the finances of an organisation in order to achieve the financial objective of the organisation. The usual assumption in financial management for the private sector is that the objective of the company is to maximise shareholder wealth. In the case of the small business it should be the maximisation of the wealth of owner or proprietor of the business.

Broadly, there are two aspects of financial management:

1. Financial planning.
2. Financial control.

Attracting financial support for the new venture is one of the entrepreneur's important tasks. However, financing the new venture can be one of the most challenging tasks facing the entrepreneur.

Business is a continuous activity and money flowing in will be used to keep the business going. The venture owner/manager needs to understand the principles of financial management. He/she will need to plan to ensure that enough funding is available at the right time to meet the needs of the business for short, medium and long term capital.

In the short term, funds may be needed to pay purchases of stocks, to smooth out changes in debtors, creditors and cash- ensuring that working capital requirements are met. In the medium or long, the organisation may have planned purchases of fixed assets such as plant and equipment, for which the owner/manager must ensure that funds to this effect are available.

The new venture owner/manager must make decisions on the uses of funds by analysing financial data to determine uses which meet the organisation's financial objectives.

The control function of the new venture owner/manager becomes relevant for funding which has been raised. He/she needs to make sure that money and other financial assets of the business are being used efficiently. To achieve these objectives, the venture owner/manager will need to develop ways to source, retain and manage finance for the business including comparing data on actual performance with forecast performance. Forecast data will have been prepared in the light of past performance (historical data), modified to reflect expected future changes.

Investments in assets must be financed somehow and the venture owner/manage must also make decisions relating to investment financing and even dividends where applicable. He/she must be concerned with the management of short term funds and how funds can be raised over the long term - taking more credits, retention of profits for investment in the business, the issue of new shares to raise capital, borrowing from banks, leasing of assets as an alternative to outright purchase, etc. The venture owner/manager as a financial manager must be concerned with how to source funds and type of funds, use of funds and financial assistance.

New ventures are frequently under-capitalised, and seldom is sufficient capital available to launch a venture optimally. Obtaining capital for the new venture is particularly difficult because it has no track record and in addition, the entrepreneur may be somewhat inexperienced. Accordingly, most lenders take a somewhat conservative approach to new venture lending, and it is appropriate that they should as most new businesses fail. However, it is possible that if those ventures were properly funded at the beginning, more would survive.

One of the most important things many potential investors look at when making investment decisions is the person – how convincing is the founder as potential entrepreneur? Then, the next thing is the quality of the idea and the robustness of the business plan – how likely it is a viable proposition? Then, is the proposition from their perspective – how likely it will help them meet their objectives?

If money is going to be raised for the business, it will be necessary for the entrepreneur as the under to convince potential investors that he/she has the requisite technical and business acumen, that the proposal is sound and that there is something it for them. The business plan will help here, but it is important to explain:

- ✓ Why the money is needed – short term capital, long term capital there are two types of financing available for such purposes i.e. equity and debt borrowing.
- ✓ The type of funding required.
- ✓ When the money will be needed.
- ✓ The deal being offered – there are five key stages in the investment process – deal origination, deal screening, deal evaluation, deal structuring, post investment activity.
- ✓ The exit routes opened for investors in the business – three options, - the business is sold when the time comes, the investor is bought out, the business is floated on the stock market or AIM

Sources of Fund

As already indicated, every small business needs money to get started and to continue if the business is to succeed

A small business can source finance:

1. Internally.
2. Externally.

1. **Internal Sources of Fund**

Personal savings, and borrowing from friends and relatives

One of the internal sources of fund for many start-ups and existing ventures is though private savings, and boogying from friends and relatives. Many small ventures start with savings - through individual saving of the proprietors who may have worked for a while and saved some capital or savings may come from employment, redundancy payments, winning a lottery or gift, etc. including borrowing from friends and relatives. Established small ventures also call for funds saved and borrowing from friends and relatives to improve financial position of the business when necessary.

Profit or retained profit

Profit or retained profit is another internal source of finance for already established ventures that may need the fund for improving the financial position of the business to progress business activities.

Retained profit is not a common way for start -up but provide an inexpensive source of fund to finance for existing ventures.

Depreciation

Another internal source of finance for existing or established ventures is depreciation - a financial provision for the replacement of worn out machinery and equipment.

Sales of assets

Existing or established ventures can also use sale of assets to source finance.

Sometimes an established venture may need to sell assets to raise finance when other sources of funds are exhausted or because assets sold are used as an investment to improve the business performance.

2. **External Sources of Fund**

External sources of finance for small business can be categorised into

- ✓ External short term sauces of finds.
- ✓ External long term sources of funds.

External Short –Term Sources

External short- term sources of funds for small businesses may include:

- ✓ Bank overdraft.
- ✓ Bank loan.
- ✓ Hire purchase.
- ✓ Trade credit.
- ✓ Leasing- operational lease, financial lease.
- ✓ Trade bills.
- ✓ Credit cards.
- ✓ Debt factoring.

- **Bank overdraft**

This is probably the most important source of fund for a very large number of business ventures. This is because bank overdrafts provide flexibility in uses and repayment.

Bank overdraft provides flexibility because the amount by which a business goes overdrawn will depend on its needs at any point in time. Requirement to standing repayment agreement and interest is only paid by the business when its account is in overdraft at a certain amount. The level of overdrafts depends on each bank overdraft policy and the entrepreneur can make manage uses and repayment as required.

- **Bank loan**

Unlike bank overdraft, a bank loan requires a rigid agreement between the venture borrower and the bank.

The amount borrowed must be paid back over a clearly stated time period, in regular instalments.

Compared with a bank overdraft, the interest charged is slightly higher and bank loans to small businesses are short term or medium term. Banks dislike long term lending to small ventures because of their need for collateral security which many small businesses are not always able to provide. Sometimes banks may change persistent overdrafts into loans so that the small venture is forced to repay.

- **Hire purchase**

Hire purchase involves buying a product, and making instalment payment of an agreed amount of the whole purchase price without owning it, until the financial instalment payment is made.

Sometimes, a hire purchase agreement requires a down payment by the borrower, who agrees to repay the remainder in instalments over a period of time. Financial houses specialise in providing funds for such agreements and the parties.

Hire purchase is often used by many ventures to buy plant and equipments. In many times, the venture involved in a hire purchase is asked to put down what is referred to a "down payment" – something like an initial deposited - with the supplier and receives delivery of the product.

The entrepreneur as the venture owner can then pay the rest of the outstanding payment in an agreed instalments or he/she may seek the assistance of the finance house that will help pay the supplier for the amount outstanding immediately. The finance house will then collect payment by instalments from the small business owner including interests.

The goods bought do not legally belong to the venture owner until the last instalment has been paid to the finance house. If the small business owner falls behind with the repayments the finance house can legally reposes the item sold.

One advantage of using finance house is that they are less selective than banks when granting loans. However the easier access to fund for the small business reflects in interest rates that are higher than the banks. They also add a servicing charge for paying in instalments which also lead to higher rates.

- **Trade credit**

Trade credit is a credit extended to a business by trade credit suppliers who let the business buy things now (products and services), and pay later. Any time an entrepreneur takes delivery of materials, equipment or other valuables without paying cash on the spot; the entrepreneur is using trade credit.

Trade credit is common for many ventures to buy raw materials, components and fuel, and they pay for them at a later date, usually between 30 to 90 days.

Paying for goods and services using trade credit seems to be an interest free way of raising finance. It is particularly profitable during periods of inflation. However, the cost of goods bought on trade credit is often higher than those paid on the spot or paid earlier.

In many cases, firms involved in giving trade credit usually encourage early payment by offering discounts.

However, entrepreneurs are advised to be careful in the handling of trade credits provided by trade suppliers because delaying the payment of trade credit bills can result in poor business relations with trade credit suppliers.

- **Leasing**

A lease is a written or implied contract in which an owner (lesser) of a specific asset grants a second party (the lessee) the right to its exclusive possession and use for specific period and under specified conditions, in return for specified periodic rental or lease payments

The entrepreneur can be involved in OPERATING and FINANCE LEASE.

An OPERATING LEASE means that the leasing company simply hires out equipment for an agreed period of time. The entrepreneur as the user never owns the equipment. But the entrepreneur could be given the option to purchase the equipment outright – in this case a FINANCE LEASE,

Leasing allows the entrepreneur as venture owner to buy plant, machinery and equipment and take a number of advantages associated with leasing such as:

- ✓ No large sums of moneys needed to buy the use of the equipment.
- ✓ Maintenance and repair costs are not the responsibility of the user.
- ✓ Access to up to date equipment.
- ✓ Useful when equipment is only required.

Limitations associated with leasing is that, over a long period of time a lease can be more expensive than the outright purchase of plant and machinery. Also, loans cannot be secured on assets which are leased.

- **Trade bills**

The entrepreneur as purchaser of overseas traded goods may sign a BILL OF EXCHANGE.

A trade bill of exchange is an unconditional order in writing, addressed by one person another, signed by the person giving it, requiring the person to which it is addressed to pay on demand, or a fixed or determinable future time, a sum certain in number or money to, or to the order of a specified person or to bearer. In other words, the small business owner/manager agrees to pay for the goods at a specified later date. Ninety days is a common period.

The seller of the goods to the entrepreneur will hold the bill until payment is due at a maturity date.

The holder can sell the trade bill at a discount before the maturity date to a specialist financial institution.

There is a well developed market for trade bills where all holders are expected to receive payment at the end of the maturity period from debtors.

- **Credit cards**

Credit cards can be a valuable source of fund for entrepreneurs.

The entrepreneur can use credit cards to meet up with regular and irregular expenses such as hotel bills, petrol or meals when travelling on business trips. Sometimes as a case of emergency the entrepreneur may use credit cards to purchase materials from suppliers who accept credit cards.

Credit cards are popular with many venture owners because they are convenient, flexible to use, and the small business owner can avoid interest charges if monthly accounts are settled within the required credit period. However, credit cards tend to have credit limits and high interest related to amount spent. This may make them unsuitable for certain purchases or long term financing.

- **Debt factoring**

Factoring is a financial transaction and a type of debtor finance in which a business sells its accounts receivable (i.e. invoices) to a third party (called the factor) at a discount.

Debt factoring can help the entrepreneur to factor its present and immediate cash needs. This usually involves specialist company (the factor) providing finance for unpaid invoices of the venture when it sells products (unpaid). These invoices will state the amount due. The invoice provides evidence of the sale and the money owed to the venture.

A common arrangement is for a factor to pay 80 percent of the value of the unpaid invoices when they are issued. The balance of 20 percent is paid by the factor when the customer settles the bill. An administrative and service fee usually charged for the whole transactions.

External Long - Term Sources

External long - term finance capital for a venture can also be in forms of the following:

1. Share capital.
2. Loan capital (debentures, mortgages, venture capitalist Business Angels).

- ✓ Bank loans.
- ✓ The money market.
- ✓ The capital market.
- ✓ Alternative Investment Market (AIM).

- **Share capital**

Entrepreneurs can source venture funds through external long term share capital. This is usually applicable to limited private ventures or companies.

Types of share capital include:

- Ordinary shares

These are called EQUITIES. They are the most common share issued. They are also the riskiest. Ordinary share holders receive dividend from profits declared and the size of the dividend depends on the profit the directors decide to retain. All ordinary shareholders have voting rights.

- Preference shares

Owners of preference shares receive a fixed rate of return when a dividend is declared. Unlike ordinary shares, they carry less risk because owners get dividend before ordinary. Shareholders. Some are CUMULATIVE -entitling the holder to divided areas from years where dividends were not declared. However, holders of preference share are not owners of the business. If a business is sold their right to dividend and capital repayment is limited to fixed amount.

- Deferred shares

These are not used often by small businesses they are usually held by founders of the large company. They only receive dividend after ordinary shareholders.

For a limited small company, share capital is likely a preferred source of fund because it can be used to raise large amount of money. The most popular share capital is the ordinary share (also called equities) which is not without risks.

Share capital is often referred to as PERMANENT CAPITAL. This is because it is not normally REDEEMED –it is not to be paid back by business. The buyer is entitled to share in the profit of the business –the DIVIDEND. It is important to remember that dividends are usually associated with risks – dividends are not always declared and sometimes business make a loss or retains its profit and therefore, no dividend is paid. However, a share holder can make a CAPITAL GAIN by selling his/her shares at a higher price. A limited small company shareholder is entitled to vote. Voting takes place annually and shareholders to the opportunity to elect or re-elect existing board members.

- **Loan capital**

Any money which is borrowed for a lengthy period of time by the business is called LOAN CAPITAL. The entrepreneur can raise loan capital in the form of:

➢ Debentures

Debentures holders in a venture are creditors of the venture, not owners. This means they are entitled to an agreed fixed rate of return, but have no voting rights. The amount borrowed must be paid back by the expiry of agreed date.

➢ Mortgage

The entrepreneur may need long term funding to buy their premises. In this instance, it may chose to take a mortgage - a long term loan from a bank or other financial institution for this purpose. The lender uses the mortgage land or property as a security for the loan.

➢ Venture capitalists

The entrepreneur can raise loan capital from a venture capitalist. Venture capitalists are specialist organisations that tend to cater for businesses, especially the small business, who have difficulties in raising funds from conventional sources. They provide funds for small firms that appear to have some potential but are considered risky by conventional sources of finance.

➢ Business Angels

They are also a source of loan capital for entrepreneurs. Business Angels are individuals who invest money often in exchange for equity stake - either individually or together with a small group of friends, relatives or business associates. Most of their investments are in start-ups or early stage of business expansions. There are several reasons people become Business Angels - excitements of the gamble involved, being part of a new developing business, tax relief offered by the government, investment opportunities for unused income, such as retired business people and lottery winners.

- **Financial intermediaries (The money market)**

Entrepreneurs can also seek the help of financial intermediaries to raise capital for their ventures.

Financial intermediaries are the institutions responsible for matching the needs of savers, who want to loan funds, with those of investors who need funds. These groups do not naturally communicate with each other.

Intermediaries provide the link between them. A number of financial institutions hold funds for savers, paying them interest.

In addition, they make funds available to investors who in turn, are charged interest. Some deal in capital i.e. permanent and long term finance while others deal in money i.e. short term loans and bills of exchange. They offer a variety of commercial and financially related services.

The money market is composed of bank and other financial institutions. The money market is dominated by the major commercial banks, such as the NatWest bank, HSBC etc. They allow payments to be made through cheque system and deal in short term loans.

Savings banks bank and finance corporations also deal with short term funds.

Building societies also provide a source of finance. They have tended to specialise in long term loans for the purchase of land and property.

At the heart of this highly complex market system is the BANK OF ENGLAND.

- **The capital market**

Already established ventures can also raise money through the stock exchange mechanisms.

The main function of the stock exchange is to provide a market where the owners of shares can sell them.

If this market did not exist, selling shares will be difficult because buyers and sellers could not easily communicate with each other. Savers would be less inclined to buy shares bad so companies would find it difficult to raise funds. A stock exchange also enables mergers and acquisition to take place smoothly. It also provides a means of protection for shareholders.

Ventures which have stock exchange listing have to obey a number of stock exchange rules and regulations which are designed to safeguard shareholders from fraud. It is also argued that the share prices reflect the health of participating ventures.

- **Alternative Investment Market (AIM)**

In June 1995, the AIM was established in UK.

Its purpose was to give small young and growing small companies the chance to raise capital and trade their shares more widely without the cost of full stock market listing.

The entrepreneur as owner of a small venture can also raise funds through the AIM.

In order to join the AIM, a nominated adviser must be appointed such as a stockbroker, banker or lawyer. The adviser must supervise the admission procedures and be responsible for ensuring that the company complies with AIM regulations. The admission procedure takes three months. The cost of listing is about £100,000 depending on the period in question.

Another market called OFEX was set up by JP Jankins, the specialist market in small company shares is not regulated by the stock exchange, but only stock exchange member firms can deal directly on OFEX. OFEX offers a market place for the shares of unlisted companies that have no interest in joining AIM. Also OFEX acts as a feeder to AIM, because floatation and other costs are less at the initial stage.

10.3.2 Government Financial Assistance Programmes and Incentives

Both central and local government have been involved in providing finance for new ventures and small business in many countries.

Governments over the world especially developed countries have developed a number of financial assistance programmes and incentives for new ventures and small business development.

The UK government for example, has introduced a number of assistance schemes to help new ventures and small businesses, and several of these are designed to encourage lenders and investors to make finance available to new ventures and small businesses.

Some examples include:

- The Loan Guarantee Scheme.
- The Enterprise Initiative Scheme.
- The Enterprise Investment Scheme (EIS).
- Development Agencies.
- Venture Capital Trust.

- The Loan Guarantee Scheme

The Loan Guarantee Scheme was introduced in 1981, intended to help small businesses get a loan from the bank, when a bank would otherwise be unwilling to lend because, the small business cannot provide the security that the bank wants.

The government however, provides some guidelines for disbursing the loan:

- ✓ The borrower's annual turnover must not exceed a limit which depends on the type of business.
- ✓ Under the scheme, which was revised in 1993, the bank can lend up to £250,000 without security over personal assets or a personal guarantee being required of the borrower.
- ✓ All available business assets must be used as security if required.

- ✓ The government will guarantee the bulk of the loan while the borrower will guarantee the remaining part of the loan.

- The Enterprise Initiative

The UK Department of Trade and Industry (DTI) offer a number of financial assistance to small businesses in a form of packages that include:

- ✓ Regional selective assistance.
- ✓ Regional enterprise grant.
- ✓ A network of business links, which are local business advice centres.

Regional selective assistance is available for investment projects undertaken by small firms in assisted areas on the condition that projects should be commercially viable, create or safeguard employment, demonstrate a need for assistance and offer a distinct regional and national benefit. The amount of grant to be given will be negotiated as the minimum necessary to ensure the project goes ahead

The regional enterprise grant scheme is specially geared to help small firms employing fewer than 25 employees in one of the development areas to expand and diversify.

Regional enterprise grants can only finance viable projects for:

1. Investments – grants of 15% of the cost of fixed assets and up to maximum grant of £15,000 are available.
2. Innovation – grants of 50% of the agreed project cost up and to a maximum grant of £25,000 are available.

- The Enterprise Investment Scheme (EIS)

The Enterprise Investment Scheme is intended to encourage investment in the ordinary shares of unquoted companies.

Individuals are encourages by many tax incentives to invest in small firms most of which are unquoted companies.

For example:

- ✓ When a qualified individual subscribes for eligible shares in a qualifying company, the individual saves tax at 20% on the amount subscribed including any share premium.
- ✓ A qualifying individual is one who is not connected with the company at any time in the period from two years before the issue or from incorporation if later, to five years after the issue
- ✓ The maximum total investment that any individual investors can qualify in a tax year is £150,000 per individual (subject to review with time period).
- ✓ Capital gains generated by the individual investor in the EIS are tax free provided the investment is held for five years.

- Development agencies

The UK government has also set up Development Agencies which has been given the task of encouraging the development of trade and industry in many areas.

The strategy of the agencies has been to encourage the start-up and development of small companies, although they also give help to larger companies.

Development agencies are set up small firm's access to:

1. Free factory accommodation, or factory accommodation at a low rent.
2. Interest relief for bank loan - development agency will agree to compensate the bank for providing a loan to a small business at a low rate of interest.
3. Financial assistance - in the form of equity finance or loan.

- Venture Capital Trust (VCT)

The UK government introduced a second measure to encourage equity investment in the form of a new kind of investment trust – VCT which came into being in 1995.

This followed critic from banks and small business groups that small companies were too dependent on short term finance.

The UK Inland Revenue is required it to invest a large proportion of its assets in unquoted companies.

Investors on in small unquoted company can gain 20% income tax relief on dividend provided shares are held in the VCT for three years, and capital gain rollover relief if the gain is invested in a VCT. However, there is an investment ceiling per period of £100,000 which is time related.

10.3.3 Uses of Fund

Apart from understanding sources of funds, the small business owner/managers also need to know the use of sourced funds - using their funds efficiently and effectively.

Generally, small business owner/managers use the money sourced to finance:

- ✓ Fixed assets.
- ✓ Current assets.
- ✓ Working capital.
- ✓ Liquidity, etc.

Fixed assets

Assets are the resources used by business. Most assets are physical in nature and are used for production . . . Some assets are not physical e.g. goodwill. Assets are usually valued at their original cost less a deduction for depreciation. Fixed assets are resources with a life span of more than a year. They can be used again and again until they wear out. Fixed assets are subject to depreciation such as machinery, but there are others such as Land and property that do not depreciate, although they have to be repaired. In the balance sheet, fixed assets may be divided into:

- ✓ Tangible – assets that can be seen such as machinery and equipment, property, land, etc.
- ✓ Intangible – assets that cannot be seen and may include goodwill, patents, copyrights and trademarks, research and development, brand names, etc.
- ✓ Financial assets - often called INVESTMENTS. If the share holding in a particular company is more than 50% then the company is classified as SUBSIDIARY. If the holding is between 20% and 50% the company is described as ASSOCIATED COMPANY. If it is less than 20% it is called TRADE INVESTMENT.

Current assets

Current assets are assets that are likely to be changed into cash within one year. The might include deposits in the bank and stocks of goods; they might also include customers who owe money to the business.

Working capital

Working capital (current asset or circulating capital) is the amount of money needed to pay for the day to day trading of business.

The working capital of a small business is the amount left over after all CURRENT DEBTS have been paid. It is normally calculated as the sum of CURRENT ASSETS minus CURRENT LIABILITIES.

It is the relatively liquid assets that can easily be turned into cash i.e. (cash, stocks, money owing from debtors who have bought goods and services) MINUS The money owed by a business which needs to be paid in the short term (to banks, to creditors who have supplied goods and services, to government in tax or shareholders' dividend payable within a year).

The small business owner/manager needs working capital to pay EXPENSES such as wages, electricity and gas charges and to buy components to make products.

Managing working for the small business owner/manager is crucial for business survival and growth. Provided that current assets are twice the size of current liability, working capital would be enough for the small business owner/manager, to avoid financial problems. However, small businesses like those in retail can operate if their working capital is less because, they have quick turnover and is usually in cash.

In some types of small business, particularly manufacturing, delays or time lags exists between different stages of business activity creating a cycle. The length of time lags can be crucial when managing working capital. The Small business owner/manager can improve working capital conditions by reducing:

- ✓ Predictive time.
- ✓ Storage time of finished goods.

- ✓ Stock holding time and improve just in time.
- ✓ Time it takes customers to settle bills by monitoring and checking late payments and offering discounts for early payments or settlements.
- ✓ Delaying payment to suppliers.

Liquidity

Cash is also a part of working capital but only a part. It is possible for a business to have adequate working capital and have insufficient cash to pay bills.

Businesses whether large or small that have difficulties in controlling cash flow and working capital often have liquidity problems. They either do not have enough cash to pay immediate debt or cannot covert liquid assets into cash quickly or are not managing debt and credit effectively which is a part of current assets. They simply suffer from liquidity problems.

Liquidity refers to the speed or ease with which assets can be converted into cash without suffering any capital loss.

Businesses that have difficulty controlling its cash flow and working capital are said to have LIQUIDITY PROBLEMS.

LIQUID ASSETS are those that are easily changed into cash. They either do not have enough cash to pay immediate debt or cannot convert the liquid assets into cash quickly enough

Sources of liquidity problems may include:

- ✓ Overtrading.
- ✓ Investing in too much fixed assets.
- ✓ Stock piling.
- ✓ Allowing too much credit.
- ✓ Taking too much credit.
- ✓ Over-borrowing.
- ✓ Underestimating inflation.
- ✓ Unforeseen expenditure.
- ✓ Unexpected change in demand.
- ✓ A tight credit control may be used to improve liquidity, reduce the risk of bad debt.

Liquidity problems can be prevented by keeping a tight control on working capital. Inevitably, there will be occasions when small firms run short of liquid resources. When this does happen, the firm main aim will be survival rather than profit.

The following measures might be used to obtain liquid resources:

- ✓ Stimulate sales for cash offering large cash discounts if necessary.
- ✓ Sell off stocks of raw materials – below costs if necessary.
- ✓ Sell off any fixed assets which may not be vital for operations.
- ✓ Sell off fixed assets and lease them back.
- ✓ Mount a rigorous drive on overdue accounts.
- ✓ Sell debts to factoring company.
- ✓ Only make essential purchases.
- ✓ Extend credit with selected suppliers.
- ✓ Reduce personal drawing.
- ✓ Negotiate additional short term loan.

Assets structure

The small business owner/manager should also understand the asset structure required by his/her business and determine the right asset structure.

Assets structure refers to the amount of capital employed in each category of asset.

Asset structure will vary according to the nature of industry and sectors- competitive, monopoly, manufacturing, construction, retail, seasonal etc.

For example,

- ✓ Manufacturing firms tend to have large amount of capital tied up in plant, machinery and equipment.
- ✓ Construction firms will have a significant amount of work in progress.
- ✓ Businesses which have seasonal demand will have large stocks of finished goods at particular times.

✓ Retail trade, public houses and restaurant will have very few debtors.

Credit control

Small business owner/managers need to have credit control system so that money owed could be collected quickly and easily.

A small business can use "Easy" or "Tight" credit terms to improve credit control.

Tight credit terms can be applied by the small to improve liquidity, reduce the risk of bad debts, exploit a seller's market or maintain adequate profit margins, etc. Easy credit terms could also be used by the small business to clear stocks, enter a new market, regular customers with financial difficulties, etc.

The small business owner/manager is expected to work closely with the credit customers since credit policy will affect the financial position of the firm and sales.

The owner/manager should set targets for the credit control in relation to bad debts or the length of time it takes to collect debts. The best way is to develop credit control procedures. When an order exceeds credit limit the credit the owner/manager must investigate. If there are persistent debts, the owner/manager must take action.

A small business will have more effective control of cash flow if the owner/manager keeps up to date business record. this will help the owner /manager always plan ahead by predicting accurate cash forecast, operate effective credit control system that helps prevent or slow down late payment. Advance information technology is now enabling small businesses to keep more up to date record and access information more quickly.

10.3.4 Factors to Consider When Financing the Venture

A number of factors are important for the entrepreneur to consider when choosing between alternative sources of funds. These include:

- ✓ Cost of fund.
- ✓ Use of fund.
- ✓ Status and size of the firm.
- ✓ Financial situation of the firm.
- ✓ Gearing.

Cost of fund

Every venture large or small prefers sources which are less expensive both in terms of interest payment and administration cost, in relation to the use of funds or investments. This is the same with the entrepreneur. He/she must always consider cost of alternative sources and uses of funds available at a particular time or future period. The choice for a particular source and use of fund needs to be linked to the cost in line with other related variables. For example, Shares usually carry high administrative costs when compared to credit cards that could be issued on line. Overdrafts tend to be relatively low in terms of interest when compared to bank loans, etc.

Use of fund

When considering the cost of funds, the entrapment is also expected to factor in the use of fund in relation to the cost. This should be linked to the type of project and period of use.

For example, if a small business decides to undertakes a heavy capital expenditure, it is expected that this project should be funded by long term source of finance - the building of a new plant should be financed by a share issue or a mortgage, revenue expenditure should be financed by short term sources, the purchase of a large amount of raw material may be funded by trade credit or bank overdraft, etc.

Statutes and size of the firm

Considering the status and size of the venture is also an important variable for the entrepreneur to consider when sourcing and using venture funds.

Small ventures especially sole traders which are limited in their choices of finance. They have limited sources of long- term and short-term financing, due to their size, and added insecurity, they cannot often demand lower interest rates from lenders.

The owner manager must therefore consider the effect of the status and size of the firms that reflects its ability to source funds which is usually a limitation. The small business owner/manager has to understand limited sources of finance available to him, /her and be able to source and use funds accordingly. If the owner/manager ignores this important variable, there is the tendency of sourcing funds wrongly for the wrong use, which might become a heavy burden for the small business as time in the short and long run that can go on and on, exposing the small business to possibility to default payment, and creating poor credit record and reference, and poor image in relation to financial stakeholders.

Financial situation

The financial situation of a venture is also an important determinant of the sources and uses of funds for the entrepreneur.

The financial situation of any business whether large or small in a normal sense, is constantly changing. The small business can find itself in a poor financial situation at one time, which can change at any time for better, depending on circumstances.

When a venture is in a poor financial situation it is likely that lenders are more reluctant to offer finance. At the same time, the cost of borrowing rises In this situation, the small business owner/ manager will need to seek and negotiate the right deals to obtain finance, and will have to consider all alternatives available before a making a decision.

Gearing

Another important factor when considering sources and use of funds for a small business is "gearing."

Gearing is the relationship between loan capital and share capital or equity of the small business.

A venture is said to be high geared if it has large proportion of loan capital to share capital or equity. This is not a good financial position for the venture because it may have to pay high interest for the borrowed loan capital which is an expense that can be avoided in the first place if the small business has a higher share capital or equity in relation to loan capital.

If the venture is highly geared, it might be difficult to raise finance in the future as lender might take into consideration its financial position and debt condition that does not appear to be good for lenders, also, the small business owner/manager may even be reluctant to raise even more finance from borrowing.

Basic rules for sourcing and using funds

The basic rules when obtaining and investing capital in a business are:

- Never borrow short and invest long.
- Always try to match the length of time you have to repay the borrowed fund with the life of the assets you are investing in.
- Long term investment (i.e. over 5 years) should be financed from long term, funds generated by business, your own capital, long term loans or mortgages.
- Modern term investment such as vehicles and plant with restricted life are generally suitable for hire purchase, leasing or medium term loan.
- The weekly fluctuating working capital can safely be financed by short term renewable sources of fund such as bank overdraft.

10.3.5 How Investors Select Investment Opportunities

1. Deal origination –is the starting of the investment process in which the entrepreneur and the investor first become aware of each other which results from a mix of searching activity by the investor or the entrepreneur.
2. Deal screening - represents the initial screening of the investment proposal to see if it fits with the investor's profile of activities. Important criteria include the mount of investment being sought, the type of technology on which the venture is based, the industry sector and the venture's stage of growth.
3. Deal evaluation – involves a more detailed evaluation of the proposal that may be carried out to capture the returns offered by the venture with the risk that it faces. Key factor to be considered is the potential of the venture in innovation and its offering, the conditions in the market it aims to develop, and the competitive pressures it will face.
4. Deal structuring – concerns decisions that must be made in relation to how initial investment will be made, and how the investor will see that the investment bears fruit. Key issues will be how much the entrepreneur is seeking and over what period thee investment is to be made, actual return, how long the investor will have to wait before return is seen.
5. Post- investment activity –this related to the degree to which investors will be involved in venture control. Inventors especially those with significant interest will usually retain a degree of involvement in their investments. Control mechanisms give the investor an active role in the venture and power to influence the entrepreneur's and the venture management decision. One common control mechanism is for the investor to be represented in the venture's management team, perhaps as a director.

10.3.6 The Questions Investors Need Answering

- Is the venture of the right type?

Every investor will naturally want to know whether the investment he/she is going into is the right venture before taking the risk.

This is because investors usually specialise in different industry sectors in which they have knowledge and expertise and focus on investment opportunities in certain technical areas. Another important dimension of specialisation is the stage of development of the business and the nature of the financing it requires. Some ventures have shifted from new start-ups to financing or investing in lower risk management buy-outs. The investor will need to be assured that the venture is in the right area and at the right stage for them.

- How much investment is required?

Investors are also interested in the amount involved in financing a given venture when required. This will be required in relation to the business the investor is in, their expertise and the cost they face in monitoring and controlling their investors. For example, retail banks usually offer loans from a few hundred to tens of thousands of pounds. Venture capitalists on the other hand are not interested in investment of less than about £250,000, and are really interested in investment of millions of pounds. Market floatation may require raising at least £5 million. The key question is, is the investor really the right source given the level of investment needed?

- What return is likely?

The return on investment is the likely financial outcome of making a specific investment.

The investor will want to know on what basis this has been calculated. They will ask how reasonable it is given the potential for the venture and of its management team. The decision to invest will be based on an assessment of the returns in relation to the risks and how the investment opportunity compared with others available . . . These comparisons may be made on intuitive rather than explicit basis.

- What is the growth stage of the venture?

This relates to what the investment capital is required for - is it to start a new business or is it to fund the expansion of existing one? Is the venture at an early stage in its growth, requiring capital to fund an aggressive growth strategy, or is the business at a mature stage with the capital to be used to use to fund incremental growth? How does this impact on the risk entailed and return offered? Is the stage of growth right for the investor?

- What projects will the capital are used for?

Investors are also interested in knowing what projects the capital their investing in a venture will be used for. This relates to how the capital will be used within the venture. For example - to cover cash flow shortfalls which result from strong growth, or to be used for a more specific project such as development of new products, funding a sales drive or marketing campaign, or for entering export markets?

The question is how does this impact on the risk, return, and specialism from the point of view of the investor?

- What is the potential for the venture?

Investors are also interested in knowing the potentials of the venture - to know what the venture can be expected to achieve in the future.

This will depend on two sets of factors:

1. The market potential - how innovative its offering is, how much value this offers the customers in relation to what is already available, and the possibilities and limitations the venture faces in delivering this innovation to customers?
2. The quality of the entrepreneur and the management teams - the skills and experience of the venture's key people and their ability to deliver the potential that the venture has. The critical question is will the investor find the venture's potential attractive?

- What are the risks for the venture?

Investors are usually interested in knowing the he risks in the venture their investing in. To an investor the risk of the venture is the probability that it will not deliver the return anticipated. Critical to judging this is an understanding of the assumptions that have been made in estimating the likely return. Some critical areas are assumptions about customer demand, the ability of the business its costs, the ability of the venture to get distributor and other key partners on board, and the reaction of competitors. The investors' judgement of risk will depend on will depend o their ability to exit the investment by liquidating their holding. An investor will ask exactly how liquid the business is and whether or not the investment can be secured against particular liquid able assets. How do the risks match up with what the investor will expect?

- How is the investment to be made?

The investor will wish to know exactly the how their investment is to be made. Is it to be a lump sum up front or will it take the form of regular series of cash injections. The entrepreneur must ask whether this is the way the investor normally operates.

- How does the investor get out?

Investors always want to know how to get their return.
Will it take the form of cash? If so, will it be single cash payment at some point in the future, or will it be a series of payment over time?
Alternatively, will it take the form of a holding of stock in the firm? If so, how can such holding are liquidated? Loans are usually paid back in cash from whereas an enquiry holding will mature as a holding in the firm.
Venture capitalists with equity holdings will insist on a clear exit strategy which will enable them to convert their equity to cash either by selling on a market or converting with the venture.

- What post-investment monitoring procedures will be in place?

An investor will want to know the means by which they will be able to keep track of their investment.

A business plan will normally be required before an injection of capital is made. The business plan is an excellent way of communicating and of managing the investor's expectations.

Regular financial reports will provide key information on performance of the business and its liquidity. The entrepreneur must consider whether the monitoring procedures on offer will be considered adequate by the investor.

- What control mechanisms will be available?

Monitoring is of little use unless the investor can use the information gained to influence the behaviour of the venture's management

Investors who hold shares can signal their approval or otherwise by buying and selling their stock in the market that changes the value of the company.

The question that must be asked is how the control mechanism on offer will influence the investor's decision.

- Communication skills?

Communication is important in any process of investment decisions

It is therefore important that the entrepreneur and investors should interact to push through a process of investment decisions.

The entrepreneurs could communicate with investors not just because they wish to tell them about their ventures but also because they want the investors to support them they can exert a positive influence on investors by backing their answer with hard evidence to increase investors' confidence on them.

Further reading

Bacharach, S. and Lawler, E. (1980), Power and Politics in organisations, San Francisco, CA: Jossey Bass.

Baumol, W. (1968), The Entrepreneur Introductory Remarks, American Economic Review, Vol. 38, pp 60 -3.

Cole, A. (1968), Entrepreneurship in Economic Theory, American Economic Review, Vol. 58, pp 64 -71.

Deakins, D. and Freel, M. (2003), Entrepreneurship and Small Firms (3rd Edition), London: McGraw Hill.

Ovian, B. And McDougall, P.(2005), "Defining international entrepreneurship and modelling the speed of internationalisation, Entrepreneurship Theory and Practice, Vol. 29, No. 5, pp.537 -53.

Parker, S. (2002), "On the dimensionality and composition of entrepreneurship", Durham Business School Working Paper.

Westhead, P. Ucbasaran, D. (2005), "Decisions, actions and performance; do novice, serial and portfolio entrepreneurs differ?" Journal of Business Management, Vol. 43, No. 4, pp.393- 417.

CHAPTER 11

THE ENTREPRENEURIAL NEW VENTURE AND LEADING

Aim

To introduce leading and its need for the new venture.

Objectives

After studying this chapter you should be able to:

- Understand the meaning of leading for the new venture
- Understand the need for leadership in a new venture.
- Describe the relationship between leadership and power.
- Understand how people respond to power in organisations.
- Understand leadership theories available to the entrepreneur.
- Understand team building in relation to a new venture.
- Understand group/team development process and performance
- Understand motivation theories and their relevance to new venture development.

11.1 Introduction

In this chapter, we shall be looking at leading in the entrepreneurial new venture, in relation to the following:

- ➤ The entrepreneur as the manager in charge of leading the new venture operations.
- ➤ The people involved in the process of leading the new venture operations.
- ➤ The method (or methods) of leading people in the new venture operations.
- ➤ The context in which leading takes place in the new venture.

Leading as described here, is about the entrepreneur as the manager and how he/she carries out the management task of leading the venture operations. It is about the leadership qualities of the entrepreneur as the manager as an individual, and the style of leadership. It is also about the people involved with the new venture development, how they behave at work as groups, and how they are motivated, to achieve goals and objectives of the new venture. Leading also takes place within a context - reflected in the business culture. It is in this respect that leading in the entrepreneurial new venture is considered.

11.2 Leadership

11.2.1 Introduction

Leadership is a "people activity". This statement captures the idea that leaders are involved with other people in the achievement of goals.

In organisational context, leadership could be described as the ability of the manager as a leader to influence people or subordinates in origination towards the attainment of organisational goals/objectives.

It usually involves the use of influence to attain these goals/objectives. In other words, leadership is the management function that involves the use of influence to motivate employees to achieve goals/objectives of the organisation. It depends on influencing others to put effort and commitment to the task- whether that is to create order or to create change.

The idea that entrepreneurship is about innovation and change, has led Wickhan (2006), to suggest that entrepreneurial leadership is concerned with creating and managing vision and communication that vision to other people. It is about motivating people and being effective in getting people to accept change

The term "effective leader" is used to describe someone who brings innovation, moves an activity out of trouble into success, and makes a worthwhile difference. In other words, an effective leader sees opportunities to do new things, takes the courage to raise the issue and do something about it. Peter Ducker (1985) wrote of the leader's ability to generate unusual or exceptional commitment to a vision, and leadership being the lifting of people's vision to a higher sight, the raising of their performance to a higher standard, the building of their personality beyond its normal limitations.

Cole (2005) also described many types of leaders -charismatic leader, traditional leader, situational leader, appointment leader, and functional leader. Charismatic leader is one who gains influence mainly from the strength of the personality. Some examples could include: Napoleon, Churchill etc. A traditional leader is usually one by birth e.g. kings, queens and tribal leaders. A situational leader is opportune by being in the right place at the right time. The appointed leader is by position and the functional leader by what he or she does.

Since most work in organisations is carried out in groups, leadership is seen as a dynamic process in a group, whereby an individual- the manager, influences the others- employees, to contribute voluntarily in the achievement of group task in a given situation. In this respect, leadership is described as human process at work in organisation, directed towards a group goal, as manager gets things done with the support of others in groups.

For the entrepreneur, managing groups (or human resources) in the venture requires generating their optimal interest, effort, and commitment through effective leadership. The entrepreneur will need to secure the willing cooperation, and commitment of other people- (individuals and groups) -whose support and perhaps approval, need to be generated, motivated, and mobilised to achieve venture desired performance. It is in this respect that the entrepreneur should address the needs of individuals and group behaviour in the new venture.

11.2.2 Leadership and Power

Power in Organisation

Leadership is dynamic and involves the use of power. In a general sense, "Power" is the potential ability to influence the behaviour of others. Power is important for influencing others because; it determines whether a leader is able to command the right influence from followers. Power is also effective if the target of an influence attempt recognises the power source as legitimate and acceptable.

In management, power represents the resource with which a manager affects changes in subordinates or employees' behaviour. However, subordinates to a manager have to recognise the source of power to be effective. If subordinates dispute the power source of a leader or manager, then the influence attempt is likely to fail. Therefore, managers who are successful influencers ensure their power sources are legitimate, and also take every opportunity to sustain or enhance them.

Entrepreneurs are managers, but they are not just any sort of manager. If we were to seek the one characteristics that distinguishes entrepreneur from there more conventional colleagues, it would not be found in their strategic or analytical insights, though these are important but in the human dimension; - the way in which they use leadership and power and their ability to motivate those around them. Any discussion of entrepreneurship should help develop an insight into the ways in which leadership, power, and motivation may be used as managerial tools in a new venture.

Power is a concept which appears to be central to successful management and which has resisted being reduced to a simple conceptual formula. To many people the term has a negative connotation. However, an emerging idea is that power is not centred on an individual at all; rather it is a result of the structural factors that define how people work together and interact with each other. However, if we define power as an ability to influence the course of action within the organisation then power becomes a necessary feature of organisational life. Power is a feature of situations in which resources are limited and outcomes are uncertain. Under thus conditions, actions must be influenced or the organisation would not be an effective organisation.

Power must be distinguished from authority. Authority represents a right not ability to influence the course of action, owing to the position that the holder has within the organisation. The right is not the same as ability. The ability relates to the way in which authority translates into power and depends on how the people who make up the organisation regard the holder's standing and the position they occupy. Entrepreneurs may be given a high degree of ostensible authority by the social system in which they operate. The venture may belong to them and is seen as the property of the individual entrepreneur. However, this in itself is no guarantee that they will actually have power over their venture.

Sources of Leader Power and Influence

French and Raven (1959), Kantar (1979), Yuki and Tracey (1992) identified various sources of power and emphasised that within organisation, managers as leaders have the following sources of power and influence:

- **Legitimate power**

Legitimate power is always associated with a formal management position in the organisation and the authority granted to it. It derives from the job the leader or manager holds. Subordinates accept the source of power as legitimate which is why they obey. This gives the manger certain forms of power e.g. to make capital expenditures, to offer overtime, to choose a supplier or to recruit.

- **Reward power**

Reward power stems from the leader's or manager's authority to bestow rewards on others. This is usually visible in an organisation when an employee's comply with the manager's request or instruction because, they expects some reward in return.

This comes from the ability that the position gives the manager to use resources of the organisation as access to formal rewards. The reward itself can take many forms – pay rise, time off, promotion or more interesting work. Managers may also have at their disposal rewards such as praise, attention, and recognition. Altogether, managers can use rewards to influence subordinates' behaviour.

- **Coercive power**

Coercive power is usually seen as the opposite of reward power. Generally, it is the ability to obtain compliance through fear of punishment. It is the capacity to harm or restrict the actions of others which they try to avoid. In originations, it may take the form of reprimands, loss of job or threats of physical force.

Aggressive language and powerful physical presence are other forms of coercive power in originations. Managers also have coercive power when they have the right to fire or demote employees, criticise, or withdraw pay increase, etc.

- **Referent power/charismatic power**

Referent power is the power that results from leader or a manager's characteristics that command subordinates' identification with, respect and admiration for, and desire to emulate the manager as a leader.

In organisations, this is visible when some characteristics of the manager are attractive to the subordinates. In this case, subordinates try to identify with the manager, and this gives the manager power over them, as they admire and respect the manager, because of the behavioural aspects of the manager that impresses them.

- **Expert power**

Expert power is the power that stems from the leader's special knowledge of or skills in the tasks performed. In organisations, this is visible when subordinates acknowledge the manager's specialised knowledge and are therefore willing to follow the manager's suggestions. This knowledge or skill may be administrative or technical or something special.

- **Position power**

Kantar (1979) observed that people are more likely to be influenced by strong and powerful managers than weak and isolated ones. She argued that managers, who want to be effective influencers, can increase their chances of doing so, by building up those sources of power that come from their position within the organisation. She identified many ways a manager's position in the organisation can relate to his or her power such as:

- ✓ Relation of job to need for approvals for non routine decisions (fewer approvals means more power).
- ✓ Relation of job to authority (central relation means more power).
- ✓ External contact (more opportunities for this means more power).
- ✓ Senior contact (more opportunities of this means more power).

All these relationships may provide the manager, access to some power, such as:

- ✓ Supply power - money and other resources.
- ✓ Information power - being in the know, aware of what is happening, familiar with plans in the organisation.
- ✓ Support power - able to get senior support or external backing for what he or she wants to do.

The more of these lines of power the manager has, the more will subordinates cooperate. They do so because they believe that the manager is in the position to make things happen.

- **Power through networking**

Another important way a manager may influence others in organisations is the ability to draw on a network of informal relationships.

In this case, networking refers to an individual's attempts to develop and maintain relationships with others, who have potential to assist them in their work or career. In organisations, a managers' ability to influence can be greatly enhanced by being connected to many networks, giving access to contacts and information that is important to organisational performance. This usually helps the manager to know what is happening in their business environment, and to extend their range of contacts to those required by the origination. It is clear, that top level managers, who deal with shaping the corporate strategic direction of their businesses, normally rely on formal and informal networks of external contacts to get things done, to the benefit of their organisations.

- **To increase power -Share it!**

Kantar (1979) proposed that managers can increase their power by sharing it. This could be done through delegating of some power to subordinates i.e. sharing it. By sharing power with subordinates managers can further increase their own power. As subordinates carry out tasks previously done by the manager, the manager has more time to build up external contacts- which further boost his or her power. Also sharing power through delegation reduces the manager's workload and the manager has more time to concentrate on major management activities and creative work that may help increase the manager's potential power.

- **Tactics and Influence**

An early example of work in this area was by Kinas et al (1980) who identified a set of influencing tactics that managers used in dealing with different groups in organisation - subordinates, bosses and worked mates. They include:

- ✓ Rational persuasion.
- ✓ Inspirational appeal.
- ✓ Consultation.
- ✓ Ingratiation.
- ✓ Exchange.
- ✓ Personal appeal.
- ✓ Coalition.
- ✓ Legitimating.

These tactics cover a variety of behaviours that managers use as they try to influence others- whether subordinates, bosses, or staff members. Yuki and Tracey (1992) extended the work by examining which tactics managers used most frequently with different target groups. They concluded that managers were likely to use:

- Rational persuasion - when trying to influence their boss.
- Inspirational appeal and pressure - when trying to influence subordinates.
- Exchange, personal appeal and legitimating - when influencing colleagues.

11.2.3 Response to Power in Organisations

Subordinates in organisations respond to the attempt to use power by managers as leaders in various ways:

- ✓ Resistance.
- ✓ Compliance.
- ✓ Commitment, /internalisation.

Resistance is a measure of response to power. Resistance means subordinates will deliberately try to avoid carrying out instruction and attempt to disobey. In other words, subordinates have no commitment to work. They do what is required grudgingly, and without enthusiasm or imagination. While it may be possible for managers to overcome resistance by using threats or coercion, this may not be the most useful reaction in a longer term.

Compliance on the other hand, means subordinates will obey orders and carry out instructions, although they may personally disagree with the instruction. They will not be enthusiastic about it, indicating that they may be willing to do what is asked but are apathetic, unenthusiastic, putting minimal effort. This is a limitation especially, if the long term success of a business depends on future innovation that relies on creative and innovative employees. It is unlikely that grudging complying subordinates will produce creative, innovative and satisfactory performance.

Commitment is also a measure of response to power. Commitment usually means that subordinates are committed to sharing the leader's or a manager's point of view, and enthusiastically carry out instruction. In this case, subordinates agree with a decision or request of a manager, and make effort to meet it. This is possible because, subordinates are fully committed, as they have internalised the source of power that leads to their commitment.

11.3 The Entrepreneurial Leader

There are numerous definitions of what makes an entrepreneurial leader.

Hit et al (2000), has suggested that entrepreneurial leadership can be defined as "the ability to anticipate, envision, maintain flexibility, think strategically and work with others to initiate changes that will create a valuable future for the entrepreneurial venture". While there is much in such definition that is good, it lacks something of the emotional nature of entrepreneurial leadership.

As Tichy and Cohen (1998) have suggested, "entrepreneurial leadership is more about thinking, judging, acting and motivating, than about strategies, methodologies and tools.

Good entrepreneurial leaders care about their organisations and their people. They do not impose solutions on their teams, or exclude or suppress potential. Rather, they encourage their staff to be creative and to find their own solutions to problems.

The authority of entrepreneurial leaders comes from their expertise and values rather than from their position, and they lead by example, empowering their teams and nurturing leaders at all levels. By so doing ensure that the venture is successful even when they are not around. They do this by the following means:

- ✓ Having a vision.
- ✓ Setting the tone.
- ✓ Developing others.
- ✓ Exhibiting and creating positive energy.
- ✓ Facing up to reality and making tough decisions.

In relation to these entrepreneurial leaders may be regarded as patient leaders, capable of instilling visions and managing for the long haul. They are identified at once a learner and a teacher, doer and visionary. If there is no immediate problem, entrepreneurial leaders will often stir things up by breaking down established bureaucratic procedures or setting new, stretching, targets and goals.

According to McGrath and McMillan (2000), the entrepreneurial leader will know he/she has succeeded when everyone in the organisation:

- ✓ Takes it for granted that business success is about a continual search for new opportunities and a continual letting go of less productive activities.
- ✓ Feels that he or she has not only the right but the obligation to seek out new opportunities and make them happen.
- ✓ Comes to work excited and is proud to be associated with it.
- ✓ When the value created with the organisation translates into stakeholders' wealth.

They suggest that, to facilitate this, the entrepreneur needs to set the work climate, orchestrate the process of seeking and realising opportunities, and become actively involved in identifying and developing new ventures.

Setting the climate involves creating a pervasive sense of urgency to be working on the next new initiative. To achieve this, the entrepreneur has to model the sort of behaviour he/she requires consistently, predictably, relentlessly, and to dedicate a disproportionate share of he/her time, attention and discretionary resources to creating new business opportunities.

Orchestrating involves defining the entrepreneurial directions that can be taken, minimising investment and launch costs until the return have been fully demonstrated, and implanting a discovery – driven philosophy into the organisation by which it is not a crime to fail, only to fail expensively and without learning.

Getting involved in identifying and developing new ventures requires that the entrepreneur is not just involved in identifying entrepreneurial insight and converting them into business propositions, but he/she:

- ✓ Builds resolve (i.e. get people to commit to the launching of the new venture initiative).
- ✓ Practices leadership by setting realistic but challenging targets, absorbing uncertainty, defining what must and cannot be accepted, clearing away any obstacles that may arise and by underwriting the proposition.
- ✓ Keeps a finger on the pulse to monitor progress.
- ✓ Constantly checks for market acceptance.
- ✓ Secures deals with key stakeholders.

- ✓ Pushes the team to initiate revenue flows ahead of costs floss, be realistic in identifying skill deficiencies.
- ✓ Orchestrates market entry.
- ✓ Keeps focus on learning.
- ✓ Makes sure all initiatives will succeed and the entrepreneurial leader's role is as critical in failure as it is to success.

Entrepreneurial leaders do not have all the answers and they are not dictators. Rather, being a successful entrepreneurial leader is about:

- ✓ Developing one's own power by making the people around you more powerful.
- ✓ Being truthful and sincere, thereby building trust and respect.
- ✓ Providing direction, not the precise route.
- ✓ Recognising that colleagues may have some of the best ideas, especially if they are doing the job every day.
- ✓ Being supportive in times of failures, and celebrating achievement in times of success.
- ✓ Learning from failures.
- ✓ Facilitating change but protecting fundamental values
- ✓ Harnessing ideas that come from unlikely encounters.
- ✓ Building relationships.
- ✓ Exposing colleagues to reality, but protecting them from danger.
- ✓ Leading by example.
- ✓ Creating more leaders.

Entrepreneurial managers are skilful at clarifying confusion, ambiguity and uncertainty. They do so in a way that builds motivation and commitment, not just too parochial interest but to cross departmental and corporate goals . . . In the process they demonstrate a willingness to relinquish their personal priorities and power in the interest of an overall goal.

They also possess an ability to ensure that the appropriate people are included in setting cross- functional or departmental goals, and in decision – making. For some more traditional managers, used to dealing with subordinates, collaborating with peers and superiors might be an uncomfortable, disturbing or confusing experience . . .

When things do not go smoothly, the most effective entrepreneurial managers work them through agreement.

Any entrepreneur that can put all these qualities described above into practices is likely to be an effective and successful entrepreneurial leader in any entrepreneurial new venture.

11.4 Theories of Leadership

A number of theories have been put forward and developed by many writers, in the area of leadership in organisation.

They are likely to be useful to the entrepreneur, for adaptation and successful application in the entrepreneurial new venture operations and management.

These theories could be categorised into:

- Traits theories.
- Style or behavioural theories.
- Contingency theories.

11.4.1 Trait Theories (Classical theories)

Trait theories include the early leadership theories that tried to identify traits that known leaders have possessed, on the assumption that some people had traits which made it more likely that they would be effective leaders. These traits as suggested could be used to select effective future leaders.

Traits are usually associated with a variety of individual attributes, including aspects of personality, temperaments, needs, motives, values, intelligence, energy, resourcefulness, appearance etc, relating to personal qualities. The foundation of thoughts in this area could be traced to the classical theorists, and the early practicing managers, like Taylor and Fayol, who were strong characters in their own rights. Part of the success of these early practicing managers is assumed to be their personal qualities. The earliest studies that were undertaken into leadership were influenced by these characters, and therefore, much attention on leadership was on them, to help determine individual qualities required for effective leadership in organisations. However, it was impossible to calculate the number of desirable traits for an effective leader which is rarely present in one person. It is also not that easy to identify the particular traits or characteristics that separate leaders from non-leaders, or to explain what particular trait contributes to effective leadership performance. These are limitation to trait theory. Nevertheless, the trait model may help to explain why some people get to position of great influence and others do not. In addition, employees of labour often include traits that are thought to be relevant to their originations in their recruitment and selection process and programmes.

11.4.2 Style or Behavioural Theories

Style or behavioural theories are essentially about a pattern of behaviour displayed by the leader or manager.

When we talk about leadership styles, we are looking at different ways that someone can lead or manage. When a particular manager is said to have a particular style, this is seen as his or her way of managing most of the time.

Style or behavioural theories described leadership as an aspect of behaviour at work, rather than traits or personal characteristics. The interest in the human factors at work which was stimulated by the researchers of human relations and taken up by social psychologists who follow them, led logically to an interest in leadership as an aspect of behaviour at work rather than of traits or personal characteristics. Many behavioural theories have been put forward. These tended to be discussed under the following:

- **Authoritarian –Democratic theory**

Main advocate of the authoritarian - Democratic theory is McGregor who developed Theory X, Theory Y.

Theory X, projects the principles of an authoritarian manager- who is autocratic i.e. tough, applying tight control with the use of punishment and reward system. Under autocratic management, the manager alone makes decisions, and employees or subordinates are told the outcome of decisions and are expected to carry out tasks accordingly. The effectiveness of autocratic leadership depends on ability of the managers as a leader, to maintain control of the subordinates, best practiced under a stable operational environment. This style of leadership is based on classical trait theory that lays emphasises on the individual- the manager. Theory Y on the other hand, projects the principles of the democratic manager, who is benevolent, participative, and believes in self control. Under democratic management, the manager as a leader consults subordinates before a decision is made. The type of leadership demonstrated is persuasive and consultative. There is also the use of delegations of authorities. This style of leadership is based on human relation's behavioural theory which emphasises relationship between individuals within an organisation as well as group relationship, and the need for communication.

- **Tannenbaum and Schmidt – The Continuum of Leadership Styles**

The continuum of leadership style ranges from the use of authoritarian behaviour at one end, to democratic behaviour at the other. In other words, managers have basic choice between been either autocratic or democratic. The leadership style emphasised that managers as leaders in organisations worked in different ways, which they presented as a continuum of styles, ranging from autocratic to democratic. The use of authoritarian or democratic style progresses with time, and under various conditions. The choice of leadership style a manager uses should reflect three forces:

1. Forces from the manager: – for examples; personality, values, preferences, beliefs about participation and confidence in subordinates.
2. Forces from subordinates: - for examples; needs for independence, tolerance of antiquity, knowledge of the problems, expectations of involvement.
3. Forces from situations: - for examples; organisation norms, size and location of work groups, effectiveness of team working, nature of the problems etc.

These forces presented above provide circumstances in which any style of leadership (autocratic or democratic styles) can be more effective than the other. The main weakness of these approaches to leadership is that it places too many emphases on the leader's behaviour to the exclusion of other elements or variables of leadership.

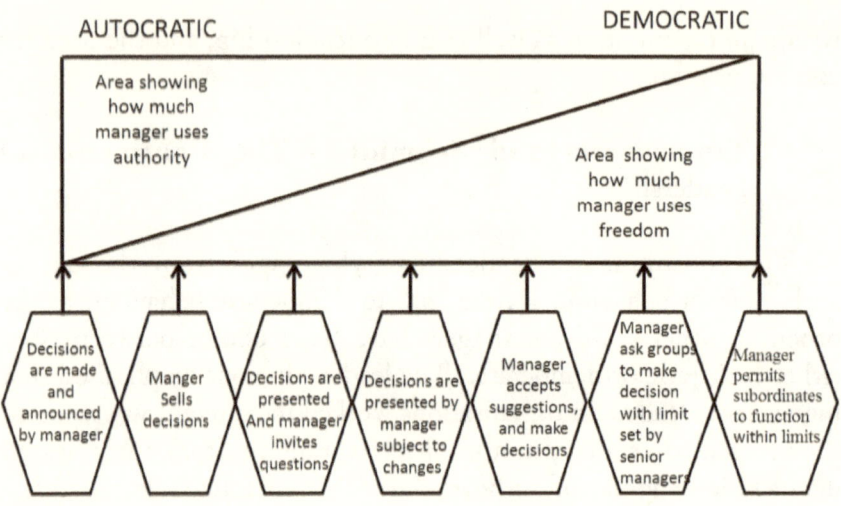

Figure 11.1 *A Continuum of Leadership Styles*

Sauce: Adapted from Tannenbaum and Schmidt, Harvard Business Review 1957

- **People - Task Orientation**

Background to this type of style or behavioural leadership could be traced to the following:

1. **The Michigan Studies**

Researchers at the University of Michigan (Liker 1967) conducted studies on manager -leadership behaviours, utilising two of the leadership variables- tasks and people. They identified some types of behaviours that distinguished effective managers from ineffective ones, which they categorised under:

> Job centered behaviours (task centered).
> Employee centered behaviours (people centered).

Job centered managers are task oriented, concentrating especially on planning and coordination of tasks and results. Employee centered managers are people oriented, with human values and are seen to be considerate, helpful, and friendly to subordinates and engaged in broad supervision rather than detailed observation of tasks that is associated with task cantered managers.

Studies carried out by the Michigan studies were centered on work activity and productivity performance. The objective was to see if any significant differences could be identified between job centered and employee centered managers that provide some clues to differences in leadership performances. The studies concluded that employee centered managers came out with the best records of performance because, they focused their primary attention on the human aspects of their subordinates' problems - paying more attention to relationship at work, building effective work groups with, less direct supervision, and encouraging employee participation in decision making. All these provided the necessary conditions for employee performance.

2. **The Ohio Studies**

Researchers at Ohio State University (Fleishman 1973) developed questionnaires that subordinates used to describe the behaviour of their supervisors or managers. When the responses to this questionnaire were analysed, two distinct groups of behaviour emerged:

1. Initiating structure.
2. Consideration.

Initiating structure refers to the degree to which managers define and organise their role and the role of followers, - that is, oriented towards goal attainment and establishment of well defined patterns and channels of communication. Managers using this approach focused on getting the work done, ensuring that everything was properly planned and worked out. As such, subordinates are asked to follow the procedures and managers made sure that they were working to full capacity. Typical manager's behaviour in this case includes:

✓ Allocating subordinates to specific tasks.
✓ Establishing standards of the requirements of the job.

- ✓ Scheduling work to be done by subordinates.
- ✓ Encouraging the use of uniform procedures.

Consideration on the other hand, refers to the degree to which a manager shows concern and respect for followers or subordinate-looking for their welfare, expressing appreciation and support. In this case, managers assume that subordinates want to work well and try to make it easier for them to do so, by placing little reliance on their formal position and power. Here, manager's behaviour may include:

- ✓ Expressing appreciation for job well done.
- ✓ Not expecting more from subordinates than they can reasonably do.
- ✓ Helping subordinates with personal problems.
- ✓ Being approachable and available for help.
- ✓ Rewarding high performance.

The result of research into the effect of leadership styles to performance showed that consideration leadership style was more effective - enabled subordinates' satisfaction and organisational performance.

3. Managerial Grid Model

Blake and Mouton (1979) developed the managerial grid model as an extension of the Ohio State research. They identified areas of manager's behaviour in organisation which they analysed in two dimensions and scales:

1. Concern for production (initiating structure).
2. Concern for people (consideration).

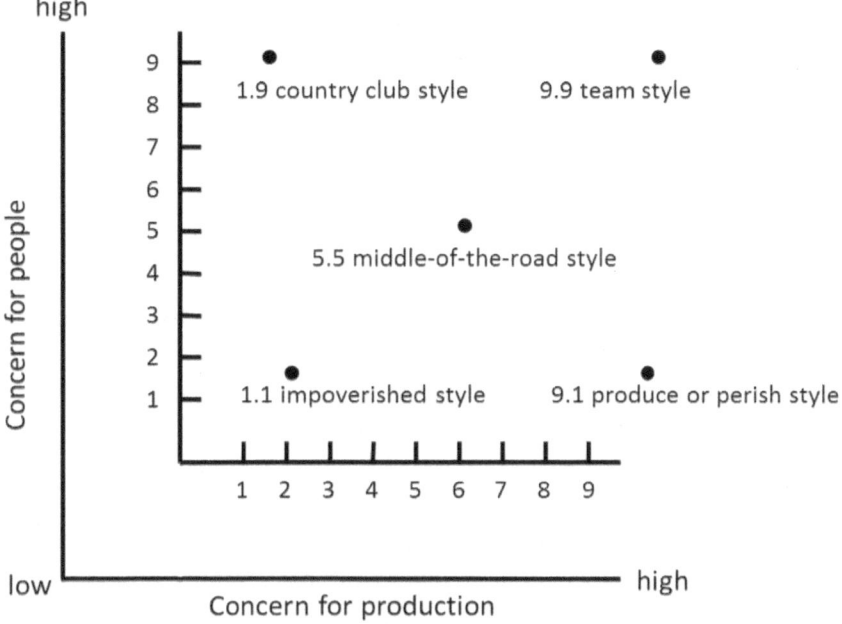

Figure 11.2 *Managerial Grid Model*

The horizontal scale in the chart above, relates to concern for production which ranges from 1(low) concern to 9 (high concern). The vertical scale relates to concern for people also ranging from 1 (low concern) to 9 (high concern).

At the lower left hand corner (1.1) is the **impoverished style** i.e. low concern for both production and people. Here, the manager uses this approach to stay out of trouble. The manager tries to avoid blames to keep his or her job, by following established system rules and procedures, and passing instruction to subordinates, so that if anything goes wrong, he or she will not be blamed.

At the upper left hand corner, (1.9) is the **country club style** i.e. high concern for people but low concern for productivity. Here, the manager assumes that subordinates will respond productively, by creating a secure and comfortable family atmosphere. The manager therefore, pays attention to the need for satisfying relationship with subordinates that should lead to a friendly atmosphere and work tempo.

High concern for production and low concern for people is found in the lower right hand corner (9.1). This is the **produce or perish style.** Here, the manager only believes in achieving objectives, using the formal authority to pressure subordinates into meeting productive quotas. Employees' personal needs are not considered as efficiency is the main focus, and employees merely have to follow instructions.

In the centre (5.5) is the **middle of the road style.** Here, the manager tries to balance the need to get work done with reasonable attention to the interests of the employees to obtain adequate performance.

In the upper right hand corner (9.9) is the **team style.** Here, the manager fosters performance through building a relationship of trust and respect. This makes it the most effective approach as the manager aims for both high performance and high job satisfaction. However, many managers have questioned whether a high level of concern for both production and people is always the best in all circumstances. For example, sudden crises that requires swift action where situation or contingency model may offer a possible answer.

4. **The Harvard Studies**

As a result of studying small group behaviour, Harvard researchers identified two distinct groups of leaders:

1. Task leaders.
2. Socio- emotional leaders.

These two types of leaders corresponded closely to those identified by the Ohio studies - Initiating structure and Consideration. However, unlike Ohio studies, the Harvard results found the two dimensions mutually exclusive. In other words, both styles of leadership are mutually exclusive – a manager could not be task leader and socio-emotional leader as well. The task leader showed concern for the structuring of activities, whereas the socio-emotional leader showed concern for supportive relationships.

11.4.3 Contingency/Situation Theories of Leadership

These are theories of leadership that describes the relationship between leadership styles and specific organisation situation. They include:

- **Fiedler's Contingency Theory**

The first theorist to use the label "contingency" explicitly was F. E. Fiedler (1967). Fielder named his leadership theory "the leadership contingency theory". In his view, group leadership performance is contingent upon the leader adopting an appropriate style, in an appropriate situation. The basic idea behind his theory is simply, to match the leader's style with the situation most favourable for success. This could be done by diagnosing and matching:

➢ Leadership style.
➢ Organisation situation.

Here, the leadership style is viewed in two dimensions:

1. Task oriented.
2. Relationship oriented.

Organisation situation is measured in three main areas:

1. Leader - Members relation- this pertains to the atmosphere that exists in a group in relation to the leader or manager- in terms of group members' attitude towards and acceptance of the leader or manager. The situation is considered favourable, when the group has trust, respect and confidence in the leader or manager.
2. Task structure- this pertains to extent to which tasks are structured i.e. defined - in terms of specific procedures, clear explicit goal. When tasks are highly structured, the situation is considered favourable.
3. Position power- this pertains to extent to which the leader or manager has formal authority on subordinates. The situation is considered favourable when the leader or manager has the

power to plan and direct the work of subordinates, evaluate it, reward or punish them.

As explained earlier, this theory suggests leadership style should be match with the situation favourable for success. Feldler suggested that relationship oriented leaders or managers are more effective situations of moderate favourability - where leader- member relationship is moderate and not very favourable. In this situation the leader may be moderately well liked, have some power, and supervise jobs that contain some ambiguity. The relationship oriented leader or manger with good interpersonal skill can create a positive group atmosphere that will improve relationship, clarify tasks structure, and establish position power.

Feldler is also of the opinion that task oriented leaders or managers are more effective when situations are either highly favourable or highly unfavourable -the task is clear, everyone is getting along well, and the leader has power. Here, all that is needed is for the task oriented leader or manager to take charge and provide direction. Also in a highly unfavourable situation a great deal of structure and task direction will be needed, and the task oriented leader or manager is needed to define task structure and establish authority over subordinates to get things done.

- **Path – Goal Theory**

Path- Goal theory is another contingency approach to leadership that describes the relationship between leadership styles, and specific organisational situation. House and Mitchell, (1974). The model is called contingency because it contains some contingencies in terms of:

➢ Leader behaviour or style.
➢ Organisation situation.

In terms of leader behaviour or style, the theory suggests some classification of behaviours or styles leaders can adopt such as:

✓ Directive leadership style – letting subordinates know what the leader expects; giving specific guidelines; asking subordinates

to fallow rules and procedures; scheduling and coordinating their work.
- ✓ Supportive leadership style– treating subordinates as equals; showing concern for their needs and welfare, creating a friendly climate.
- ✓ Achievement oriented leadership style- setting challenging goals and targets; seeking performance improvements; emphasising excellence in performance; showing confidence that subordinates will attain high standards.
- ✓ Participative leadership style – consulting subordinates; taking their opinions into account.

In terms of organisation situation, House suggested that the appropriate style would depend on the situation such as:

- ➢ Personal characteristics of group members - ability, skills, needs and motivation -which the leader has to consider and provide help.
- ➢ Work or task environment- which include the degree of task structure i.e. how tasks are defined, job description and procedures, the formal authority system, the amount of legitimate power used by the leader.
- ➢ Work group characteristics - in terms of the educational level of subordinates and the quality of relationship among them.
- ➢ Use of rewards- intrinsic or extrinsic.

The manager as a leader has the responsibility to increase subordinates motivation to attain personal and organisation goals. Subordinates motivation could be increased by:

- ✓ Clarifying the subordinates' path to reward that is available.
- ✓ By increasing the rewards that the subordinates value and desire.

Effective managers as leaders are those who clarify "path" to rewards available to subordinates, or ensure that rewards available have value to them. Path clarification means the manager as a leader, works with subordinates (using any appropriate leadership styles –supportive, directive, achievement oriented, participative styles) to help them identify and learn the behaviour that will lead to successful task accomplishment and organisation's reward. Increasing reward means that managers should talk with subordinate to learn which rewards are important to them i.e. whether they deserve intrinsic reward from the work itself or extrinsic reward such as praises or promotion. The leader's job is to make the path to payoff clear and easy to travel.

House suggested that appropriate leadership style would depend on the situation s such as the work environment and characteristics of the subordinates. A directive style will work best in a work environment where the task is ambiguous and subordinates lack flexibility – the manager as a leader absorbs uncertainty for the group and shows them how to achieve this task. A supportive style will work well in a work environment with highly repetitive tasks or those that are frustrating or physically unpleasant – subordinates respect the leader who joins in an unpleasant or difficult task. An achievement oriented style works well in a work environment when a group faces non repetitive ambiguous tasks, which will challenge their ability- so they need encouragements to use their abilities to the full, and encourages them by showing confidence in those abilities. Imitative approach is likely to work best when the task is non repetitive and the subordinates are confident that they can do the work. Leadership style should also consider subordinates situations. For example, if an employee has little confidence or lack of skill, then the supportive oriented style should be appropriate, and need to be adopted by the manager, such as providing coaching, training and other support. If the subordinate is one who lacks clear direction then directive oriented style should be appropriate. On the other hand, a highly skilled subordinate will be influenced more, if the manager as a leader uses a participative or achievement oriented style.

11.4.4 Helping, Coaching and Resolving Conflicts

The most effective entrepreneurial managers are creative and skilled in handling conflicts, generating consensus decision and sharing their power and information. They:

- ✓ Are able to get people to open up and share their view.
- ✓ Get problems aired and identified.
- ✓ Acknowledge without being defensive, the view of others
- ✓ Are aware that high quality decisions require information flowing in all directions.
- ✓ Are comfortable with knowledge, competence, logic and evidence prevailing over official status or formal rank.
- ✓ Are able to get potential adversaries to be creative and to collaborate by reconciling viewpoints.
- ✓ Are constantly blending views, often risking their own vulnerability in the process by giving up their own power and resources?

In the short form, the benefits of such an approach are often difficult to identify and it appears a painful way to manage. Longer term, however, the gains from the motivation, commitments and teamwork can be considerable, especially when grounded in consensus.

As mentioned earlier, the entrepreneurial leader gets a task completed by developing relationship with his/her colleagues and harnessing their combined resources. According to Appell (1984) it is the leaders task to arounse and unit followers to a common goal. A true leader fulfils this function by being aware of the changing group needs, by arousing these needs so that they become transformed into demands and by organising the group so that these demands can be met through group action.

He/she arouses and unites his/her colleagues/employees by:

- ✓ Listening to them and gaining their respect and trust.
- ✓ Being friendly and approachable but remaining sufficiently distant to exert authority.
- ✓ Treating them as equals without losing the capacity to exert authority.

- ✓ Paying attention to their individual as well as their collective needs.
- ✓ Involving them in agreeing objectives, reviewing results, solving problems, etc.
- ✓ Representing their interests.

These resources are harnessed by ensuring colleagues/ employees:

- ✓ Fully understand their goals and objectives and, as far as possible, are involved in determining them.
- ✓ Know how they are going to achieve their objectives, and are party to deciding and agreeing the course of action to be taken.
- ✓ Are empowered to make decisions.
- ✓ Know and agree the control to be exercised over them.
- ✓ Are aware of the rewards and penalties of not achieving their objectives.
- ✓ Trust and respect the leader's judgement.

11.4.5 Leadership Development

As with entrepreneurship, there is considerable debate over whether leaders are born or made.

While it is generally accepted that the natural, truly inspirational leaders are probably born, there is a growing acceptance that leadership capability, as in other areas, can be developed and /or enhanced. Handy (2000) suggests that leaders are grown not made.

Clearly, leaders need followers. In any organisation aspiring leaders can secure the hearts and minds of their employees quite easily using a series of recognised currencies:

- ✓ Economic currencies – rewarding loyal colleagues fiscally with promotion and /or with peaks.
- ✓ Political currencies – rewarding loyal colleagues through protection or patronage.
- ✓ Psychological currencies – using anger and threats to create climate of fear that encourages loyalty.
- ✓ Empowerment currencies – rewarding desired behaviour with increased authority and power.

11.5 Group and Team Building

As already indicated in chapter 9, growth is an important area in entrepreneurial development since this is one essential factor that differentiates the entrepreneurial new venture from a small business.

As the venture grows, the need for involving, as well as efficient organisation of more individuals in the venture operations becomes paramount.

It is therefore imperative that entrepreneurs should understand the process of group and team building in their ventures and how this could be managed effectively.

11.5.1 Groups in Organisation

A group could be described as a collection of individuals contributing to some common aim, under the direction of a leader, sharing a sense of common identity. This description identifies a group as more than an aimless crowd of people, but one with a purpose, temporary or permanent, and a degree of self awareness as a group.

Organisations make use of groups to serve its purposes, as well as that of individuals in the organisation. Most tasks in organisations are usually undertaken by groups and teams rather than individuals. Groups are used for creating new ideas, solving problems, making decisions, as well as coordinating tasks to fulfil organisational goals. In addition, individuals themselves need groups, as groups provide stimulus, protection, assistance and other social and psychological requirements. Groups can therefore work in the interest of organisation as well as that of individuals.

Organisations are also made up of formal and informal groups, a distinction arising from Hawthorn experiment (explained earlier in chapter 2). Formal groups are those set up by management to undertake duties in the pursuit of organisations goal. They are sometimes described as official groups, to avoid the confusion that will arise when describing operations in an informally structured organisation, which may be informal in the sense they have few rules, enjoy participative leadership and have flexible roles, nevertheless they are completely official. Unofficial groups on the other hand, are those which the employees themselves have developed in accordance with their own needs.

Working as group may bring benefits:

- ✓ Increase efforts and motivation - as working in a group help increase level of effort and motivation among group members as well as their performance in terms of social facilitation.
- ✓ Individual satisfaction – as working in group help satisfy individual needs of members - need for belongingness and affiliation. Creating an atmosphere that encourages group identity, group belonging and affiliation.
- ✓ Diversity of resources - as working as a group help tap the advantages of diversity of resources in the group such as

knowledge, ability, skills brought in by several or diverse members, offering alternatives points of view for discussions, decisions and feedbacks.

However, working as a group may create limitations:

- ✓ Free riding or social loafing – this refers to limitations by some group members who benefit from group membership, but do not do a proportionate share of the work -members do not exert equal effort as some people are likely to work less.
- ✓ Coordination costs – group coordination usually require much effort in time and energy, to achieve task performance. Groups must spend time getting ready to do work and may lose productive time in deciding who is to do what and when.
- ✓ Individual dominant – a group may be dominated by individuals. This may be the leader of the group in a hierarchical organisation, where people do not challenge those in a position of authority. It may be a technical expert who takes over, when others hesitate and show their lack of knowledge. This can lead to unproductive experience.
- ✓ Diffusion of responsibility – because each person may be expected to do a part of the task, no one is to blame if the group fails and no one gets the credit if it succeeds.
- ✓ Succumb to groupthink – individuals succumb to group think, when they are so keen to be seen as team players and as such, refuse to say things that might end their membership of the group. Janis (1972) research analysis on social psychology traced back bad decisions among groups to groupthink- why able and intelligent people in a group could make bad decisions. He observed the inability of the group to consider a range of alternatives rationally, or to see the likely consequences of the choice made as a phenomenon of "succumb to groupthink".

11.5.2 Group Development

- **B. Tuchman's View**

A useful way of looking at group development was devised by B. Tuckman (1965), who saw group development as moving through key stages:

1, Forming

This is the earliest stage in group development. The group is forming by going through the process of knowing new group members, finding out about the task, rules and methods, acquiring information and resources, testing one another for friendship possibilities, and task orientation. The process allows group members to find out behaviours that are acceptable with members. Uncertainty is high during this stage of group formation, and members usually accept whatever power or authority is offered by either formal or informal leaders. Members are dependent on the group until they find out what the ground rules are, and what is expected of them. It is important at this stage that the manager or group leader, provides time for members to get acquainted with one another, and encourage them to engage in informal social discussions.

2, Storming

The group is trying to settle at this stage. Storming is likely evident, as the group goes through a storming period of development. The personalities of individual group members do emerge, as individuals within the group now become more assertive, in clarifying their roles. The tendency for disagreement among group members becomes high, and members try to position themselves within the group with the formation of coalitions or subgroups. The group is not yet a cohesive team and may be characterised by a general lack of unity. Unless a group can successfully move beyond this stage, it may get dismantle or never progress further. It is important that the manager or group leader encourage group member participation at this stage that allows members propose ideas to help the group work through the storming period.

3, Norming

This is the stage in group development when conflict is settled, cooperation develops, views are exchanged, and new standards (norms) are developed. A group norm is usually a standard conduct that is shared among group members that guides their behaviour. Norms begin to develop in the first interaction among members of a new group. In most cases, they are informal and are not written down as rules and procedures. However, they are valuable because they define boundaries of acceptable behaviour. They make life easier for group members by providing a framework of reference for what is right or wrong. Identify key group values, clarify role expectations, and facilitate group survival.

Group norms could develop out of:

- ✓ Critical events – critical events in group history that establish an important precedent leading to the creation of a norm.
- ✓ Primacy - primacy means that the first behaviours that occur in a group often set a precedent for later group expectations.
- ✓ Carryover behaviours – carryover brings norms or learned behaviour into the group from other groups.
- ✓ Implicit statements - with explicit statements, leaders or group members can initiate norms by articulating them to the group.

Norms are influenced by organisational factors such as policies, management style, rules and procedures. They are also influenced by unofficial norm of individual employees whose standard may or not be in line with those of the official norms of the organisation that may require harmonisation by the manager or leader of the group.

4, Performing

This is the stage when the group is fully settled and developed. Members now know each other enough to be aware of individual characters of group members and their positions in the group.

Interaction between group members is now frequent through direct discussions. Members are now committed to group mission and goal after going through the storming period successfully. The group starts performing as expected because, group task is now clearly defined and well coordinated, and the group is well focused to achieve group desired goal. Any distracting group problem can be confronted and resolved in the interest of task accomplishment. The perfuming stage is also associated with a mature, well managed team character. The major emphasis during this stage is on problem solving and accomplishing the assigned task. However, a group may move to the performing stage only to revert to the storming stage when it is infused with new members. It is important that the manager or leader of the group concentrate on managing socio-emotional conditions in the group to develop high task performance.

5, Adjourning

This is the stage when groups disperse on completion of tasks. The adjourning stage may occur through the use committees, task forces and teams that help to smoothen the adjournment process. This stage may also see some low feeling, depression or even a sense of regret generating among group members due to emotion of departure. At the same time, individual group members may feel happy about mission accomplishment, or sad about loss of friendship and associations. It is important that the manager or leader of the group at this stage signify group ending with a ritual or ceremony, or giving out awards for competences or achievements to signify closure for group members.

- **Teams**

A team according to Adair (1986), is more than just a group with a common aim. It is a group in which contribution of individuals are seen as complementary. The key to team activity is collaboration, working together. Adair suggested that the test of a good team i.e. effective team is whether its members can work as a team while they are apart- contributing to a sequence of activities, rather than to common task which requires their presence in one place at one time. Basic features of effective teams include:

➢ Small number - most effective teams have between two and ten people- with between four and eight probably being most common range.
➢ Common purpose - they need to express it in clear performance goals.
➢ Common approach - this includes deciding who does which jobs, what skills members need to develop, and how the group should make and modify decisions.
➢ Mutual accountability - a team cannot work as one until its members willingly hold themselves to be collectively and mutually accountable for the result of the work.

A team can also be effective when:

✓ Objectives are clear and goals are agreed.
✓ Openness and confrontationist observed within the team.
✓ There are team support and trust.
✓ Cooperation and conflicts are reasonably accommodated.
✓ Sound procedures are in operation.
✓ Appropriate leadership is in force.
✓ Regular review is practised.
✓ Individual development is the key.
✓ Sound intergroup relations is accepted and practised.

- **Woodcock's View- Team development**

Tuchman's analysis of group development can be compared with that of Woodwork (1979) who had made a particular study of teams and their development. Like Tuchman, Woodcock produced similar stages with group development, but with different underpinning themes, descriptions, and interpretation in stages of development.

1. The underdeveloped team

Woodwork described the earliest stage in team development as undeveloped. During this stage, the team could be described as underdeveloped, as feelings are unclear, objectives uncertain, the leader takes most of the decision.

2. The experimenting team

The second stage sees the team progress in development as experimental. Here team issues are faced more openly, listening takes place; the group may become temporally introspective.

3. The consolidating team

At this stage the team starts consolidating as a team, as personal interaction is established on a cooperative basis, the task is clarified, objectives agreed, and tentative procedures implemented.

4. The matured team

The team grows to maturity at this stage, as feelings are open, a wide range of options considered, working methods are methodical, leadership style is contributory, individuals are flexible and the group recognises its responsibility to the rest of the organisation.

11.5.3 Entrepreneurial Team Working

As already explained, successful entrepreneurs are not those who display autocratic leadership, but can work with and through others, to achieve goals/objectives of the venture.

According to Belbin (1981) effective team working requires that the team members fulfil various roles. These, he suggested are as follows:

- Chairperson.
- Plant.
- Shaper.
- Monitor-evaluator.
- Resource investigator.
- Team workers.
- Company worker.
- Completer-finisher.
- Specialist.

Clearly, for task to be progressed, all of these roles are needed. Hence, the successful entrepreneur, while frequently possessing many of the qualities him/herself, frequently joins in partnership with others to ensure that the idea/concept or the venture for change is brought to fruition.

Timmons (1999) has suggested that, the capacity of the entrepreneur to craft a vision, and then to lead, inspire, persuade and cajole key people to sign up for and deliver the dream, makes an enormous difference between success and failure. It is the role of the entrepreneur to bring this about. To do this, Peters (1982), suggested the entrepreneur need to:

- ✓ Involve all personnel at all levels in all functions.
- ✓ Ensure there are no limits on their ability to contribute.
- ✓ Engage staff who are committed, properly selected and well trained, appropriately supported, organised into self managed teams.

Also, the capacity to be very effective in this endeavour will depends on how much he/she is able to:

- ✓ Recognise and cope with innovation.
- ✓ Take risks.
- ✓ Respond quickly.
- ✓ Cope with failure (absorb setbacks).
- ✓ Find chaos and uncertainty challenging and stimulating.

To achieve this, the entrepreneur needs interpersonal/team working skills that involves the ability to:

- ✓ Create a climate and spirit conducive to high performance, including rewarding work well done and encouraging creativity, innovation, initiative and calculated risk taking.
- ✓ Understand the relationships present among tasks, and between the leader and followers.
- ✓ Lead in those situations where it is appropriate, including a willingness to manage actively, to supervise and to control the actions of others.

These interpersonal skills are normally termed "entrepreneurial influencing skills" since they have to do with the way the entrepreneur exerts influence over others through leadership/ vision/ influence; helping, coaching and resolving conflict; team work and people management.

Entrepreneurs build confidence by encouraging creativity, innovation and calculated risk-taking, rather than by criticising and punishing. They encourage independent thinking by expecting and encouraging others to find and correct their own errors and to solve their own problems. This does not mean they are abandoning their colleagues to their own, rather they are perceived by others as:

- ✓ Accessible and willing to help when needed.
- ✓ Facilitators, providing the resources that enable others to do their job more effectively.
- ✓ Champions who defend their peers and subordinates even when they know they cannot always win.
- ✓ Hero-makers, who ensure that others receive the credit for their efforts rather than accepting the credits themselves.

Through such actions, they have the capacity to generate trust. They reinforce this by being:

- ✓ Straight forward – doing what they say they are going to do.
- ✓ Open and spontaneous.
- ✓ Honest and direct.
- ✓ Creative problem solvers.
- ✓ People developers.

The most effective entrepreneurial managers are creative and skilful in handling conflicts, generating consensus decision, sharing power and information. They:

- ✓ Are able to get people to open up and share their view
- ✓ Get problems aired and identified.
- ✓ Acknowledge, without being defensive, the views of others.
- ✓ Are aware that high quality decisions require information flowing in all directions.
- ✓ Are comfortable with knowledge, competence, logic, and evidence prevailing over official status or formal rank.
- ✓ Are able to get potential adversaries to be creative and to collaborate by reconciling viewpoints.
- ✓ Are constantly blending views, often risking their own vulnerability to the process, by giving up their own power and resources.

11.6 Motivation

11.6.1 Introduction

Motivation could be described as the arousal, direction, and persistence of behaviour. According to Body (2008), "motivation refers to the forces within or beyond a person that arouse and sustain commitment to a course or action". It is a psychological process through which unsatisfied wants or needs lead to drives that are aimed at goals or incentives. The process of motivation could be clearly described by introducing the basic model of motivation.

Stimulus >	Response >	Outcome
Physical needs/drive Social needs/drive	Behaviour	Satisfaction/Frustration

Figure 11.3 Basic *Model of Motivation*

The model introduced above is the most useful way of explaining the meaning and process of motivation. It suggests that a stimulus (e.g. in the form of physical drive or some social needs), gives rise to a response (i.e. behaviour of some kind) which leads to outcome, that either satisfies or fails to satisfy the original situation and therefore, leads to satisfaction or frustration. This simple model has been very helpful for the theoretical understanding of motivation. In practice the process may be a complex matter. This is so because sometimes a person's motives may be clear to him, but not clear to others. Also, a person's motives especially, where stress is involved may be unclear him, and the individual concerned may be totally unaware of his or her motives, while others may see them quite clearly. This explains the complexity of motivation. Managers should be aware of this complexity in their efforts to motivate their subordinates.

11.6.2 The Entrepreneur Motivation Challenges

Self motivation

Understanding the entrepreneur and motivation process in the entrepreneurial new venture does require, depth knowledge of what motivates the entrepreneurs as an individual, and his/her ability to motivate others involved in the entrepreneurial new venture.

As has been discovered in chapter 1, the entrepreneur is not just a creative or innovative individual, but someone who can make things happen. The entrepreneur is a doer - motivated by many factors.

A number of factors described as pull and push forces have been identified as some of the self motivating factors for entrepreneurial option. Pull forces encourage individuals to become entrepreneurs by attractiveness of the option, and they include:

- ✓ The freedom to pursue a personal innovation.
- ✓ The freedom of work for oneself.
- ✓ The potential to achieve personal goal
- ✓ The sense of achievement to be gained from running one's venture.
- ✓ The financial reward or entrepreneurship
- ✓ A desire to gain a social standing achieved by entrepreneurs.

Push forces on the other hand, force individual into entrepreneurial venture due to unacceptable circumstances and lack of alternative option, and they include:

- ✓ Limitations of financial rewards from conventional jobs.
- ✓ Being unemployed in the established economy.
- ✓ Ned for job security.
- ✓ Career limitations and setbacks in a conventional job.
- ✓ Being a "misfit" in an established organisation.
- ✓ The unfulfilled.
- ✓ The displaced persons.

Insight into how you can motivate yourself and achieve high level of personal productivity can be obtained from the study of what is termed "Personal peak performance."

According to Garfield (1986) personal peak performance does not result from specific personal talent or trait, nor from a particular set of behaviour rather, does it appear to be a result of a combination of traits and attributes that include:

- ✓ A sense of personal mission (results orientation).
- ✓ The ability to work both independently and as part of a team
- ✓ A capacity for a self correction and change management.

Two outstanding conditions that stimulate personal peak performance according to the work of Adams (1984) include:

1. Commitment.
2. Challenge.

Commitment is important because:

- ✓ It shields people from workload stress.
- ✓ High level of performance requires a significant involvement of time and emotion.
- ✓ Perk performers are known to care about the tasks they perform.

It is this concept of commitment that is behind the concepts of ownership and empowerment. It is argued that if individuals believe they own an idea or are empowered to make decisions, they are more likely to be committed.

Challenge is important because perk performers need, or desire an appropriate challenge:

- ✓ Constantly search for new opportunities to "stretch" themselves.
- ✓ Set themselves targets or goals that are achievable but ambitious.
- ✓ Emphasise actions – outcomes, results, and solutions.

Another outstanding factor that stimulates self motivation has to do with the power of imagination.

Given that personal peak performance does not result from a personal talent or trait, it can be developed. Thus, the starting point for enhancing our personal performance and motivating ourselves to achieve more and better is our imagination.

As human, our lives are not so much determined by our environment or by physical limitations but by our imagination.

As humans, our lives are not much determined by our environment or by physical limitations but by our imagination – "we can because we think we can" to quote slogan from former president of America Obama – "Yes we can."

What we become and achieve is what we imagine ourselves becoming and achieving. Essentially our only limits are those we place upon ourselves.

According to Appell (1984), to increase our personal performance we need to engage our imagination by setting goals for ourselves. Once we have set our goals, we need to visualize them as already achieved. Visualisation does not relieve us of working to achieve our goal, it will guide us towards achieving them.

Motivating others

Once self motivation has been achieved, the entrepreneur is in a strong position to start motivating others.

Motivation is a behavioural phenomenon. Individuals are motivated by the way people act towards them. This behaviour is an integral part of leadership.

To motivate others effectively, the knowledge and understanding of popular theories of motivation will be very helpful to the entrepreneur.

Entrepreneurs can motivate others by adapting popular theories of motivation to suit venture situation to help them among others:

- ✓ Understanding needs that motivate people.
- ✓ Processes needed to achieve best motivation.
- ✓ Set goals that are realistic and achievable.

- ✓ Offer support to individuals to achieve their targets and goals.
- ✓ Using rewards to encourage performance.
- ✓ Monitor outcomes to ensure that individuals or groups are accountable for achieving their targets and goals.
- ✓ Ensure that the reward system is transparent- performance will be rewarded.
- ✓ Adopt positive approach to sanctioning – when people underperform, they should try to understand the cause or source, and provide adequate support for improvement.

11.6.3 Motivation Theories

Managers 'approaches to motivation in organisations could be based on motivation theories such as:

1. Content theory of motivation.
2. Process theory of motivation.

1. Content Theories of Motivation

The content theorists are usually described as the early motivation theorists. They provided a group of theories that emphasise the needs that motivate people i.e. needs that trigger behaviour, or motivation in terms of what arouses, energizes, or initiates employee behaviour in organisations. They argue that at any point, people have basic needs for example, - food, achievement, monetary; reward, etc.

These needs usually translate into desire that motivate behaviour.

Contributors to these theories include:- Schein, Maslow, Alderfer, McGregor, Herzberg, Likert, Argyris, and McClleland.

- **Schein**

Schien (1995) developed a classification of managers' views and assumptions of employees in organisations in relation to motivation.

The basis of his classification is human motives that are directed towards desired ends and how behaviour is selected consciously or sometimes unconsciously to satisfy these desired ends.

1. Rational Economic Man

The idea of a rational man is based on the assumption that a human being usually behaves in a rational economic manner and therefore, is a rational man. This view of human motivation could be traced to the economic theory of Adam Smith. It suggests that the pursuit of self interest and maximisation of gain is the prime motivator of individuals as a rational man.

2. Social Man

This view of social aspect of human behaviour is based on conclusion of human relation theory, from the Hawthorne experiment. It suggests people are motivated by social needs and need for personal relationship (human relations).

3. Self actualising Man

This view could be associated with Maslow's human needs, stressing the individual's needs for self fulfilment as prime motivator, and that people need challenging responsibility and autonomy in work to work effectively.

4. Complex Man

This view of complex man reflects the fact that understanding people's motivation is a complex thing that involves several interrelated factors at work, in terms of the organisation, employees, and their relationship. One particular aspect of the relationship between the individual and organisation is the concept of "psychological contract" - a form of contract between the organisation and its employees, based on their contributions to each other. It implies series of mutual expectation and satisfaction of needs from organisation to its employees and vice versa. It covers a range of expectation of rights and privileges, duties and obligation which do not form part of formal agreement, but still has important influences on organisational behaviour.

- **Maslow's Hierarchy of Needs**

Maslow hierarchy of needs is one of the early content theories of motivation the theory proposes that people are motivated by five categories of needs, that exists in a hierarchical order of ascendance, beginning with the most basic at the bottom of the hierarchy:

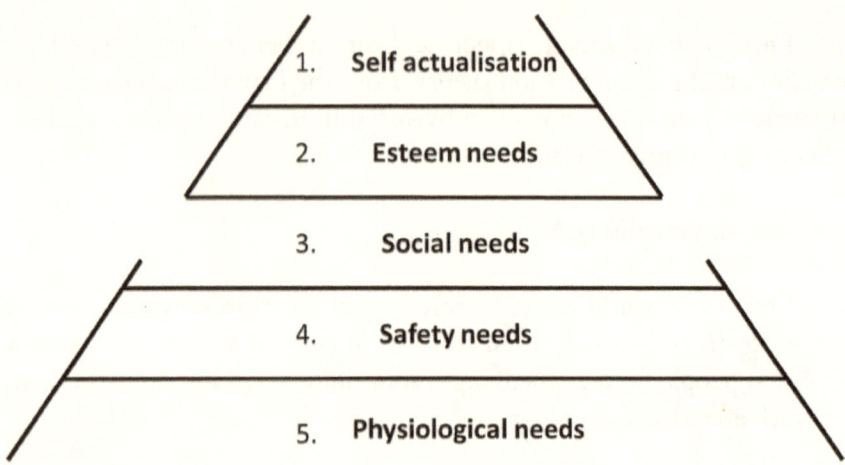

Figure 11.4 *Maslow's Hierarchy of Needs*

1. **Self actualisation needs** - the desire to reach one's full potential by becoming everything one is capable of becoming.
2. **Esteem needs** - the need for power and status.
3. **Belonging-/social-needs** - the need to interact and affiliate with others and to feel wanted by others.
4. **Safety needs** - the desire for security, stability and the absence of pain.
5. **Physiological needs** - food, clothing, shelter and other basic physical needs.

The starting point of Maslow's hierarchy theory is that people are motivated by a desire to satisfy a specific group of needs, and that people tend to satisfy their needs systematically, starting with the basic physiological needs, and then moving up the hierarchy. Until a particular group of needs is satisfied, a person's behaviour will be dominated by them, thus a hungry person is not going to be motivated by consideration of safety or affection, until after his or her hunger has been satisfied.

This assumption in Maslow's theory has not been without criticism. The most criticism is that systematic movement up the hierarchy does not seem to be consistent form of behaviour for many people. Alderfer (1972), argued that individual needs were better explained as being on a continuum, rather than in hierarchy and that people were likely to move up and down in continuum in satisfying needs at different levels. For example, in some developed and even developing countries, a consumer may go without food in order to buy a refrigerator and therefore, satisfy the dominant need of social status before physical satisfaction. A study identified that self-esteem needs were most important to Chinese consumers with the least important being physiological needs (Johnson 2002). Despite these criticisms, Maslow's hierarchy of needs has received a great deal of attention from management researchers, who have attempted to identify the value in understanding employee motivation. It has provided useful framework for the discussion of the variety of needs that people may experience at work and the way their motivation can be met by managers.

Many established firms like IBM, Tesco, and John Lewis, have all adopted Maslow's principles to motivate employees, by considering their needs according to management levels and departments - associating top management and middle management with social, self esteem and self actualisation needs, and lower management with physical and safety needs. The need hierarchy theory also explains why sales departments in these organisations and other sales oriented organisations have shifted from commissions to salaries for compensating sales people. Commission puts the emphasis on making money to meet safety and physiological needs, but expose sales people to high risk during period of economic or business downturn. Fixed salaries guarantee that basic needs will be met, thus freezing individual members of the sales force from worries of basic needs.

- **Alderfer -ERG –(Existence, Relation and Growth needs)**

Aldermen's ERG -needs is similar with Maslow's needs because both are in hierarchical form. However, Alderfer proposed a modification of Maslow's hierarchy of needs theory in an effort to simplify it and respond to criticism of the lack of empirical verification, by reducing the number into three categories:

1. Growth needs - the development of human potential and the desire of personal growth and increased competence.
2. Relation needs - the need for satisfactory relationship with others.

3. Existence needs - the needs for physical well being.

Alderfer proposed that the movement up the hierarchy of needs is more complex than assumed by Maslow. This complexity reflects a frustration- regression principle; - meaning that usually the failure of an individual to meet a higher need, may trigger a regression to an already fulfilled lower need. For example, a worker who cannot fulfil a need for personal growth or relationship may revert to lower order of need such as redirecting effort towards making enough money to exist, suggesting that individuals may move up and down the hierarchy of needs in continuum, depending on ability to satisfy needs.

- **McGregor Theory X and Theory Y**

These theories were based on a manager's assumption about people and management behaviour towards people. The theory assumes that there are two different set of assumption made by managers about people or subordinates, and placed these assumptions into two theories- theory X and theory Y.

Theory X
Theory X assumes that managers regard people or subordinates as being inherently lazy, avoiding responsibility, only seeking security and requiring coercion and control. This relates to the theory of scientific management with emphases on control and rewards. It also shares the idea of rational economic man.

Theory Y
Theory Y is based on the believe that managers see people or subordinates in more favourable light, as liking work- which is as natural as rest or play, needing no control or coercion and committed to organisation's goals/objectives. Managers believe that under proper condition, subordinates will accept and seek responsibility, are able to exercise imagination and ingenuity at work. This relates to Maslow's higher level of needs and Schein's concept of self actualisation.

- **Motivators/Hygiene Theory by Herzberg**

Motivators /Hygiene theory developed in 1959 by Herzberg, originated from his study on satisfaction at work by identifying factors affecting job attitudes. In his study, a number of 200 accountants and engineers were asked in an interview to recall when they had experienced satisfactory and unsatisfactory feelings about their work. The studies were later extended to various groups to include manual and clerical workers. The conclusion was that certain factors tend to lead to satisfaction and dissatisfaction at work which he grouped under:

- Motivators
- Hygiene factors

Motivators are factors that influence job satisfaction such as:

- Achievement.
- Recognition.
- Responsibility.
- Advancement or opportunity for growth.

These are related to content of work, with intrinsic challenges, interests, and individual responses generated by them. Attentions to motivators tend to improve work satisfaction and performance.

Hygiene factors are those that trigger the presence or absence of job dissatisfaction in organisations such as:

- Company policy and administration.
- Supervision.
- Salary.
- Interpersonal relationship.
- Working condition.

These hygiene factors are most related to context of work or work environment, and are usually associated with dissatisfaction at work. Dealing with hygiene factors will only remove dissatisfaction, but will not be a major employee motivator, as they serve to prevent dissatisfaction. For example, unsafe working conditions or a noisy work environment will cause people to be dissatisfied; their correction will not lead to a high level of motivation and satisfaction. Motivators need to be in place for employees to be highly motivated and excel at work.

- **Rensis Likert - Supportive Relations Theory**

Likert's theory combines structure and supportive relationship. It describes the importance of supportive relation that assumed management will achieve high performance when employees see their membership of work group to be supportive (i.e. experience of sense of personal worth and belonging).

The theory was developed at the time he was director of social research University of Michigan.

He suggested that managers who achieve high productivity, low cost, high employee motivation tend to build success on interlocking and tightly knit groups of employees, whose cooperation is achieved through motivating forces of economic and security, ego, creativity and self actualisation.

The idea of supportive relationship is built into Likert view of ideal organisation structure. He maintained that supportive relationship which leads to effective workgroups was a result of interacting with other groups in an overlapping form of organisation.

In this form of organisational structure, certain key roles perform a linking pin function. For example, the head of a section is a member not only of his own group but also of superior group, and his superior also a member of group higher. Such organisation structure has a basic shape of classical hierarchy or organisation pyramid, but operates in practice on basis of interlocking teams instead of separate specialisation.

For Likert, participative – group is the ideal system in relation to autocratic system.

Under participative system, the keynote is participation, leading to commitment to the organisation's goals in a fully cooperative way, as well as good communication upwards, downward and laterally. Motivation is obtained through participation. Productivity is excellent with less human resource turnover and absenteeism.

He distinguished between different styles of management- (exploitative -authoritative, benevolent -authoritative, consultative, and participative).

He identified participative style of management in group as ideal, leading to commitment to the organisation's goals in a fully cooperative way.

- **Chris Argyris – Maturity/Immaturity Theory**

Professor Argyris theory suggested reasons why much employee aparthy in organisations are not due to laziness, but because employees feel they are been treated like children.

This observation led to his developing what he called- "immaturity and maturity theory"- that suggest human personality develop from immaturity to maturity in continuum, within which a number of key changes takes place and influence their behaviour and motivation.

Immaturity > > > > Maturity	
Behave passively	Behave actively
Dependence behaviour	Relative independence behaviour
Behave in few ways	Behave in many ways
Display erratic, shallow interest's	Display deeper, clear interests
Have short term perspective	Have long time perspective
Accepts subordinate position	Demand equal or superior position
Lack self awareness	Have full self awareness

In his model of immaturity/maturity, Argyris set out features of the typical classical organisation: - task specialisation, chain of command, unity of direction and chain of control.

The underlying assumption surrounding this type of business environment is the expectation that employees will be passive, dependent and subordinate in their behaviour, i.e. employees are expected to behave immaturely.

For employees who are relatively mature, this environment is a major source of frustration at work. This frustration leads to employees seeking informal ways of minimising their difficulties, such as creating informal groups, which work against the formal hierarchy, or becoming lazy at work in protest.

Managers need to understand human needs and the importance of integrating the needs of employees with those of the organisation that will lead to cooperative behaviour of employees and improvement in work performance.

- **McClelland -Achievement Motivation Theory**

McClelland (1961) carried out a study on how people think and react in a wide range of situations in line with their needs.

The study led to three categories of human needs which individuals possess in different amounts.

1. Need for achievement.
2. Need for power.
3. Need for affiliation or belonging.

He isolated need for achievement as key human motive and argued that people with high need for achievement tend to have the following characteristics:

- ✓ Their need for achievement is consistent.
- ✓ They seek tasks in which they can exercise personal responsibility.
- ✓ They prefer tasks which provide a challenge without being too difficult and which they see as within their mastery.
- ✓ They are less concerned about their social affiliation needs.

McClelland theory of achievement is not based on common features like other theories, but on differences between individuals.

He observed that high need for achievement is not only influenced by personality, but also by environmental development - developed by childhood experiences and cultural settings. This implies that needs are influenced by environment and not purely by inherited factors, indicating the possibility of developing motivation training programmes in organisations.

The major disadvantage of persons with high achievement is that by definition, they are task-oriented and less concerned with relationships.

This characteristics are not always suitable for those whose responsibility is to get things done through people, i.e. managers and supervisors, but may not be a problem for entrepreneurs, as individual achievers.

2. **Process Theories of Motivation**

Process theories present another perspective of motivation that focus mainly on the process of motivation rather than the content. They describe those processes - both instinctive and rational, by which people seek to satisfy the basic drives, perceived needs and personal goals which trigger human behaviour, such as - how employee behaviour is initiated, redirected, and halted. They also try to explain how people in organisations select needs that trigger behaviours, and determine whether their choices were appropriate. This involves the process of judging the merit of needs. Notable theories in this area include: Equity theory, Goal theory, Attribution theory, Reinforcement theory, Expectancy theory.

- **Equity Theory**

Equity theory developed by Stacey Adams focused on peoples' perception of how fairly they are treated relative to others in a work context. The theory suggests that people make comparisons between themselves and others, in terms of what they invest or contribute in their work (inputs), and what compensation or outcome they receive from it (output). In other words, people value equity by a ratio of inputs and outputs or outcome. Inputs could include education, experience, effort, ability etc. Outputs could include pay, recognition, benefits, promotion etc. which make up needs.

If people perceive their compensations are equal to what others receive for similar contribution, they will believe their treatment is fair and equitable. Inequality occurs when input/outcome are conceived by an individual to be out of balance. Such individual may experience "equity tensions" that may lead to inappropriate behaviour.

Robbins (1993), in a review of research, suggests that when people in organisations perceive an inequitable situation for themselves, they can be predicted to make one of six choices:

1. Change their inputs (e.g. not exerting as much effort).
2. Change their outcome (e.g. individual paid on a piece rate basis increase their pay by producing a higher quantity of units even if of a lower quality).
3. Distort their perception of self (I used to think I work at a moderate pace but now I realise I work a lot harder than everyone else).
4. Distort perception of others (e.g." X's job in not as desirable as I first thought").
5. Choose a different reference point (e.g. "I may not be doing as well as my brother, but I am doing better than our father did at my age").
6. Leave the job.

Equity theory suggests that people are not only interested in rewards, but are also interested in the comparative nature of rewards. Thus, part of the attractiveness of rewards at work is the extent to which they are seen to be comparable to those available to the peer group. This can best be applied to extrinsic rewards, such as pay, promotion, pension arrangements, company car and other similar benefits. This theory however, cannot be applied in the same way to intrinsic rewards such as interest, personal achievement and excise of responsibility which by their very nature are personal to the individual, and entirely subjective. Nevertheless, managers could reflect on the ideas of Equity.

- **V. H. Vroom -Expectancy Theory**

V. H. Vroom Expectancy theory proposes that motivation depends on individual's expectations about their ability to perform tasks and receive desired rewards. It indicates the components of efforts that can lead to relevant performance and appropriate rewards. Key is that an individual's behaviour is formed not on objective reality, but on his or her subjective perception of the reality. It is concerned with the thinking process that individuals use to get rewards that is normally based on relationship between "effort – performance –outcome/ reward". In other words, the expectancy that putting effort will lead to performance and reward. The author focused especially, on the factors involved in stimulating an individual to put effort into something, since this is the basis of motivation. He concluded that there were three such factors that affect motivation, each based on individual's personal perception of the situation.

1. Expectancy

This is the perception that effort will lead to effective performance. It could also be explained as the extent of the individual's perception or belief that a particular act will produce a particular outcome. For expectancy to be high, the individual must have the ability, previous experience and necessary machinery/tools and opportunity to perform.

2. Instrumentality/ performance

This is the perception that effective performance will lead to awards. It could also be explained as the extent to which the individual perceives that effective performance will lead to desired reward.

3. Valence

This is perception that attractive rewards are available. Rewards could be intrinsic or extrinsic rewards. Intrinsic rewards – are those gained from fulfilling higher level personal needs such as self esteem, personal growth etc. These rewards are more likely to be perceived as producing job satisfaction. This has led to development of work design, where emphasis has been laid on intrinsic job satisfaction within the control of the individual. Extrinsic rewards on the other hand, are those provided by the organisation and thus outside the control of the individual, such as pay, promotion and working conditions. These rewards are less likely to be perceived as producing job satisfaction.

- **Reinforcement Theory**

The theory by B.F. Skinner (1970) suggests that a given behaviour is a function of the consequences of earlier behaviour (based on relationship between a given behaviour and its consequences). He argued that all behaviour is determined to some extent by the reward or punishments obtained from previous behaviour, which has the effect of reinforcing current efforts. The theory focuses on changing or modifying behaviour through use of rewards or consequences, and reinforcement. Reinforcement is anything that causes a given behaviour to be repeated or inhibited. This could be achieved through:

- ✓ Positive reinforcement – positively reinforce desired behaviour.
- ✓ Avoidance learning– ignoring undesirable behaviour, so far as possible.
- ✓ Punishment -as a means of achieving desired performance.
- ✓ Immediate reinforcement - as soon as possible after the response.
- ✓ Extinction-withdrawal of positive reward.

The underlying assumption behind reinforcement approach is that people are there to be controlled, and that management's task is to provide the right conditions to encourage high performance. It is suggested that the timing or schedules of reinforcement impacts on the speed of employee learning. Timing or Schedules pertain to the frequency with, and intervals over which reinforcement occurs. A reinforcement schedule can be selected to have maximum impact on employees' job behaviour. There are five basic types of reinforcement schedules:

- ✓ Continuous schedules- every occurrence of the desired behaviour is rewarded.
- ✓ Fixed ratio schedules – reinforcement occurs after a specified number of desired responses.
- ✓ Fixed interval schedules – reinforcement is administered at random times.
- ✓ Variable ratio schedules –reinforcement is based on random number of desired behaviour rather than time periods.

Continuous reinforcement schedule is most effective for establishing new learning. Partial reinforcement schedule is more effective for maintaining behaviour over extended time period. Variable-ratio schedule is a more permanent way of maintaining desired behaviour is rather than for a time period.

- **Job Design for Motivation**

Job Design for motivation relates to designing or structuring of work process to motivate employee's attitude and engagement to work and improvement in productivity. Notable approaches include:

- ✓ Job simplification.
- ✓ Job enlargement.
- ✓ Job rotation.
- ✓ Job enrichment.

Job simplification is about reducing the complexity of a job by designing the job to be simple, repetitive, and standardized. The aim is to create a routine job process that reduces job complexity, that motivates an employee job interest and increase efficiency, by reducing the task an employee must do in a job. This allows the employee more time to concentrate on doing more of the same routine tasks in the job. The simplification of tasks also allows the use of low skill employees to perform a particular task routinely, producing high level of proficiency and efficiency. However, people dislike routine and boring jobs and may react in a number of negative ways, including sabotage, absenteeism, and unionization.

Job rotation is about moving employees from one job to another in a systematic way. The aim is to increase the number of different tasks an employee performs without increasing the complexity of any one job. Job rotation has great motivational potential when the jobs are challenging, rather than simplified. The opportunity to try new and different jobs is usually fascinating to employees. The exposure to unfamiliar areas usually gives employees opportunity to expand their knowledge of corporate operations in many other areas, through hands on experience. Employees can also develop multi-skills in the process. However, there are the dangers that that employees' interest and novelty may wear off as repetitive work is mastered.

Job enlargement is about combining a series of tasks into one new broader job. Instead of only one job, an employee may be responsible for three or four and will have more time to do them. It is a response to dissatisfaction of employees with oversimplified jobs. However, this normally creates greater challenge for employees.

Job enrichment represents the idea that managers can change specific job characteristics to promote job satisfaction and so motivate employees. It is a job design that incorporates high level motivators into work, including responsibility, recognition, and opportunities for growth, learning, and achievement. For example, employees have control over the resources necessary for performing it, makes decision on how to work, experience personal growth and take control their own work pace. In this way, achievement, recognition, and other high level motivators are incorporated into the job design.

Richard Hickman and Greg Oldman job enrichment model (1980) extended the work of earlier theorists, by proposing that managers could change specific job characteristics to motivate employees and promote job satisfaction. The model identifies three critical psychological states that must be present to achieve high motivation. If any are low, motivation will be low:

1. Experience meaningfulness – the degree to which employees perceive their work as valuable and worthwhile. If workers regard a job as trivial and pointless, their motivation will be low.
2. Experienced responsibility – how responsible employees feel for the quantity and quality of work.
3. Knowledge of results – the amount of feedback employees receive about how well they are doing the job. Those who do not receive feedback will careless about the quality of their performance.

These psychological states are influenced by five job characteristics:

- Skill variety – the number of diverse activities that comprise a job and the number of skills used to perform it. For example, a routine administrative job is low in variety, whereas that of a marketing or customer support assistant is likely to require a wide variety of analytical and interpersonal skills. A routine repetitious assembly line job is low in variety, while an applied research position that entails working on new problems every day is high in variety.
- Task identity – the degree to which an employee performs a total job with a recognisable beginning and ending. For example, a nurse who organises and oversees all the treatments for a hospital patient has more task identity than one who provides a single treatment to many different patents. A chef who prepares an entire meal has more tasks identity than a worker on a cafeteria line who handles mashed potatoes.
- Task significance – the degree to which the job is perceived as important and having impact on the company' consumers or society. For example, people who can see that there job contributes directly to performance, or that it is a major help to others, will feel they have a significant task. People who distribute penicillin and other medical supplies during times of emergencies would feel they have significant jobs.
- Autonomy – the degree to which the job has freedom, discretion, and self determination in planning and carrying out tasks. For example, a sales agent in a call centre following a tightly scripted and recorded conversation with potential customer has much less autonomy than a sales agent talking face to face to a customer. A house painter can determine how to paint the house. A paint sprayer on an assembly line has little autonomy.
- Feedback – the degree to which doing the job provides information back to the employee about performance. For example, a football coach knows whether the team won or lost, but a basic research scientist may have to wait years to learn whether a research project was successful. Modern manufacturing systems can provide operators with very rapid information on quality, scrap, materials use etc. Operators can

then receive high degree of feedback, on the level of the result of their work.

The model also suggested that management increase employees' motivation by improving enrichment through:

1. Task combination – staff can combine tasks, so they use more skills and complete more of the whole task. For example, an order clerk could receive orders from a customer and arrange transport and invoicing instead of having these done by different people.
2. Workgroups –groups could be created that carry out a complete operation. In order to give more responsibility and enable sharing and skills. For example, instead of a product passim down the assembly line, with each worker performing one operation. A group may assemble the whole product sharing out the tasks amongst themselves.
3. Customer relations involvement– customer relations could be improved from people doing parts of the whole job for all customers, to looking after all that allows establishment of closer relationship and better understanding customer needs.
4. Vertical loading – this happens when employees take on some responsibilities of supervision to solve problems and develop workable solutions, thus adding to their autonomy. For example, operators may be given responsibility for checking the quantity and quality of incoming materials and reporting any problems. They use more discretion over the order in which they arrange a week's work.
5. Maintaining feedback channels – this is to make sure that employees receive feedback on their performance from internal or external customers. For example, operators can attend meetings at which customers give their view on the service provided as a basis for improving performance and building client relationships. It also helps in building for public recognition for achievement, contributes to a positive psychological state of employees as well as improving their performance and satisfaction.

The model also included growth desire or strength, as a feature of job characteristics i.e. the extent to which an individual desires personal challenges, accomplishment and learning on the job. Employees have different needs, or desire for growth and development. Those with high needs for challenge, growth and creativity will respond more positively to job enrichment than those with low growth needs.

- **Goal Theory**

Locke (1968) first proposed the idea of Goal theory where he suggested that working towards goals was in itself a motivator.

Goal theory assumes that motivation is driven primarily by goals /objectives set by individuals for themselves. The goal itself provides the driving force. It suggested that performance improves, when individuals set specific goals for themselves. Performance also improves, when individuals set specific, rather than vague goals for themselves.

Other factors essential for achieving goals include:

- ✓ Feedback - receiving feedback is necessary to increase motivation. Feedback provides information on past performance to allow employees to use it in adjusting their performance.
- ✓ Goal commitment - which is the extent to which the individual is committed to pursuing the goal when things get tough. Participation allows employees to take part in setting goals, to increase commitment.
- ✓ Self efficacy - which is the perception that one has on the ability to achieve the goal. Managers should set goals that are hard enough tom stretch employees, but not so difficult as to be impossible to accomplish.
- ✓ Management by Objectives (MBO) – this happens when goals are set with employees, rather than imposed externally i.e. concept of goal ownership. The sense of ownership encourages commitment and motivation to achieving the goals.

- **Attribution Theory**

Attribution Theory presents the basis on which people judge each other's behaviour, in or out of an organisational settings. The theory suggested that, people judge other people's behaviour by attributing meaning to the behaviour.

The behaviour could be a result of internal and external forces or causes. Internal caused behaviour is perceived to be under the control of the individual. The individual has made the choice in selecting the behaviour. External caused behaviour is perceived to be from environmental forces that are perceived to influence people's behaviour (e.g. organisation's rules, machinery breakdown etc) and over which the individual has little or no control. Kelley (1972) suggested that when people make attribution, they do so with three major criteria in mind:

1. Distinctiveness - how distinctive or different or typical the behaviour is to the individual.
2. Consensus- how far the behaviour is typical of others in the same situation.
3. Consistency - how consistence the behaviour is over time with the individual.

Attributes Theory is as much an issue of perception between individuals as is a theory of motivation. Nevertheless, by providing another way of looking at people's behaviour, it can add to the understanding of motivational process. The theory has connection with achievement theory since people attributed with primarily internal sources of behaviour, have strong similarities with those showing high achievement needs i.e. behave in their own internal strength. People attributed with external sources are likely to see their working lives dominated by external forces for example, production system, action of management etc.

- **The Japanese Approach - Theory Z**

Theory Z describes approach to employee motivation based on Japanese management practices. The phrase was coined by an

American exponent of Japanese approach to management, W Ouchy (1981). He used it to describe attempts to adopt Japanese practices to western firms. Consideration was given to the success of Japanese management industries.

One of the key factors in the Japanese success according to Ouchy has been their approach to management of resources, especially people, which centres on human related factors:

➢ High degree of mutual trust and loyalty between management and employee.
➢ Lifelong job relation or career path.
➢ Shared decision making at all levels.
➢ Long term performance appraisal.
➢ Collective responsibility for success than individual.

Ouchy believes that certain features of Japanese management could be applied in a westerner context. In his view this requires a" new" philosophy of managing people based on a combination of the following features of Japanese management:

✓ Lifelong employment prospects.
✓ Shared form of decision making.
✓ Relationships between boss and subordinate based on mutual respect.

According to Ouchy, the successful implementation of the above proposed management features would require embracing of the ideas of security of employment, shared decision making, career development, team spirit, acknowledgement of individual contribution within the team as an organisation's philosophy. The implementation of new approach should be carried out through the basis of consultation and communication with the workforce, and with full training support to develop relevant skill for managers, supervisors and their teams.

Research carried out in Japanese manufacturing factories (manufacturers of colour television (Johnso2002) revealed that the Japanese personnel policy was directed at maximising the contribution of each employee through training, job rotation, use of quality circles and individual council ling. The emphasis on learning about, and being committed to the company culture was striking.

Critics of Japanese management approach have pointed to the slow processes of decision making, the lack of risk- taking, the reliance on a myriad of small firms and part time employees, the docile nature of trade unions, and the imprisoning effect of lifetime employment in one company. It is precisely because of these criticisms that the Japanese management practices have to be adapted if they are to be employed successfully elsewhere.

Further reading

Cole G A (2004) Management Theory and Practice (6th Edition) Thomson

Daft, R. A. (2010), New Era of Management (9th Edition), South Western.

Daft, R. L. [2000], Management (5th edn), The Dryden Press, Fort Worth, TX.

Ducker, P. (1954), the Practice of Management, Hamper, New York

Drucker, P. (1999), Management Challenges for the 21th century, Butterworth, London

Fayol, H. (1949), General and Industrial Management, Pitman, London.

Handy, C. (1988), Understanding voluntary organisations, penguin Harmondsworth

Hates, C. (2002) Bureaucracy and continuities in managerial work, British journal of Management vol. 13, No. 1, pp.51-66

Magretta, J. (2002), what management is (and why it is every one's business), Profile Books, London Thompson, P. and McHugh, D. (2002), Work organisation: A critical introduction, (3rd edition) Macmillan, Basingstocke

Roddick, A. (2000), Business as Usual, Thorsons, London

CHAPTER 12

THE INTREPRENEURIAL NEW VENTURE CONTROL

Aim

To introduce management controlling and explain why it is a key management function for the entrepreneurial new venture.

Objectives

After studying this chapter you should be able to:

- Understand the meaning of controlling in management.
- Describe the range of steps the entrepreneur can use to ensure effective control in the new venture development.
- Explain the various control focus for the entrepreneur.
- Explain different control methods available to the entrepreneur.
- Describe and understand management control systems relevant for the new venture effective control and development.

12.1 Introduction

Controlling is an important management activity for entrepreneurial new venture development and sustainability.

Controlling as a management activity could be described as the systematic process through which managers regulate organisational activities, to make them consistent with expected performance standards. It involves monitoring employee activities, keeping organisation on tracks toward goals/objectives, and making necessary corrections.

In other words, controlling is the process through which standards of performance in organisations are set, communicated, monitored, controlled, and corrected, as may be required, to achieve performance standards.

The entrepreneurial new venture needs some degree of control at various areas and levels of its activities, and at varied times, if it is to achieve what is intended.

From time to time the entrepreneur needs to check where the development process of the new venture is, in relation to the required destination.

The sooner the entrepreneur does this, the better he/she will be on track, and the more confident he/she will be. Frequent checks ensure that corrective action can be taken quickly or on time to avoid wasting effort and resources and time.

The method of controlling that takes place in the venture may vary according to the size, operating activities, and the leadership style of the entrepreneur.

In a micro or very small business with one or very few employees, the owner/manager can often exercise control by personal observation with limited paperwork and then take decision about corrective action. This is not the case for a larger venture with more employees involved in the venture, where it becomes necessary that a process of controlling is introduced. It is now difficult to know the current position, as work goes on in many separate places at the same time and mangers as well as employees in separate management areas may differ about their precise objectives and targets. Thus, the entrepreneur can apply a range of steps to ensure effective process of controlling in their organisations. These include:

1. Establish standard of performance.
2. Measure actual performance.
3. Compare performance standard.
4. Take corrective action.

1. **Establish standard of performance**

The first step in the controlling process is to establish standards against which results or performance can be measured. Managers first define goals/objectives for the organisation and departments in specific, operational terms as standard of performance. The standards which managers desire to obtain in key desired areas should be measured in quantitative, verifiable and in clearly stated terms such as:

- ✓ Physical standards (e.g. specific units or outputs in machine production, labour productivity, etc.).
- ✓ Cost standards (specific cost areas and unit such as direct costs units or indirect cost per unit, material cost per unit, labour cost per unit, etc).
- ✓ Revenue standards (e.g. specific unit or average numbers such as average sales per customer, sales per capital employed etc),
- ✓ Capital standards (e.g. specific rate unit rate such as rate of return on capital employed, rate of return on current assets employed, etc),
- ✓ Intangible standards (e.g. specific or average standards on competence of manager per department, or marketing success on public relations programmes, etc).

Where standards are rather qualitative, it is important that they are expressed in terms of end results. Numeric and non numeric standards should be balanced.

2. **Measure actual performance**

Standards of performance need to be measured to make sure of their achievements.
Measurement of performance can be done by personal observation a in the case of subordinates being observed at work and by a study

of various summaries of figures, such as reports (spoken and written reports), charts and statements.

Quick comparisons of these figures with standards are possible. Managers can develop quantitative measurement standard that can be reviewed on a daily, weekly or monthly basis, that makes it easy for them to measure and manage performance.

The possibility of developing an effective quantitative performance measurement standard, usually depends on, the relevance, adequacy and timeliness of information available for managers to use.

The single most important source of information is the management accounting department, which is responsible for the regular production of operating statements, expenditure analysis, profit forecast, cash flow statements and other relevant control information explained in details later in this chapter.

3. Compare performance to standard

The comparison of performance with standard is meant to help managers dictate deviation where it occurs and action taken where necessary, and at the right time. This is enhanced by developing an established quantitative standard of measurement that provides the basis for standard of control, enabling managers to compare actual performance to standards.

Managers may use many methods as they deemed suitable, to compare performance to standards, as well as interpretation.

Some managers have targeted performance standard right on the computer printout along with the actual performance for the previous week and the previous year. This makes the comparison easy for them. Other may use reporting system to monitor performance and compare actual performance against standards.

4. Take corrective action

As explained, the essence of making comparison is to dictate progress or deviations where they occur. By comparing standard with performance, managers are able to identify "Gaps" and need for corrective actions.

Corrective action is a change in work and activities to bring them back to acceptable performance standard. Also, corrective actions should be taken without wasting time so that the normal position can be restored.

Managers should determine the causes for deviation, for example, inadequate or poor equipment and maintenance, inadequate communication systems, lack of motivation of subordinates, poor training of personnel etc. The remedial actions managers should take depend on types and merits of deviations for control. They need to exercise their formal authority to make necessary changes needed to adjust management tasks.

In order to exert effective control over the whole organisation that meets desired corporate goals/objectives, managers need to integrate control with strategic planning – that monitors both internal and external business activities and performance standards.

If control simply monitors internal activities (internal control), it may not help the organisation achieve its strategic objectives (external control).

The linkage of strategy to control is important because strategy reflects changes in external environment that create opportunity and threats for the organisation.

Absence of this linkage may leave the firm concentrating on internal control activities that does not reflect current external environment changes for achieving successful performance standards.

In is important to recognise that each control step - established standard, measure performance and takes corrective action, is continually changing and thus, demands flexibility in the control process. The process should encourage adjustments that lead to new plans, new standard of performance, new activities, etc.

12.2 Control Methods

Whether the entrepreneur focuses control activities on input, process/procedure, output, or individual, it must also decide on the method of control, that include the use of bureaucratic, or clan control methods or both.

The entrepreneur needs to use a control system that will enable the new venture retain its creativity and innovativeness in order to maintain the process of change.

Bureaucratic control seemed not to be entrepreneurial and not appropriate as a control method since it is based on rules, regulations and procedures and therefore not flexible and adaptive to the environment and change. It assumes that targets can be defined, and that employees' work behaviour will conform to those targets if formal rules and regulations are provided.

Clan control on the other hand, appear to be entrepreneurial and is likely to be appropriate control method for the entrepreneur since it is based on trust, and not on rules, regulation or supervision of employees to achieve venture performance, and therefore gives room for flexibility and adaptability to the environment and change. Employees are trusted, and the entrepreneur believes they are willing to perform correctly without much rules or supervision. Giving minimal direction and standards, employees are assumed to perform well. They are even encouraged to participate in setting standards and designing of the control systems.

This method of control is usually implemented through the use of:

- ✓ Corporate culture.
- ✓ Peer group.
- ✓ Self control.
- ✓ Selection and socialisation.

Corporate culture is a powerful control devise. The basis of cultural control strategy is the acceptance and willing compliance of employees with the requirements of management. This works well in organisations with established values consistent with its goals.

Provided employees have the necessary skills and ability, they can be given wide freedom of action in deciding how to undertake their responsibilities.

Firms also use Peer groups as control instrument. This could happen through work group and cohesive group influence on employees. Where peer control is established, less top down bureaucratic control is needed, and groups are likely to pressure members into adhering to group norms and achieving business objectives.

Since no organisation can control employees 100 percent at a time, there is need for self control in organisation. It is assumed the most employees bring to the job a belief in doing a fair day's job and a desire to contribute to the organisation's success in return for rewards and fair treatment (theory Y). To the extent that managers can have greater advantage of employee self- control, bureaucratic control can be reduced. Employees that are high in self control are often those who had several years of training and hence, have internal standard of performance. It is common to see this among attorneys, researchers, or doctors. It is also common to see this attributes existing in employees of large corporations. The experience, training, and socialisation of professionals in these large firms provide internal standards of performance that allow self-control.

The clan methods of selection uses personal evaluations rather than the formal testing procedures associated with bureaucratic control. There is likely to be careful selection, training and socialisation of staff in order to permit the use of semi-autonomous methods of working, with only limited formal controls. This approach tends to be exemplified by organisations offering professional services and staffed by professional people.

It is advisable that entrepreneur need to adopt tight and lose control methods which should be applied accordingly. They should use tight, centralized control for the venture's crucial core values as no exceptions are made to core values (e.g. quality). Yet in other areas employees should be free to experiment, to be flexible, to innovate, and to take risks in ways that will help the entrepreneurial venture achieve its goal. In other words, employees should not be allowed to deviate from basic cultural values but have great freedom while working within them.

12.3 Control Systems

Every organisation needs basic management control systems, necessary to steer the organisation towards its goals. Research into the makeup of control system across organisations revealed the existence of core management control systems that include:

Entrepreneurs use resources to achieve their aims in that they combine resources in a way which is innovative in the pursuit of opportunity.

In order to achieve desired performance, the entrepreneur needs to establish control systems that will help measure outcome of performance in various areas – financial and non financial.

To help steer the venture towards achieving its goals, the following controls and system are inevitable:

- ✓ Financial control.
- ✓ Budgetary control.
- ✓ Performance appraisal
- ✓ Total Quality Control.
- ✓ Information Systems for Management Control.

12.3.1 Financial Control

A major performance yardstick for many businesses is usually the financial standard of performance. Financial standard of performance is an indicator of the financial health condition of a firm, without which it risks being denied the resources needed to achieve desired goals/objectives, such as growth, survival, profit maximization, shareholders' returns, etc.

Firms develop financial control systems to help them control financial management activates and achieve overall organisational performance.

Key financial control tools include:

- ✓ Strategic plan.
- ✓ Financial statements.
- ✓ Financial forecast.
- ✓ Financial analysis.
- ✓ Financial audits.

Managers need all these tools to control the financial health condition of the firm. The starting point for financial control is the strategic plan. This consists of the organisation's strategic objectives, as discussed in chanter 4. It is based on in –depth analysis of the organisation's industry position, internal strengths and weaknesses, and environmental opportunities and threats. The written plan typically discusses company products, competition, economic trends, new business opportunities, resources etc.

The overall strategic plan is top management responsibility, and presents the blueprint of overall corporate direction and as well as the financial standard of performance that could be measured in financial terms. Top management control systems concern performance for the organisation as a whole and include financial statements.

Financial statements provide the information needed for financial control of a firm's assets, liabilities and cash flows. Major financial statements – the balance sheet, the income statements, and the cash flow forecast – are the starting points for financial control. The balance sheet shows the firm's financial position with respect to assets and liabilities at a specific point in time. The income statement or profit and loss accounts summarizes the firm's financial performance in terms of revenues, expenditures, profit and loss, for a given time interval, usually one year.

An important step towards financial control is preparation of a financial forecast and comparing actual financial statement with forecasted financial statements. The financial forecast consists of a one- to five years projection of company financial statements. This is the company's financial projection based on overall strategic plan. The controller's office can calculate income statement and balance sheet forecast based on anticipated new products, sales and expansion. Companies use projected financial statements to estimate their future financial position.

Managers carry out financial analysis through ratio analysis that will reveal in detail how a firm is performing. A financial ratio is the comparison of two financial numbers. Several financial ratios can be used to illustrate a firm's performance. Most frequently used ratios are liquidity, leverage, activity, and profitability ratios. Actual ratios are compared to budget targets and to industry averages to evaluate company performance.

Financial audits are independent appraisals of the organisation's financial standing through records. Audits are of two types- external and internal. An external audit is conducted by experts from outside the organisation, typically certified public accounting firms. An internal audit is handled by experts within the organisation. Both external and internal audits should be thorough. Their purpose is to examine every nook and cranny to verify that the financial statement represents actual company operations that should reflect the firm's performance and guide to management control.

The financial control by top management follow the control steps described eelier in this chapter. Targets are set, actual performance is measured, and performance compared to targets. A more difficult control function is corrective action. Managers need to look beneath the financial figures to dictate financial problem and find solutions. They need to make an accurate diagnosis. The diagnosis must be followed with action plan that will change activities so as to meet financial standards.

12.3.2 Budgetary Control

Budgetary control systems are developed and established in organisations as a primary control devise, especially for middle management, with top management involvement during the process of developing and sanctioning of budgets for the company as a whole.

A budget is a plan which is agreed in advance. It must be a plan and not a forecast – a forecast is a prediction of what might happen in the future whereas a budget is a planned outcome which a firm hope to achieve. Budgets are the most widely used control system by middle management.

Budgetary control systems are therefore, designed to help managers think ahead, improve co-ordination and take responsibility for the budget performance of their departments, as well as being accountable for their decisions in this regard. Middle level managers use them to plan and control the money value of resources that are essential for the strategic and operational performance, and success of the organisation. These include planned and actual departmental cash income, expenditure, assets, raw materials, salaries, and other materials that need to be budgeted.

There are many types of budgets in this regard such as,

- ✓ Revenue budget.
- ✓ Expense or Expenditure budget.
- ✓ Profit budget.
- ✓ Financial budget.
- ✓ Zero based budgeting.
- ✓ Top down or Bottom up.

A revenue budget identifies the revenues required by the organisation. The revenue budget is the responsibility of a revenue centre, such as marketing or sales. Many organisations apply the use of " responsibility centres" to foster proper management control, by defining each departments as a "responsibility centre" and creating a budget for every department within the organisation, no matter how small, so long as it performs a distinct project, programme, or function. A responsibility centre is any organisation department under the supervision of a single individual who is responsible for its activity.

A revenue centre arises, when a budget is based on generated revenue or income i.e. the department has a revenue goal or revenue budget e.g. sales and marketing department budgets.

An expense budget outlines the anticipated expenses for each responsibility centre and for the total organisation. Expense budget apply to cost centres. A cost centre is a responsibility centre, in which the manager is held responsible for controlling cost inputs (e.g. salaries, supplies etc). Three different kinds of expenses normally are evaluated in the expense budget- fixed costs, variable cost, discretional costs.

A profit budget combines both expense and revenue budgets into one statement to show gross net profit. Profit budgets apply to profit and investment centres. A Profit centre arises when control is based on profit target. Here the budget measures the difference between revenue and costs. For budget purpose, the profit centre is defined as self contained unit to enable a profit be calculated. Investment centre is based on the value of assets employed to produce a given level of profit. For control purpose, managers are concerned with return on investment (ROI). Cost and revenue centres typically exist in a functional structure. Profit centres exist in divisional structure and each self contained division are valued on total cost minus total revenue (TR-TC = profit) basis . . . Every large organisation whose division is autonomous uses investment centre.

Financial budgets define where the organisation will receive funds and how it intends to spend it. Three important financial budgets are:

1. Cash budgets.
2. Capital expenditure budget.
3. Balance sheet budget.

The cash budget estimates cash flows on daily or weekly or monthly basis to insure the organisation has sufficient cash flow to meet its obligations. The cash budget shows the level of funds flowing through the organisation and the nature of cash disbursement. The capital expenditure budget plans future investments in major assets such as building, trucks, and heavy machinery etc. Capital expenditure are major purchases that are paid for over several years, Capital expenditure must be budgeted to determine their impact on cash flow and whether revenues are sufficient to cover capital expenditures and annual operating expenditure. The balance sheet budget plans the amount of assets and liabilities for the end of the time period under consideration. It indicates whether the capital expenditure and cash management, revenues, and operating expenses will melt into the financial results desired by senior management. The balance sheet budget shows where future financial problems may exist. Financial ratio analysis is performed on the balance sheet and profit budgets to see whether important ratio targets, such as debt to total assets etc, will be met.

Some firms also demand Zero budgeting when the manager responsible for a centre is required to calculate its resource needs based on coming year priorities i.e. starting from zero rather than on previous year budget/figures.

The budgeting process adopted by a firm can be either "top down" or "bottom up "showing how budgets are usually formulated and implemented by middle management in an organisation. Top down budget process exist when middle and lower level managers set department budgets targets in accordance with overall organisation revenue and expectation specified by top management. The problem with this type of budgeting is that lower managers are not usually committed to it, because they feel they were not involved in the budgeting of resources and decision making specified by top management. Bottom up budget process exists when lower level managers budget the department resource needs and pass it to the top management for approval. This has the advantage of more process involvement and ownership of the middle managers and subordinates.

12.3.3 Performance Appraisal Systems

A performance appraisal system is usually designed to provide the systematic description of job relevant strength and weakness of employees, and system for rewarding and developing employees in all departments. It typically includes standard forms and rating scales that evaluate employee skills and abilities. Middle managers can use it to control their departments, as it provides a formal method of evaluating and recording of the performance of managers and employees. As a sensor in a control system, managers need to gather information about unit performance, for comparison with the unit's plans and budgets. This may be done in two basic ways:

1. Performance monitoring - Keeping an eye on the progress.
2. Performance review - Taking a look at results and or methods used in a given period.

Performance monitoring methods may include:

- ✓ Observation - monitoring performance by watching operations as they are carried out by employees. This maybe through task inspection or activity sampling.
- ✓ Reports – monitoring performance via reports from operators and others involved in the task. Reports can be in form of time sheets, surveys, and operational data.
- ✓ Method study"- this is the systematic recording and critical examination of existing and proposed ways of doing work as a means of developing and applying easier and more effective methods and reducing costs. It is concerned with how work could and should be done more efficiently.
- ✓ Management By Objectives (MBO) - performance appraisal in which management defines objectives for each department project and employee and use them to control subsequent performance. It focuses on the achievement of explicit objectives.
- ✓ Statistical Process Control- involves the use of carefully gathered data and statistical analysis to evaluate and appraise productivity and quality of employee activity. It could be

used in any department in which output can be defined and employee's tasks can be subdivided into discrete, measurable elements, but more popular with manufacturing departments, where worker activities are measurable.

In general terms, there are certain attributes of successful organisational performance which can be appraised. They all begin with "E". The desirable "Es" factors of organisational performance are as follows:

- Effectiveness - this relate to the firm's ability to serve the needs of its owners and chosen market- market share of the specific market, quality of product, financial performances etc.
- Efficiency – this has to do with how resources should be used to achieve the goals of the firm- materials and energy and waste rates, speed of response to customer enquiries and order, completion of projects on time, productivity etc.
- Economy - is concern with the financial aspects of the firm's operations and flows in relation to objectives- cost per unit, contribution per unit etc.
- Elegance – this is about doing things the right way- appearance of business premises and staff, punctuality/professionalism of service etc.
- Ethicality – this concerns the firm's adherence to its social responsibilities and to business ethics -impact of operations on environment, hiring and minority groups, non reliance on contracts etc.

12.3.4 Total Quality Control

Apart from financial, budgetary and appraisal control methods that focus on financial values, another control method is the "Total Quality Control" that focuses on physical values.

Total Quality Control is a control concept that gives workers rather than managers responsibility for achieving standards of quality. The role is to ensure that appropriate standard of quality are set and that variances beyond the tolerances are rejected.

The burden of quality proof rests on the makers of the part with a concurrent control focus during the process. Everyone in the organisation must make quality control happen.

The approach targets of zero defects -everyone strives for perfection. This instils habit of continuous improvement. Quality control thus becomes part of the day to day business of every employee. Employees are trained to think in terms of prevention, and given the responsibility of correcting their own errors and exposing any quality problems they discover.

The measurement of quality is the price of non conformity. This approach to control was successfully implemented by Japanese companies that gave Japanese products an international reputation. The Japanese had borrowed the ideas that Americans had ignored for years. "Do it right the first time "is the motto.

Quality Circles

Firms create quality circles to implement total quality control philosophy effectively.

A quality circle is a group from six to twelve volunteer employees who meet regularly to discuss and solve problems that affect their common work activities.

The driving force is that the people who do the job know better than anyone else. Quality circles also push control decision making to lower organisational level.

When task skill demands are high, the use of quality circle can further enhance control functions and productivity. Also when quality circle serves to enrich jobs and improve motivation, quality circles will be a success. In addition, when quality circle improves workers problem solving skills, the use of quality circle will usually be a success.

However, when task demand is low and simple, the use of quality circle will unfortunately have little impact on control function and productivity.

12.3.5 Information Systems for Management Control

Introduction

Managers need information systems - a mechanism that will collect, organise, and distribute data to individuals and departments, and help foster control and measurement of standard performance in the organisation.

The information necessary to carry out control functions effectively, are produced from a variety of sources, and often in a variety of forms - processed by computer technology, or of judgemental nature.

Characteristics of useful Information include:

- ✓ Quality- the degree to which information accurately portrays reality.
- ✓ Timeliness- the degree to which information is available soon after events occur.
- ✓ Completeness- the extent to which information contains the appropriate amount of data i.e. too much lead to information overloads.
- ✓ Relevance- relevance to problem, decision or task.

Management activities differ according to top management and middle management levels in the hierarchy. The hierarchical differences mean that managers need different kinds of information.

For example, strategic planning is a primary responsibility at the top level, while operational control is a primary responsibility of the middle managers. Top managers work on nonprogrammable problems such as new product development, marketing plan, acquisition of other companies etc. Information they use pertains mostly to the external environment. It is broad in scope, to cover unanticipated problems that may arise, and is oriented toward the future, including trends and forecasts.

Middle managers in contrast, deal with programmable decisions, arising from well defined problems such as inventory control, production scheduling, and sales analysis. They need information for internal operations that is narrowly focused on specific activities with reference to past performance. Most management data used by all these managers are now computer based.

A computer based information system is a system that uses electronic computing technology. To meet different information needs of managers along the hierarchy, various types of computer based information systems have evolved.

They include:

- ✓ Transaction Processing System (TPS).
- ✓ Decision Supporting System (DSS).
- ✓ Management Information System (MIS).

Transaction Processing System

At the lower organisation level, transaction processes systems (TPSs) assist first line supervisors with record keeping, routine calculations, and data sorting. The transaction processing system performs the organisation's routine, recurring transactions. Examples of transactions include sending bills to customers, depositing cheques in the banks, placing orders, recording receipts and payments etc. Transactions processing systems are thus used, when there are many transactions and when transactions are repeated several times during the day.

Decision Support System (DSS)

A decision support system is an interactive, computer based information system which retrieves, manipulates, and displays information needed for making specific decisions. It provides computers-based facilities for conducting analyses, simulations etc.

The objective of DSS is to support managers in their work, especially decision making and control. They acquire much of their basic data from routine transaction processing and the result of analysis performed on such data.

Top managers use DSS to provide information for strategic and non programmable decisions. DSS may also be used by middle managers. It allows managers to make enquiries and receive answers to pressing questions rather than periodic reports (an interactive processing that allows rapid responses). It also gives managers access to any multiple data depending on the immediate information needs. For example, some Airlines use decision support system for pricing and route selection. Petroleum companies use it for corporate planning and forecasting, and some Banks use it for investment evaluation etc. A number of decision support packages are now available to manager such as, simulation, spreadsheets, forecasting, non linear and linear programming, and regression models.

Management Information system (MIS)

MIS is a system that convert data from internal and external sources into information, and to communicate that information in an appropriate form to managers at all levels, in all functions, to enable them managers make effective decisions for which they are responsible. This may encompass all the systems describe earlier in this section.

MIS include:

- ✓ Database systems - which process and store information, which can be drawn upon as a kind of organisational memory bank.
- ✓ Enquiry systems - based on either internal or external databases, for carrying out investigations into the performance of departments, product lines, competitors, etc.
- ✓ Control systems - which monitor the organisation's activities and report on them egg production output, sales revenue etc.

To be successful, MIS must be designed and operated with due regard to organisation and behavioural principles, as well as technical factors.

MIS is available for all levels of management, but mostly used by middle managers. Its reports are composed of statistical data, relevant to the performance of department or division. Their exact content depends on the nature of task activities and available resources.

Further reading

Alexander, D. Noble, C. (2004,) International introduction to financial accounting, Financial Times/ Prentice Hall, Harlow.
Coggan, P. (2002), Money machine Penguin, Harmondsworth
Drury, C. (2004), Management and Cost accounting, Thompson Learning, London.
Hangmen, et al, (2002), Cost Accounting (10th Edition), Financial Times/Prentice Hall, Harlow.

REFERENCES

Baumol, W. (1968), The Entrepreneur: Introductory Remarks, American Economic Review, Vol. 38, pp 60 -3.

Baumol, W. (1967), Business Behaviour, Value and Growth, Harcourt Brace.

Bolton Report (1971), Report on the Commission of Enquiry on Small Firm, HMSO.

Burns, P. et al, (1996), Small Business and Entrepreneurship, Second Edition, Macmillan Business.

Cannon, T. (1991), Enterprise Creation, Development and Growth, Butterworth – Heinemann.

Casson, M. (1982), The Entrepreneur; An Economic Theory, Martin Robertson.

Churchill N.C. and Lewis V. L. (1983), The Five \Stages of Small Business Growth, Harvard Business Review, May/June 1983.

Cole, A. (1968), Entrepreneurship in Economic Theory, American Economic Review, Vol. 58, pp 64 -71.

Curran, J. et al, (2000), The Survival of the Small Firm, Gower.

Davis J. R. and Kelly, M. (1972), Small Firms in the Manufacturing Sector, Report of the committee of Enquiry on Small Firms, Cmnd4811, HMSO.

Deakins, D. and Freel, M. (2003), Entrepreneurship and Small Firms (3rd Edition), London: McGraw Hill.

Drucker, P. (1985), Innovation and Entreprenurship, London: Heinmann.

Ganguly, T. (1983), UK Small Business Statistics and International Comparisons, Harper & Row.

Kakabadse, A. (1983), The Politics of Managing Growth.
Kirby, D. (2003), Entrepreneurship, London: McGraw Hill.
Kuratko, D. and Hodgetts, R. (2001), Entrepreneurship: A contemporary Approach (5th Edition), New York: Dryden.
Morris, M. (2000), "Revisiting "who" is the Entrepreneur", Journal of Developmental Entrepreneurship, Vol.7, No. 1, pp2.10.
O'Farrel, F. N, (1986), Entrepreneurs and Industrial Change, Irish Management Institute
Ovian, B. And McDougall, P.(2005), "Defining international entrepreneurship and modelling the speed of internationalisation, Entrepreneurship Theory and Practice, Vol. 29, No. 5, pp.537 -53.
Parker, S. (2002), "On the dimensionality and composition of entrepreneurship", Durham Business School Working Paper.
Ray, G. H. And Hutchinson, P. J. (1983), The Financing and Financial Control of Small Enterprise Development, Govern.
Stanworth, J, et al, (1991), The Small Firm in the 1990s, Paul Chapman
Storey, D. et al, (1987), The Performance of \New Firms, Croom Helm.
Storey, D. J. (1982), Entrepreneurship and the new Firm, Croom Helm
Utton, M. A. et al, Small Business Theory and Policy, The Action Society, Croom Helm
Westhead, P. Ucbasaran, D. (2005), "Decisions, actions and performance; do novice, serial and portfolio entrepreneurs differ?" Journal of Business Management, Vol. 43, No. 4, pp.393- 417.
Wynarczyk, P. K. Et al, (1993), The Managerial Labour Market in the Small firm Sector, Rutledge.

Bandara, A. (1997), Self Efficacy; The Exercise of Control, Freeman, New York.
Barile A. (1983)The captive insurance company: An emerging profit centre. Best review in property, and casualty insurance, 7th Edition New York.
Bass, P. (2000), Changing The Culture of a Hospital From Hierarchy to Netwoked Community, Public Administration London.
Batt, P. (2000), Managing Customer Services: Human Resource Practices London.

Bearshaw, et al (2004) Economics: A student's Guide (5th edition), Pitman Publishing.
Becker, B. Huselid, M. The Human Resource Scorecard, Harvard Business School Press, Boston.
Bucanan, D. and Badham, R. (1999), Power, Politics and Organizational Change: Wining the turf game, Sage, London.
Bucanan, D. and Bobby, R. [1992], The Expertise of the Change Agent, Prentice Hall International, Hamel Hempsted.
Bucanan, D. and Huczynski, A.A [2004], Organizational Behaviour: An introductory text [50th edn], Financial Times/Prentice Hall, Harlow.
Burnes, B. [1996], Managing Change, Pitman, London.
Burns, J.M. [1978], Leadership, Harper & Row, New York.
Burns, T. [1961], 'Micropolitics: mechanisms of organizational change', Administrative Science Quarterly, vol.6, no.3, pp. 257 – 281.
Burns. T. and Stalker, G.M. [1961], The Management of Innovation, Tavistock, London.
Butt, J. [1971], Robert Owen: Prince of cotton spinners, David &Charles, Newton Abbott.
Cairncross, F. [2001], The Death of Distance 2.0: How the communications revolution will change our lives, Orion, London.
Campbell, A. [1997], 'Stakeholder: the case in favour', Long Range Planning, vol. 30, no.3, pp. 446 – 449.
Camuffo, A., Romano, P. and Vinelli, A. [2001], 'Back to the future: Benetton transforms its global network', MIT Sloan Management Review, vol. 43, no. 1, pp. 46 – 52.
Cannon, T. [1996], Basic Marketing: Principles and practice [4th edn], Cassell, London.
Cappelli, P. [2000], 'Managing without commitment', Organizational Dynamics, vol. 28, no. 4, pp. 11 – 25.
Carlson, S. [1951], Executive Behaviour, Stromberg Aktiebolag, Stockholm.
Carr, N.G. [2004], 'In praise of walls', MIT Sloan Management Review, vol. 45, no. 3, pp. 268 – 295.
Carroll, A. (1999), 'Corporate social responsibility'- Business and Society, Vol. 38, pp. 268 – 295.

Caster A. (1984), Handbook of risk management,- London Harron handbooks.
Catterick, P. [1995], Business Planning for Housing, Chartered Institute of housing, Coventry.
Certo SL et al (2007) Modern Management Concerts and Skills (11th Edition) Prentice Hall.
Chaffey, D. [ed.] [2003], Business Information Systems [2nd edn], Financial Times/Prentice Hall, Harlow.
Champy, J. and Nohria, N. [1996], Fast Forward, Harvard Business School Press, Cambridge, MA.
Chandler, A. (1962), Strategy and Structure, MIT Press, Cambridge, MA.
Chapman, D. and Cowdell, T. (1998]), New Public Sector Marketing, Financial Times Management, London.
Chen, M. [2004], Asian Management System, Thomson, London.
Cherns, A. [1987], 'The principles of sociotechnical design revisited', Human Relations, vol 40, no. 33, pp. 153 – 162.
Cherysalides, G.A.D. and Kale, J.H. [1993], An Introduction to Business Ethics, Chapman & Hall, London.
Child, J. [1972], 'Organizational structure, environment and performance: the role of strategic choice', Sociology, vol. 6, pp.1 – 22.
Child, J. [1984], Organisation: A guide to problems and practice [2nd edn], Harper & Row, London.
Chow, I. (1994), 'An opinion survey of performance appraisal practice- in Hong Kong and the People's Republic of China', Asia Pacific Journal of Human Resources, vol. 32, pp. 62 – 79.
Christensen, C.M. and Raynor, M.E. [2003], The Innovator's Solution, Harvard Business School Press, Boston, MA.
CIPD [2002], Pensions and HR's Role, Charted Institute of Personnel and Development, London.
Clarke, F.L. [2003], Corporate Collapse: Accounting, regulatory and ethical failure, Cambridge University Press, Cambridge.
Clutterbuck, D. [1994], The Power of Empowerment, Kogan Page, London.
Coggan, P. [2002], The Money Machine, Penguin, Harmondsworth.
Cole G A (2004) Management Theory and Practice (6th Edition) Thomson

Cooke, B. [2003], 'The denial of slavery in management studies',- Journal of management Studies, vol. 40, no. 8, pp. 1895 – 1918.

Cooke, S. And Slack, N. [1991], Making management Decisions [2nd edition], Prentice Hal Hemel Hempstead.

Coombs, R. and Hull, R. [1994], 'The best or the worst of both worlds: BPR, cost reduction, and the strategic management of IT', paper presented to the OASIG seminar on Organizational Change, London, September.

Cornfield, R. [1999], Successful Interview Skills, Kogan Page, London.

Cravens, D.W. [1991], Strategic Marketing [3rd edn], Irwin, Chicago, IL.

Critchley, W. and Casey, D. [1984], 'second thoughts on team building', Management Education and Development vol. 15, no 2, pp. 163 – 175.

Crosby, P. [1979], Quality is Free, McGraw-Hill, New York.

Cusumano, M.A. and Nobeoka, K. [1998], Thinking Beyond Lean, the Free Press, New York.

Cusumano, M. [1997], 'How Microsoft makes large teams work like small teams', MIT Sloan Management Review, vol. 39, no.1, pp. 9 – 20.

Cyert, R. and March, J.G. [1963], A behavioural theory of the firm, Prentice Hall, Englewood cliffs, NJ.

D Stokes (2006) Small Business Management (4th Edition) Continuum

Daft, R. A. (2010,) New Era of Management (9th Edition) South Western.

Daft, R.L. [2000], Management [5th edn], The Dryden Press, Fort Worth, TX.

Daniels, J.D. and Radebaugh, L.H. [1998], International Business [8th edn], Addison-Wesley, Reading, MA.

Davenport, T.H. [1998], 'Putting the enterprise into enterprise system', Harvard business review, vol. 76, no. 4, pp. 121 – 132.

David Boddy (2012_essentials of Management, A coincise Introduction

David, B. (2012), Essentials of Management, A coincise Introduction, Pearson Education, Prentice Hall.

Davis, K. [1960], 'Can business afford to ignore social responsibilities?' California management review, vol. 2, no. 3, pp, 70 – 76.

Davis, K. [1971], Business Society and Environment: social power and social response, McGrew Hill, New York.

Day G. (1985) Strategic market planning, the pursuit of competitive advantage

De wit, B. And Meyer, R. [2004], strategy: process, content and context, and international perspective, international Thomas Business, London.

Deal, T.E. and Kennedy, A.A. [1982], corporate Culture: the rites and rituals of corporate life, Addison-wesley, Reading, MA.

Delaney, J.T. and Huselid, M.A. [1996], 'the impact of human resource management practices on perceptions of organizational performance' Academy of management journal, vol. 39, no. 4, pp. 949 – 969.

Delmar, F. and Shane, S. [2003], 'Does business planning facilitate the development of new ventures?', strategic management journal, vol. 24, no. 12, pp. 1165 – 1185.

Deming, W.E. [1988], out of the crisis, Cambridge University Press, Cambridge.

Dent, C.M. [1997], the European Economy: the global context, Routledge, London.

Department of trade and industry [1996], the rewards of success: flexible pay systems in Britain, DTI, London.

Dibb, S., Simkin, L., Pride, W.M. and Ferrell, O.C. [1997], marjeting: concepts and strategies [4th edn], Houghton Mifflin, New York.

Dicken, P. [1992], global shift: the internationalisation of economic activity, PCP, London.

Dimbleby, R. and Burton, G. [1992], more than words: and introduction to communication [2nd edn], Routledge, London.

Dobson, P. Starkey, K. Richards, J. [2004], Strategic management issue and cases, Blackwell, Oxford.

Domasio, A.R. [2000], The Feeling of What Happened, Heinemann, London

Donaldson, L. [1996], For positive organization theory, Sage, London.

Donaldson, L. [2001], The contingency theory of organization, Sage, London.

Drucker, P.F. [1954], The practice of management, Harper, New York.

Drucker, P.F. [1985] Innovation and entrepreneurship, Heinemann, London

Drucker, P.F. [1999], Butterworth- Heinemann, (2nd edition)Oxford.

Drummond, H. [1996] escalation in decision-making, Oxford university Press, Oxford.

Drury, C. [2004], management and cost accounting, Thomson learning, London.

Druskat, V.U. and Wheeler, J.V. [2004], 'how to lead a self-managing team' MIT, Sloan management Review, vol. 45, no.4, pp. 65 – 71.

Dutta, S. Segev, A. [1999], 'Business transformation on the internet' European management journal, vol. 17, no. 5, pp. 44 – 476.

Dutton, J.E., Dukerich, J.M. and Harwuail, C.V. [1994],'organizational images and member identification', administrative science quarterly, vol. 39, no. 2, pp. 239 – 263.

Economist intelligence unit [1992], making quality work: lessons from Europe's leading companies, economist intelligence unit, London.

Egan, J. and Wilson, D. [2002], private business – public battleground, Palgrave, Basingstoke.

Elliot, B. And Elliot, J. [2003], financial accounting and reporting [6th edn], Financial Times/Prentice Hall, Harlow.

Engel, J. Kollatt, D. and Blackwell, R. [1978], Consumer behaviour, Dryden Press, Boston.

Equal opportunities commission [1999], "facts about women and men in Great Britain", EOC, Manchester.

Ezzemel, M. Lilley, S. and Wilmott, H. [1994], 'the new organization and the managerial work", European management jounal, vol.12, no. 4, pp. 454 – 461.

Fayol, H. [1949], General and Industrial Management, Pitman, London. General and industrial management, Pitman, London.

Feigenbaum, A.V. [1993], Total quality control, McGrew-Hill, New York.

Fenton, E. M. and Pettigrew, A.M. [2000],'theoretical perspectives on new forms of organization', in A.M. Pettigrew and E. Fenton [eds.], the innovating organization, sage, London.

Fieldler, F.E. and House, R.J. [1994],'Leadership theory and research: a report of progress', in C.L. Cooper and I.T. Robertson [eds.], key reviews of managerial psychology, Wiley, Chichester.

Finkelstein, S. [2003], Why smart Executives fail: and what you can learn from their mistakes, penguin, New York.

Fleishman, E.A. [1953], the description of supervisory behaviour, journal of applied psychology, vol. 37, no. 1, pp. 1 – 6.

Flores, S.L and Pearce, S.L. [2000], the use of an expert system in the M3-competition, international jounal of forecasting, vol. 16, no. 4, pp. 485 – 493

Flynn, N. [2002], Public Sector Management [4th edn], Financial Times/Prentice Hall, Harlow.

Fogel, R.W. [1989], without consent or contract: the rise and fall of American slavery, Norton, New York.

Follet, M.P. [1920], The new state: Group organization, the solution of popular government, London.

Fombrun, C.Tichy, N.M and Devanna, M.A. [1984], strategic human resources management, Wiley, New York.

Ford, H. [1922], My life and work, Heinemann, London.

French, J. and Raven, B. (1959), "the bases of social power", in D. Cartwright (ed.), Studies in Social Power, Institute for Social Research, Ann Arbor, MI.

Friedman, M. (1962), Capitalism and Freedom, University of Chicago Press, Chicago.

Gabrial, Y. (1988), Working Lives in Catering, Routledge, London.

Gerwin, D. (1979), "Relationships between structures and technology at the organizational and job levels", Journal of Management Studies, vol. 16, no.1, pp. 70-79.

Ghoshal, S. And Bartlett, C.A. (1998), The Individualized Corporation, Heinemann, London.

Gilbreth, L.M. (1914), The Psychology of Management, Sturgis & Walton, New York.

Gillespie, R. (1991), Manufacturing Knowledge: A history of the Hawthorne experiments, Cambridge University press, Cambridge.

Gitman L. (1985) Managerial finance 4th edition.

Glaister, K.W. (1991), 'Virgin Atlantic Airways', in C. Clark-Hill and K. Glaister, Cases in Strategic Management, Pitman, London.

Glaister, K.W. and Falshaw, J.R. (1999), 'Strategic Planning: still going strong?' Long Range Planning, vol. 32, no. 1, pp. 107-116.

Glass, N. (1996), 'Chaos, non-linear systems and day-to-day management', European Management Journal, vol. 14, no. 1, pp. 98-106.

Goldratt, E. and Cox, J. (1989), The Goal, Gower, Aldershot.

Goold, M. (1997), 'Institutional advantage: a way into strategic management in not-for-profit organizations', Long Range Planning, vol. 30, no. 2, pp. 291-293.

Govindarajan, V. And Gupta, A.k. (2001), 'Building an effective global business team'. MIT Sloan Management Review, vol. 42, no. 4, pp. 63-72.

Graham, P. (1995), Mary Parker Follett: Prophet of management, Harvard Business School Press, Boston, MA.

Grant S T (2004) Introduction to Economics (6th Edition) Longman.

Grant, S. T. (2004) Introduction to Economics (6th Edition) Longman.

Grant, R. (2002), Contemporary Strategy Analysis (4th edn), Blackwell, Oxford.

Grant, R.M. (1991), 'The resource-based theory of competitive advantage: implications for strategy formulation', California Management Review, vol. 33, no. 3, pp. 114-135.

Greem, Mark. (1983), Risk management, Text and Cases N Y.

Greenberg, J. (1990), 'Employee theft as a reaction to underpayment inequity: the hidden costs of pay cuts', Journal of Applied Psychology, vol. 75, no. 5, pp. 561-568.

Greenwood, R.G., Bolton, A.A. and Greenwood, R.A. (1983), 'Hawthorne a half century Later: relay assembly participants remember', Journal of Management, vol. 9, Fall/Winter, pp. 217-231.

Greer, C.R. (2001), Strategic Human Resource Management, Prentice Hall, New Jersey.

Gronroos, C. (2000), Service Management and Marketing: A customer relationship management approach (2nd edn), Wiley, Chichester.

Guest, D. (1988), 'Human resource management: a new opportunity for psychologist or another passing fad?' The Occupational Psychologist, February.

Guest, D.E. (1987), 'Human resource management and industrial relations', Journal of Management Studies, vol. 24, no. 5, pp. 502-521.

Guest, D.E. and Conway, N. (2001), Organisational change and the Psychological Contract: An analysis of the 1999 CIPD Survey, Chartered Institute of Personnel and Development, London.

Guirdham, M. (1995), Interpersonal Skills at work, Prentice Hall International, Hemel Hempstead.

Gyory Robert. The future of risk management, in risk management V11

Habermas, J. (1972), Knowledge and Human Interests, Heinemann, London.

Hackham et al. (1975), 'Development of the job diagnostic survey', Journal of Applied Psychology, vol. 60, no.2, p. 161.

Hackham, J.R. (1990), Groups that Work (and those that don't), Jossey-Bass, San Francisco, CA.

Hackham, J.R. and Oldham, G.R. (1980), Work Redesign, Addison-Wesley, Reading, MA.

Hage, J. and Aiken, M. (1967), 'Program change and organizational properties: a comparative analysis', American Journal of Sociology, vol. 72, pp.503-519.

Hagman, E. (2000), Keynote address to Arthur Anderson European Business and Environment Network Annual Conference, 15 September.

Hales, C. (2001), Managing through Organization, Routledge, London.

Hall, W. (1995), Managing Cultures, Wiley, Chichester.

Hamel, G. And Prahald, C.K. (1996), Competing for the Future, Harvard Business School Press, Boston, MA.

Handbook of Management (2004,) (3rd Edition), FT Prentice

Handy, C. (1988), Understanding Voluntary Organizations, Penguin, Harmondsworth.

Handy, C. (1993), Understanding Organizations (4th edn), Penguin, Harmondsworth.

Hannagan, T. (2008), Management Concepts and Practices (5th) Edition FT Prentice Hall.

Hanson Edward.(1986) Reducing Insurance cost through risk management

Hardaker, M. and Ward, B. (1987), 'getting things done', Harvard Business Review, vol. 65, no. 6, pp. 112-120.

Hargie, O. et al (2004), Communication Skills for Effective Management, Palgrave.

Hargie, O.D.W. (1997), Handbook of Communication Skills, Routledge, London.

Harris, P.R. and Moran, R. (1991), Managing Cultural Differences, Gulf Publishing, Houston, TX.

Harrison, E. F. (1999), The Managerial Decision. Making Process (5th edn), Houghton Mifflin, Boston, MA.

Hartley, J. Bennington, J. and Binns, P. (1997), 'Researching the roles of internal change agents in the management of organizational change', British Journal of Management, vol. 8, no. 1, pp. 61-74.

Hawcult, P. (1982), Captive insurance company. Establishment, Operation, and Management, NY.

Heil, G., Bennis, W. and Stephens, D.C. (2000), Douglas McGregor, Revisited, Wiley, New York.

Helgesen, S. (1995), The Female Advantage: Women's way of leadership, Currency/Doubleday, New York.

Heller, R. (2001),'inside Zara', Forbes Global, 28 May, pp. 24-25, 28-29.

Hellriegel, D. and Slocum, J (1988), Management (5th edn), Addison-Wesley, Readig, MA.

Hellriegel, D., Jackson, S.E. and Slocum, J.w. (2002), Management: A competency-based approach, South Western College Publishing, Cincinatti, OH.

Henderson, D. (2001), Misguided Virtue: False notions of corporate social responsibility, Institute of Economic Affairs, London.

Herzberg, F. (1959), The Motivation to Work, Wiley, New York.

Herzberg, F. (1987), 'One more time: how do you motivate employees?' Harvard Business Review, vol. 65, no. 5, pp. 109-120.

Heydebrand, W.V. (1989), 'New organisational forms', Work and Occupations, vol. 16, no. 3, pp. 323-357.

Hill, C.W.L. and Pickering, J.F. (1986), 'Divisionalization, decentralization and performance of large United Kingdom companies', Journal of Management Studies, vol. 23, no. 1, pp. 26-50.

Hill, T. (2004), Operations Management (2nd edn), Palgrave Macmillan, London.

Hiltrop, J.M. (1995), 'The Changing psychological contract: the human resources challenge of the 1990s', European Management Journal, vol.13, no. 3, pp. 288-294.

Hofstede, G. (1980) Culture's Consequences: International differences in work-related values, Sage, Beverley Hills, CA.

Hofstede, G. (1989), 'Organizing for cultural diversity', European Management Journal, vol. 7, no. 4, pp. 390-397.

Hofstede, G. (1991), Cultures and Organisations: Software of the mind, McGraw-Hill, London.

Honderich, T. (ed.) (1995), Ethical Reasoning:The Oxford Companion to Philosophy, Oxford University Press, Oxford.

Hoppe, M.H. (1993), 'The effects of national culture on the theory and practice of managing R&D professionals abroad', R&D Management, vol. 23, no. 4, pp. 313-325.

Horngren, C.T., Foster, G. And Datar, S.M. (2002), Cost Accounting (10th edn), Financial Times/Prentice Hall, Harlow.

House, R.J. (1996), 'Path-goal theory of leadership: lessons, legacy and a reformulation', Leadership Quarterly, vol. 7, no.3, pp. 323-352.

House, R.J. and Mitchell, T.R. (1974), 'Path-goal theory of leadership', Contemporary Business, vol. 3, no. 2, pp. 81-98.

Howard, J.A. and Sheth, J.N. (1969), The Theory of Buyer Behaviour, Wiley, New York.

Howard, P. (1999), 'Fair play is better businesses, Business Review Weekly, March.

Huczynski, A.A.(2004), Influencing Within Organizations (2nd edn), Routledge, London.

Hueber S, (1982) Insurance development, in annuals of the American academy of political and social science, Philadelphia.

Huselid, M.A. (1995), 'The impact of human resource management practices on turnover, productivity and corporate financial performance', Academy of Management Journal, vol. 38, no. 3, pp. 635-672.

Ibbott, C. and O'keefe, R. (2004), 'Transforming the Vodafone/Ericsson relationship', Long Range Planning, vol. 37, no. 3, pp. 219-237.

Ichniowski, C., Kochan, T.A., Levine, D., Olson, C. and Strauss, G. (1996), 'What works at work: overview and assessment', Industrial Relations, vol. 35, no. 3, pp. 299-333.

IPD (1999), Organisational development: whose responsibility? Institute for Personnel and Development, London.

IRS (1997), 'The state of selection: an IRS survey', Employee Development Bulletin, 51, pp. 5-8, Industrial Relations Services, London.

Isobel, l Dole & Robin Lowe (2004), International Marketing Strategy (4th Edition) Thomson.

Jackson, T. (1993), Organizational Behaviour in International Management, Butterworth/ Heinemann, Oxford.

Janis, I. L. (1977), Decision Making: A psychological analysis of conflict, choice and commitment, The Free Press, New York.

Janis, I. (1972), Victim of Groupthink, Houghton-Mufflin, Boston, MA.

Jennings, D. (2000),'PowerGen: the development of corporate planning in a privatized utility', Long Range Planning, vol. 33, no. 2, pp. 201-219.

Jobber, D. (2004), Principles and Practices of Marketing (4th edn), McGraw-Hill, London.

John, K.A., Northcraft, G.B. and Neale, M.A. (1999), 'Why differences make a difference: a field study of diversity, conflict and performance in work groups', Administrative Science Quarterly, vol. 44, no. 4, pp. 741-763

Johnson, G, (1986) Strategic Change and the Management Process, New York,

Johnson, G. and Scholes, K. (2001), Exploring Corporate Strategy (6th edn), Financial Times/Prentice Hall, Harlow.

Johnson, G. and Scholes, K. (eds.) (2002), Exploring Public Sector Strategy, Prentice Hall, Harlow.

Johnston, R.A., Kast, F.E. and Rosenweig, J.E. (19667), 'people and systems', in -The Theory and Management of Systems, McGraw-Hill, New York.

Jones, J. R., George J. M. (2010). Contemporary Management (3rd Edition), McGraw Hill.

Judd, V.C. (2003), 'Achieving customer orientation using people power- the 5th P', European Journal of Marketing, vol. 37, no. 10, pp. 1301-1313.

Judge, T.A. Piccolo, R.F. and Ilies, R. (2004), 'The forgotten ones? The validity of consideration and initiating structure in leadership resaerch', Journal of Applied Psychology, vol. 89, no. 1, pp.36-51

Juran, J. [1974], quality control Handbook, McGrew-Hill, New York

Kakabadse, A. [1993], 'the succecsss levers for Europe: the Cranfield executive competence survey', journal of management development, vol. 12, no. 8, pp.12 – 17.

Kanter, R.M. [1979] 'Power failure in management circuits' Harvard business review, vol. 57, no. 4, pp. 65 – 75.

Kanter, R.M. [1983], the change masters, Unwin, London.

Kaplan, R.S. and Norton, D.P 1996], the balanced scorecard: translating strategy into action, Harvard business school press, Cambridge, MA.

Kaplan, S. [2000], 'E-Hubs: the new B2B marketplace', Harvard business review, vol. 78, no.3, pp. 97 – 113.

Katzenbach, J. R. and Smith, D.K 1993a], "the discipline of teams", Harvard business review, vol. 71, no.2, pp. 111– 120.

Katzenbach, J. R. and Smith, D.K 1993b]," wisdom of teams", Harvard business school press, Boston.

Kay, J. [1993], foundations for corporate success: how business strategies add value, oxford university press, oxford.

Kay, J. [1996], "the business of economics", Oxford University Press, Oxford.

Keaveney, P. and Kaufmann, M.[2001], marketing for the voluntary sector, kogan page, London.

Keef, S.P. [1998], 'the casual association between employee share ownership and attitudes', British jounal of industrial relations, vol. 36, no.1, pp. 73 – 82.

Keegaan, warren (2004) Global Marketing (4th Edition) Prentice hall.

Keen, P. [1981], 'information systems and organisation change', in E. Rhodes and D. wields [eds], implementing new technologies, Blackwell/open university press, oxford.

Klien, G. [1997], courses of power: how people make decisions, MIT press, Cambridge, MA.

Klien, N. [2000], "No logo": Taking aim at the brand bullies, Flamingo, London.

Kliener, A. [2003], who really matters: the core group theory of power privilege and success, Doubleday, New York.

Kloman, H. (1984)Captive insurance company; in risk management report

Knapp, M. L. and Hall, J [2002], Non-Verbal Communication in Human Interactions, Thomson learnig, London.

Knights, D. and Murray, F. [1994], managers divided: organisational politics and information technology management, Wiley, Chichester.

Kochan, T.A. [1992], "Principle for a post new-deal employment policy", Sloan School of Management, MIT, working paper 5.

Kochan, T.A. et al. [2003] 'the effect of diversity on business performance: report of the diversity research network', Human resource management, vol. 42, no.1, pp. 3 – 21.

Kolb, D. Rubin, E. and Osland, J. [1991], organisational psychology, Prentice Hall, Englewood Cliffs, NJ.

Komaki, J. [2003], 'Reinforcement theory at work: enhanced and explaining what workers do', in L.W. porter, G.A. B igley and R.M steers [eds], motivation and work behaviour [7th edn], Irwin/McGrew-Hill, Burr Ridge, IL.

Komaki, J.L. Coombs, T. Redding, T.P. and Schepman, S. [2000],'A rich and rigorous examination of applied behaviour analysis research in the world of work', in C.L. Cooper and I.T. Robertson [eds], international review of industrial and organisational psychology, Wiley, Chichester, pp. 265 – 367.

Kotler, P. [2003], Marketing Management [11th edn], Pearson Education, Upper Saddle river, NJ.

Kotler, P. Armstrong, G. [1997], Marketing: An introduction [4th edn], Prentice Hall International, Hemel Hampstead.

Kotler, P. Armstrong, G. Saunders, J. and Wong, V. [2002], Principles of Marketing [3rd European edn], Financial Times/Prentice Hall, Harlow.

Kottasz, R. [2004], 'how should charitable organisations motivate young professionals to give philanthropically?', international journal of non- profit and voluntary sector marketing, vol. 9, no.1, pp. 9 – 27.

Kotter, J.P. [1982], The General Manager, free press, New York.

Kotter, J.P. [1991], A force for change: how leadership differs from management, the free press, New York.

Kotter, J.P. and Heskett, J. [1992], corporate culture and performance, free press, New York.

Kotter, J.P. and Schlesinger, L.A. [1979], 'choosing strategies for change', Harvard business review, vol. 57, no.3, pp. 106 – 114.

Kotter, J. and Cohen, D. [2002], the heart of change: real life stories of how people change their organisations, Harvard business school press, Boston, MA.

Krackhardt, D. and Hanson, J.R. [1993],' informal networks: the companies behind the charts', Harvard business review, vol. 71, no.4, pp. 104 – 111.

Lancaster, G. and Messingham, L. [1993], Essentials of Marketing [2nd edn], McGrew-Hill, New York.

Laudon, K.C and Laudon, J.P. [2004], management information systems: managing the digital firm [8nd edn], Principle Hall, Upper Saddle River, NJ.

Laurie, J. Mullins (2010), Management and Organisational Behaviour (9th edition) FT Prentice Hall.

Linstead, S. et al (2004), Management and Organisations- Palgrave.

Mintzberg (1973), The Nature of Management Work, Harper&Row.

Naylor J (2004) management – An Introduction (2nd Edition) Pearson

Needle, D. (2002), Business in Context (3th Edition), Thompson.

NHS constitution (2011) NHS Publication.

Philip, Kotler (2006), Marketing Manage net (6thEdition) Prentice Hall

Philip, Kotler (2004) Principles of Management (5th Edition) Prentice hall

Rosebaum, D. (1981), Captive Insurance Company Report VIII, Property and Liability Insurance- Captive insurance Company Review 1981.

Stokes, D. (2006), Small Business Management (4thEdition) Continuum.

Sutherland, J. et al (2004), Key Concepts in Management, Palgrave.

Vaughan E (1986), Fundamentals of risk management and insurance (4th Edition) New York.